SECURITY IN
SOUTH AMERICA

SECURITY IN

SOUTH AMERICA

The Role of States and Regional Organizations

Rodrigo Tavares

FIRST**FORUM**PRESS

A DIVISION OF LYNNE RIENNER PUBLISHERS, INC. • BOULDER & LONDON

Published in the United States of America in 2014 by
FirstForumPress
A division of Lynne Rienner Publishers, Inc.
1800 30th Street, Boulder, Colorado 80301
www.firstforumpress.com
www.rienner.com

and in the United Kingdom by
FirstForumPress
A division of Lynne Rienner Publishers, Inc.
3 Henrietta Street, Covent Garden, London WC2E 8LU

Library of Congress Cataloging-in-Publication Data
Tavares, Rodrigo.
  Security in South America: the role of states and regional organizations/
Rodrigo Tavares.
  Includes bibliographical references and index.
  ISBN 978-1-935049-92-0 (hc: alk. paper)
  1. Security, International—South America. 2. National security—South America.
3. Human security—South America. 4. South America—Foreign relations—21st
century. 5. Non-state actors (International relations)—South America.
6. International agencies—South America. 7. Regionalism—South America.
I. Title.
JZ6009.S63T38 2014
355'.03308—dc23   2014003634

British Cataloguing in Publication Data
A Cataloguing in Publication record for this book
is available from the British Library.

This book was produced from digital files prepared by the author
using the FirstForumComposer.

Printed and bound in the United States of America

∞   The paper used in this publication meets the requirements
     of the American National Standard for Permanence of
     Paper for Printed Library Materials Z39.48-1992.

5 4 3 2 1

To my son Gabriel
Por me ensinar que o amor supera a biologia

Contents

Tables and Figures

Tables

Figures

Foreword

Since the end of the Cold War, the necessity of amplifying the concept of security and distinguishing between "traditional" and "human" security threats has been increasingly accepted. Organizations such as the European Union and NATO have been very vocal in adopting policies that integrate a wide concept of security and that underline how traditional and human security threats overlap and in many ways reinforce each other.

In 2003 the European Union adopted the European Security Strategy, a comprehensive document that analyzes and defines the EU's security environment, identifying key security challenges and subsequent political implications for the EU. The document lists five key threats to Europe: terrorism, the proliferation of weapons of mass destruction, regional conflicts, failing states, and organized crime. All of these threats are interlinked, and they can be found in different combinations in situations of severe insecurity. As the strategy points out, "none of the new threats is purely military; nor can any be tackled by purely military means."

South America suffers from these same threats and provides a good example of how traditional and human security are interlinked. Drawing from a pool of empirical resources, Rodrigo Tavares has successfully made it his mission to show readers these connections. This book provides an extensive analysis of the traditional and human security threats affecting the countries of South America. In addition, it assesses what roles states and regional organizations can and should play in maintaining both traditional and human security in South America. The result is a comprehensive and far-reaching book that will certainly be very useful for scholars and policymakers alike.

—Javier Solana

Former European Union High Representative for the Common Foreign and Security Policy and Former Secretary-General of NATO

Acknowledgments

This book is the last piece of a four-volume study. The overall goal was to provide an analysis of the security dynamics in all regions of the world, namely by looking at how international organizations operate in each region and how the UN is sponsoring this process of decentralization.

The three initial books were *Understanding Regional Peace and Security: A Framework for Analysis*, *Regional Security: The Capacity of International Organizations*, and *International Organizations in African Security*. These three books provided new theoretical understandings on regional security and empirically assessed the security profiles of Europe; South, Southeast, and Central Asia; Africa; the Middle East; Oceania; and North America.

Until now, the remaining empty spot was South America. Although it is one of the most talked-about regions when the issue is security (or insecurity), we generally focus on how problems are handled in specific countries or emphasize specific challenges (such as drugs). But what is the global picture? And what are the comparative advantages and disadvantages of intergovernmental organizations vis-à-vis sovereign states in the provision of security?

Several people were fundamental in supporting my fixation with regional security, a passion that probably started in 2002 when I was accepted at Gothenburg University in Sweden. I will always be indebted to Professor Emeritus Björn Hettne and to my friend Associate Professor Fredrik Söderbaum. Luk Van Langenhove (at United Nations University) and Professor Emeritus Edwin Epstein (whom I met as a visiting research scholar at the University of California, Berkeley) were also unending sources of inspiration and support.

But this current book would have never come to fruition if it were not for the involvement of Professor Emeritus Albert Fishlow at Columbia University, who supervised this undertaking from the beginning. Beyond tutoring me at Columbia University, where I was a visiting scholar in 2010, he generously maintained his support after I left New York. I will never be able to repay his altruism.

I was awarded a grant by the Portuguese Foundation for Science and Technology (SFRH/BPD/66180/2009), which provided fundamental and exclusive funding for the research. I am also grateful to the UN University (UNU-CRIS) for providing continuous support to the book. UNU-CRIS has established itself as one of the world's leading organizations for the analysis of regional integration, and I was honored to count on its support throughout the book's production and publication.

Finally, the greatest thanks go to my family in Portugal and to my wonderful wife, Mirna, and son, Gabriel. Although the book took away time that could have been spent with them, my wife and son showed an immense tolerance and affection. I love you, too.

.

South America

1

South America: An Island of Peace?

The end of the Cold War remains endlessly attractive as a turning point in international relations. As the world changed when the Soviet Union collapsed and the Berlin Wall fell, so did South America.[1] Until the late 1980s, the region was characterized by militarism, hyperinflation and slow development. Although by international standards it has been relatively free from interstate violence, some armed conflicts such as the Chaco War (1932-1935) and the wars between Ecuador and Peru (1941 and 1981) caused thousands of deaths. This bleak picture was accentuated by the emergence of military regimes in the 1960s, most of which were unparalleled in their brutality and suppression of civil society and political movements. The United States' support to these right-wing authoritarian regimes contributed further to the emergence of conflict, guerrilla movements, death squads, and polarization.

The end of the Cold War was a breaking point. Authoritarianism was replaced by democratic regimes and the "evil of inflation" was exorcized. The end of military regimes in the 1980s enabled rapprochements processes and marked a new trend towards democratization and economic stability. The United States also had to overhaul its posture vis-à-vis the region in the post-Cold War and establish new relations of power with its southern neighbors.

This new context brought about a metamorphosis in security. Gradually, the focus expanded from traditional security concerns – with the stress on the state's ability to deter or defeat an attack – to include also human security. Urban criminality, drug trafficking or environmental degradation started to be regarded and studied as major threats. Human security does not obviate state security, however, nor does it encompass all of the security agenda. It does not imply that the military must dilute its focus on defense and melt into the purveyor of

1

primary education, hospital building, and drug control. In fact, both traditional and human security are valid, and in some way they are complementary. Both develop systematic, comprehensive, durable, and coordinated institutional responses to selected threats. Collaboration with state security forces could be essential to human security at the national level. States are critical in providing opportunities for people, creating and supporting a stable environment so that livelihoods can be pursued with confidence, and offering measures to protect people when livelihoods contract. Human security may be an opportune extension of the state security framework, one that explores the newer issues that are already on the boundaries of the security agenda.

This comprehensive perspective of security is, however, not the rule. The exclusive focus on traditional security, as often seen in political discourse and some academic work, has often led us to believe that South America is an island of peace. For instance, the heads of state of the South American Union of Nations (UNASUR) together at an ordinary session in 2013 in Paramaribo, Suriname, emphasized their "determination" to build a South American identity based on the "consolidation of South America as a zone of peace."[2] In some way they are right. If we look at security in a conventional way, it is fair to observe that the last open conflict between two South American countries was in 1995 (Ecuador and Peru). But the region is still affected by critical and pervasive threats to the vital core of people's lives. Presently, the homicide rate is more than twice the world's average, and public security is considered by South Americans to be the most important problem in their countries, ahead of unemployment, poverty or poor education (Corporación Latinobarómetro, 2011:65).[3]

In this environment of insecurity, it is also inevitable that we discuss which players are better suited to handle threats to security. The assumption of traditional security postulates that when conflicts do emerge, it is up to states to resolve them. The state operates solely to ensure its own survival. Decision-making power is centralized in the government, and the execution of strategies rarely involves the public. Traditional security also assumes that a sovereign state is operating in an anarchical international environment, in which there is no world governing body to enforce international rules of conduct. By this token, since South America is primarily a state-driven region and issues of national sovereignty still rank high in the political agenda, international organizations should play a slim role in conflict management.

But this view is far from universal. The realization of human security involves not only governments but also a broader participation of different actors. Indeed, some traditional and nontraditional threats in

South America do not respect geographical demarcations and have a regional outreach, calling for a reexamination of the state as the sole and effective agent in security management. The end of the Cold War unleashed powerful forces of political liberalization and democratization and sparked the emergence or the reform of regionalist projects. Several states in the region no longer benefited to the same extent from superpower protection and had to develop collective capacities to respond to a challenging new environment. Consequently, international organizations gained new clout in the political game.

The metamorphosis in security triggered by the end of the Cold War meant, all in all, the expansion of threats (traditional plus human security threats) and the expansion of security providers (states plus international organizations). This is the most relevant mutation in the security profile of South America since the end of colonialism in the nineteenth century. To grasp this reconceptualization of the meaning and practice of security, the book is guided by two questions:

- What type of threats and violence affect South America?
- What role do states and international organizations play to ensure the security of South American citizens?

Debate 1: Is South America a Secure Region?

As mentioned in the introduction, South American heads of state are eager to portray the region as peaceful and secure. Gathered in Guayaquil, Ecuador, on the occasion of the Second Meeting of Presidents of South America in July 2002, they adopted a declaration proclaiming "South America to be a Zone of Peace and Cooperation, a historical event that reflects the best traditions of understanding and peaceful coexistence among the peoples of the region."[4] This assumption is also reflected in some academic work. In a well-received volume on geopolitics in the Southern Cone published in 1988, most authors believed that the region was moving toward "a harmony of national interests" (Kelly and Child, 1988:4). Others claimed that the region "no longer represents a global threat in terms of security" (Narich 2003:1) and it "contributes to international peace and security" (Aravena, 2005:209). These views derive from the fact that the continent enjoys considerable religious and ethnic homogeneity. Other authors have depicted the region as a "pluralistic security community" – a transnational region composed of sovereign states whose people maintain dependable expectations of peaceful change (Kacowicz, 2000:216; Kacowicz, 1998:121; Domínguez, 2007:111-112; Jervis,

2002:9; Hurrell, 1998; Oelsner, 2003). Even Simón Bolívar, leader of the independence movements in South America, had appealed to the region's common cultural heritage to seek the union of American states in 1826.

This view is far from being unanimous. As Mares and Bernstein pointed out, "Contrary to common belief, the use of force in Latin American relations has occurred throughout the region's history" (Mares and Bernstein, 1998:29). The military culture fostered by the authoritarian regimes of the 1960s to 1980s put a stress on military expenses and war preparations. Although it has subsided, it has not been fully eliminated (Hirst, 1996:156). By the same token, Saavedra argues that the region's relatively favorable context has not meant that "confidence among neighbors is a hallmark of international relations between and among Latin American states. The region is traditionally one of considerable distrust and the fact that this lack of confidence does not break out into open conflict more often should not lead us to the conclusion that this is a zone of peace" (Saavedra, 2004:158).

Several statistics covering traditional threats back this argument. Solís argues that between 1945 and 1990, eleven international armed conflicts and thirty-eight internal armed conflicts have occurred in Latin America: fourteen of which were in Central America, thirteen in the Caribbean, and twenty-two in South America (Solís, 1990:98). Morris and Millan (1983:2) identified more than thirty conflicts in the region during the 1980s concerned with ideology, hegemony, territory, resources, and migration. Child (1984:25) identified twenty interstate conflicts in the 1980s, most of which concerned territory, borders, resources, or migration. Huth (1996) lists eighteen territorial conflicts between 1950 and 1990 in the region, many of which have resource and ethnic dimensions. According to Mares, between 1990 and 2001, there were close to seventy militarized conflicts in Latin America, all occurring between countries with border disputes. In five conflicts, there was only one threat of use of force. In thirty-one cases the verbal threat turned into military deployment. The use of force (an exchange of fire along the border, capture of people or goods) took place on twenty five occasions. Only one militarized conflict ended in war, in 1995, between Ecuador and Peru (Mares 2003: 67-69). In the same vein, Thompson's (2001) classification of strategic rivalry finds tenty-six rivalries between Latin American states (Thies, 2008).

This dichotomy in academic views – leading towards a more positive or negative vision of the security profile of the region – should not overshadow the fact that both are predicated on a traditional concept of security. What it is looked at are classical military threats to the state, perpetrated generally by other states or by internal guerilla groups. This view is not necessarily erroneous, but it is certainly insufficient. As stressed by Kaldor, there is a real security gap today, but "our security conceptions, drawn from the dominant experience of the Second World War, do not reduce that insecurity" (Kaldor, 2007:10). This book claims that it is also important to incorporate the well-being of individuals and hence to include nontraditional threats into any analysis. Human security has surpassed conventional notions of security, which are generally thought of as being geographically confined by a nation's frontiers. Because nontraditional threats are not limited to military activity, sheer force is not enough to contain them (see Table 1.1.).

Urban criminality presents a good illustration of the importance of adding a human perspective to the security equation. The homicide rate in South America is 20 per year per 100,000 inhabitants, the fifth largest in the world after Southern Africa (30.5), Central America (28.5), Eastern Africa (21.9), and Middle Africa (20.8). As a comparison, the world's rate was 6.9 intentional homicides per 100,000 populations in 2011, more than two times lower (UNODC, 2013).[5] According to the UN, between 2000 and 2010, the murder rate in Latin America grew by 11 percent, whereas it fell or stabilized in most other regions in the world. In the last decade, more than one million people have died in Latin America and the Caribbean as a result of criminal violence (UNDP, 2013). Drug trafficking, organized crime, and the legacy of political violence are the principal factors behind rising criminality levels in the subregion. Although it is neither directed at states nor military in nature, urban criminality still affects the well-being of South American citizens.

This broader definition of security first emerged in the 1980s (see Independent Commission on Disarmament and Security Issues, 1982; Ullman, 1983) and was soon highlighted by scholars congregating around what was loosely labeled critical security studies (Tickner, 1995; Krause and Williams, 1996, 1997), who argued that narrow definitions of security had proven insufficient for analyzing the post-Cold War security concerns of states, regions and even the global system, let alone the concerns of nonstate actors such as nations, minorities and individuals (Oelsner, 2009: 196). The focus of human security is squarely on human lives. But in order to protect human lives effectively, actors must deliberately identify and prepare for distinct threats. Threats to human security are critical – that is, they threaten to cut into the core activities and functions of human lives (Alkire, 2003). This vision of security has become mainstream in the 1990s with a flurry of publications sustaining its validity and its distinctiveness vis-à-vis traditional security concerns (Acharya, 2001; Axworthy, 1997; Kaldor, 2007; Haq, 1995; Goucha and Crowley, 2009).

Table 1.1: The Distinction Between Traditional and Human Security

	Traditional National Security	Human Security
Security for whom (referent object)	Primarily states	Primarily individuals
Security by whom	Exclusively states	States, international organizations, NGOs
Values at stake	Territorial integrity and national independence	Personal safety and individual freedom
Security from what (threats)	Traditional threats (military threats, border disputes, coups and civil unrest)	Nontraditional (urban crime, environmental hazards, drug trafficking, terrorism, etc.)
Security by what means	Force as the fundamental instrument of security. Balance of power also plays an important role. Cooperation between states is tenuous beyond alliance relations.	Human development and humane governance as key instruments of individual- centered security.

At policy level most countries tend to make a conceptual and even institutional distinction between these types of threats. Traditional threats and violence are generally handled by the military establishment, whereas threats to human security are normally confronted by the police.[6] This generally leads to a duality of strategies, timings, concepts and institutions. Although it is conceptually necessary to make a distinction between traditional and nontraditional means of security, in reality, they are intricate and mutually reinforcing. Drug trafficking illustrates this view. In Colombia and Peru, the guerilla groups that threaten the authority of the state and use violence to implement a new revolutionary order have largely fed on revenues originated in drug trafficking to sustain the armed conflict. In urban areas, drug trafficking also fuels violent criminality. In the major cities of Brazil, Colombia or Venezuela, criminal organizations have developed with the primary purpose of promoting and controlling drug trafficking operations. They range from loosely managed agreements among various drug traffickers to formalized commercial enterprises. In addition to drug trafficking, these cartels have been tied to both human and arms trafficking, assassinations, auto theft, and kidnapping. They form urban guerillas whose violent operations defy classical demarcations between civil war and urban violence.

The book assesses these two types of threats singly, but acknowledges the ties between both whenever necessary. At the same time that it looks at armed and nonarmed conflicts, it also assimilates the nontraditional outlook by examining such threats as drug trafficking, urban criminality, illegal small-arms trade, Islamic terrorism, and environmental threats. The task of a critical approach is not to deny the centrality of the state in security, but "to understand more fully its structures, dynamics, and possibilities for reorientation" (Krause and Williams, 1997: xvi). The referent object is transported back to the individual and the emphasis is put on his/her emancipation.[7] Human security does not negate traditional security. Naturally, extreme stressing of one of them leads us to exposing conceptual differences. But the right of the state and the right of the individual somehow coexist in the security environment and influence each other.

To refine its analytical capacity, the book also makes a fine distinction between security and peace. In the arena of international relations, where the *lingua franca* is often marked by buzz words and capturing messages, both concepts are sometimes used interchangeably without proper investigation on their adequate meaning. Even the United Nations Charter, probably inspired by the Preamble of the Covenant of the League of Nations Charter, uses these terms almost synonymously, as a unified formula, without pausing for reflection on their substantive conceptual value. However, no matter how symbiotically linked they may be, they reflect a basic distinction. Security is primarily about the management of threats,[8] whereas peace is about the management of violence.[9] The first is associated with a statement of intention, a menace. It involves a cognitive and subjective interpretation derived from a latent and potential action. Peace, on the other hand deals with the absence of physical violence, i.e., it presupposes absence of real damage or adverse effect. Whereas threat is related to the expression of an *intention*, violence is the *observable materialization* of that threat. Very often, the literature selects only peace (or absence of violence) as a benchmark to examine the region, leading to the natural conclusion that South America is fairly peaceful. This book adds to its analysis the idea that the intention or the threat is equally decisive to people's welfare. Therefore, beyond armed conflicts, where violence is manifestly used, we will also examine non-armed conflicts such as territorial disputes and domestic political crises. Illustratively, it is as important to assess the five times the Peru-Ecuador border conflict built up to violence (1828-1829, 1857-1860, 1941, 1981, 1995), as it is to examine the dormant periods when there was only a menace to act bellicosely. Both feed into each other and both generate a negative impact on the welfare of the population.

Debate 2: Who Are the Security Providers in the Region?

Agents of peace and security are actors who may provide a voluntary or involuntary contribution to the successful transformation of violence and insecurity. Their role derives from their shared commitment to a set of overarching shared values and principles, the ability to identify policy priorities and to formulate coherent policies, and the capacity to effectively negotiate with other actors in the international system (Bretherton and Vogler, 1999:38). The book will examine two actors: states and international organizations.

In traditional security discourse the state is the most instrumental agent in promoting external peace in a world of anarchy, and in guaranteeing internal order and security to its citizens. National security refers, hence, to the public policy of maintaining the integrity and survival of the state through the use of political, economic and military power and the exercise of diplomacy, in times of peace and war. The operative capacity of the state in peace and security is therefore twofold:

Externally, the state maneuvers to maximize its national interests by resorting primarily to balances of power, nuclear deterrence, alliances, and war. In an anarchical world war can indeed be regarded as an instrument of state policy to shape the international system by carving international order and stability. To neorealists, survival is presupposed to be the single and most fundamental goal of states (Waltz, 1979: 92/134). In contrast to classical security studies, liberal institutionalism appoints to the state the external capacity to foster norms, values, and identities that would provide its citizens with peace and security. This would be achieved by participating in international regimes or institutions. And unlike realist theories that emphasize the competitive over the benevolent nature of state behavior, states can serve, for instance, as mediators in international disputes or as stabilizers in regional arenas.

Internally, the state is still believed to be the main entity responsible for granting security and peace to its population. Although in a globalized world punctuated by failed states and breaches in sovereignty this is a disputed postulation, it is nonetheless still a commanding principle in international relations. The thought is, to some extent, inspired by the social contract. In Rousseau's view, the people agreed to cede authority to some group in order to gain the benefits of community and safety. If those in power refused to guarantee community and safety, the governed were free to disobey and establish a new political contract.

According to Giddens, the modern nation-state can be characterized by fixed borders, extended administrative control of the population and the permanent existence of class conflict as a result of the relation between capital and wage-labor. Relative to pre-modern states, the state form in modernity displays a massive concentration of power: increased surveillance, control by the state power, monopoly of the means of violence via control of the army and police, intensified industrialization often subsidized by the state and the expansion of capitalism (Giddens, 1987). The state Westphalian order, epitomized by Richelieu's notion of *raison d'etát* or Metternich's and Bismark's concept of *real politik*, is thus based on the territorial equality of states, on the principle of nonintervention in internal affairs as result of respect for sovereignty and on the polarized idea that the hierarchical internal composition of a state is opposed by anarchy in the external sphere (Miller, 1990).

But this traditional view is under dispute. In a globalized world punctuated by failed states and breaches in sovereignty on the one hand, and by drug trafficking-related violence carried out by substate forces (criminal gangs and guerrillas) on the other, the conflict management instruments traditionally available to states – ranging from balances of power to cooperative security – are irrelevant (Domínguez, 1988:17). Autarchy leads to marginalization and an increase in vulnerability. Indeed, the proliferation of security concerns at all levels of national and international life and obvious institutional failures to cope with them has led to a new focus on the obligations of the state and on the role of other security players. In the words of Centeno (2002: 6-7):

> "With regard to the maintenance of social or civil order, citizens living in any Latin American city increasingly find themselves victims

to crime and are turning to some form of privatized protection.... In some cities, where the safety of even the most powerful political figures is not assured, daily life has assumed an almost predatory quality. Nowhere, again with the possible exception of Chile, can one rely on the state to provide a reasonable assurance of protection."

Public surveys reflect this view. In 2011, only 61 percent of South Americans believed the state could fix the problem of criminality and only 57 percent were confident about its capacity to handle the problem of drug trafficking (Corporación Latinobarómetro, 2011:91).

International organizations may offer complementary options. As argued by Keohane, "Globalization has occurred within the context of the dramatic institutionalization of foreign policy" (Keohane, 2001:211). Unlike twenty years ago, one cannot talk about foreign policy without talking about international institutions. Due to their cultural and geographical proximity to the conflict, regional organizations are deemed more likely to understand the factual background of disputes and to share the applicable norms and procedures. In fact, for more than two decades now the UN has shown a strong proclivity to empower regional and other intergovernmental organizations to handle political crises within their regions – as enshrined in Chapter VIII of the UN Charter. In the words of Secretary General Ban Ki-moon, "Regional actors are often better positioned to detect potential crises early and to mobilize coordinated international responses. They have unique influence on, leverage over and access to crisis situations in their respective regions." He added that international organizations are well equipped to confront transnational threats "such as organized crime, pandemics, terrorism and the effects of climate change."[10] Currently, there are thirty-eight organizations worldwide with a security mandate (Tavares, 2010:5). In Africa, Australasia, Central Asia, Central America and Europe regional organizations play a valuable role in the security field (Tavares, 2010; Graham and Felício, 2006; Diehl and Lepgold, 2003; Pugh and Sidhu, 2003; Boulden, 2003; Alagappa and Inoguchi, 1999; Weiss, 1998).

But if the role of international organizations in managing traditional disputes has been amply acknowledged, their capacity to handle non-traditional threats still needs to be better assessed. Indeed, most of the critical issues today – from transnational crime to drug trafficking – are indeed transnational and regional problems that cannot be successfully solved except through cooperative regional efforts. This is not an easy task, however. Susan Strange alerted that the chances of an international regime for the management of containment of transnational crime are likely to be poor because it would strike at the "very heart of national sovereignty – the responsibility for maintaining law and order and administering criminal justice" (Strange, 1996:20). Even so, international organizations have been able to adopt common programs and strategies to disrupt transnational criminal organizations or drug trafficking. The OAS, for instance, adopted in 1997 the Inter-American Convention against the Illicit Manufacturing of and Trafficking in Firearms, Ammunition, Explosives, and Other Related Materials. It was the first multilateral treaty designed to prevent, combat, and eradicate illegal transnational trafficking in firearms, ammunition, and explosives.

But what do we mean by international organizations? They are of two kinds: agencies and arrangements. The distinction between them concerns the degree of formality of the entity in question. A regional agency is a recognized organization with legal personality and an organizational structure (i.e., secretariat) located in a member country. A regional arrangement, on the other hand, is a mere grouping of states united under a common purpose often without a permanent secretariat or a constitutional treaty. Presently, South American states are member of twelve international agencies and six arrangements (see Table 1.2.). Nowhere else in the world is the institutionalization web so thick.[11] There are more organizations than countries in the region.

Some of them have been strictly formed around economic or political objectives (mostly during the Cold War) and have, thus, neglected hardcore security issues. Also, after the fall of the military regimes the focus of South American countries was put on economic development (and democratization) and therefore the organizations that were established also reflected this objective. That notwithstanding, other organizations – such as the Organization of American States, the Andean Community of Nations, the Union of South American Nations and others – have exercised their legal mandate to handle traditional and/or nontraditional security threats.

Selection of Cases

South America is currently composed of twelve sovereign states and eighteen international organizations (agencies and arrangements) have South American states as members (see Table 1.2.). Out of these twelve states, the book concentrates its analysis on five: Argentina, Brazil, Chile, Colombia and Venezuela. Economic and political factors have dictated this selection. It can be argued that these are the countries that

Table 1.2: Hemispheric Organizations with South American Countries

Organization	Year Founded	Total Number of Members / South American Members	Legal Capacity in Security Issues	Operational Experience In Security
INTERNATIONAL AGENCIES				
Amazon Cooperation Treaty Organization (ACTO)	1978 (treaty signed), 1995 (ACTO established)	8/8	No	No
Andean Community of Nations (CAN)	1969 (as Andean Pact) and 1996 (as CAN)	4/4	Yes	Yes
Association of Caribbean States (ACS)	1994	25/4	No	No
Caribbean Community (CARICOM)	1973	15/2	Yes	Yes
La Prata Basin Treaty	1969	5/5	No	No
Latin American and Caribbean Economic System (SELA)	1975	28/12	No	No
Latin American and Caribbean Summit on Integration and Development (CALC)	2008 (it was replaced by CELAC in 2011)	33/12	No	No
Latin America Integration Association (LAIA/ALADI)	1980	12/10	No	No
Latin American Parliament (Parlatino)	1964	22/11	No	No
Organization of American States (OAS)	1948	35/12	Yes	Yes

continues

Pacific Alliance	2012	5/3	No	No
Southern Common Market (Mercosur)	1991	4/4	No	No
Union of South American Nations (UNASUR)	2008	12/12	Yes	Yes

INTERNATIONAL ARRANGEMENTS				
Africa-South American Summit (ASA)	2006	65/12	Yes	No[1]
Bolivarian Alliance for the Peoples of our America (ALBA)	2004	8/3	No	No
Ibero-American Summit	1991	22/10	Yes	Yes
Rio Group	1986 (it was replaced by CELAC in 2011)	23/11	Yes	Yes
Community of Latin American and Caribbean States (CELAC)	2011	33/12	Yes	Yes (Rio Group)
Summit of South American-Arab Countries (ASPA)	2005	34/12	Yes	No[2]
Summit of the Americas	1994	34/12	No	No

---

[1] The first ASA Summit ended with the adoption of the *Abuja Declaration* and the *Plan of Action*, which left no doubt about the aspirations of regional leaders to discuss security issues. The *Nueva Esparta Declaration,* adopted at the Second Summit, is a bolder document spread over twenty-eight pages and containing ninety-six points, twelve of which are specifically on peace and security. But despite this legal capacity, ASA has not made any intervention in the security field.

[2] The juridical basis of ASPA lies upon the *Brasília Declaration*, a document approved at the First ASPA Summit. It is divided into thirteen chapters, the most important being the one on biregional cooperation, peace, and security. Three years later the Declaration adopted by the Foreign Ministers of ASPA gathered in Buenos Aires included a loyal reproduction of the same principles included in the Brasilia Declaration. The *Doha Declaration*, adopted at the end of the Second ASPA Summit (March 2009) did the same. It is actually surprising that the wording of these three declarations – regarding the political and security dimensions – are fairly the same. Several sentences are even repeated. But despite this legal framework, APSA has not had any operational experience in the security field.

primarily mold the South American regional cluster or security complex. They represent not only the five largest economies in the region (led by Brazil and followed by Argentina, Colombia, Venezuela and Chile) but they are deeply involved with the security issues in the region. Brazil is the traditional contender for regional leadership, whereas Argentina plays a fundamental role in the Southern Cone. They are the main actors in the security festival of the Southern Cone, with their animosity oscillating from a nuclear race and military tension (up until the late 1970s), to commercial disputes or mere football hostility (present days). Chile has equally been equipped to play a larger role due to its steady growth since 1990 and to its democratic credentials – the most solid in the region. Colombia is also an interesting case study because it has battled its drug problem without much international support (except from the U.S.) and has been locked in a bilateral security contention with Ecuador and mainly Venezuela for at least one decade now. The latter would have wished to play a more decisive role in the region, but its frail domestic economy in recent years has frustrated that ambition. Part III of the book assesses the foreign policy patterns of each country since the end of the Cold War before zooming in on their specific contributions to traditional and human security.

Of the eighteen existing hemispheric agencies and arrangements that include South American states, eight have legal capacity to undertake security-related activities: the Andean Community of Nations (CAN), Caribbean Community (CARICOM), Community of Latin American and Caribbean States (CELAC), Organization of American States (OAS), Union of South American Nations (UNASUR), Africa-South American Summit (ASA), Ibero-American Summit, and the Summit of South American-Arab Countries (ASPA). All of them, with the exception of ASA and ASPA, have exercised their legal capacity to operate in the security field. The book assesses the contribution of all these organizations that have operational experience in security, except for CARICOM, given that its operational focus is dominated by Caribbean affairs (and not South American). These five organizations vary widely in terms of institutional capacity and represent varying levels of power, influence and capacity. Therefore, we will look at the legal capacity, organizational capacity and operational experience of each to assess their real contribution to peace and security.

Book Structure

To be able to determine the security profile of South America and to identify the actors that may provide a contribution to regional order, the book is divided in five parts. The first places the book vis-à-vis the current theoretical debate. It assesses the academic debates by putting its focus on the dichotomy between traditional and human security. The chapter also provides an introductory overview of the region by pinpointing the rationale behind conflicts and peace and by describing the important impact the end of the Cold War had on the region. The second part concentrates on the regional security profile. It identifies the traditional security threats (armed and nonarmed conflicts) and the human-security ones, which include drug trafficking, urban criminality, illegal small arms trade, Islamic terrorism and environmental threats. Parts III and IV of the book examine the providers of peace and security. Firstly, they look at the foreign policies and the contributions to the security of Argentina, Brazil, Chile, Colombia, and Venezuela in the post-Cold War era, and then they progress to determining the legal and organizational capacity and the operational experience of five international bodies: the Andean Community of Nations (CAN), the Organization of American States (OAS), the Union of South American Nations (UNASUR), the Ibero-American Summit, and the Community of Latin American and Caribbean States (CELAC). Part V presents the final conclusion.

Notes

[1] It includes twelve countries (Argentina, Bolivia, Brazil, Chile, Colombia, Ecuador, Guyana, Paraguay, Peru, Suriname, Uruguay, and Venezuela) and three dependencies – Falklands/Malvinas (United Kingdom), South Georgia and the South Sandwich Islands (United Kingdom) and French Guiana (France).

[2] "Declaration of Paramaribo" (30 August 2013), Preamble.

[3] 28 percent of the 19,000 people surveyed replied that public security was the most important problem in their countries, whereas 16 percent replied that it was unemployment.

[4] See *Consensus of Guayaquil on Integration, Security, and Infrastructure for Development,* adopted in 2002. This notion was preceded by the signature of the Treaty for the Prohibition of Nuclear Weapons in Latin America and the Caribbean (Treaty of Tlatelolco, 1967), and the formation of the South Atlantic Peace and Cooperation Zone (1986).

[5] Using a different methodology, the Geneva Declaration on Armed Violence and Development states that South America's average homicide rate from 2004 to 2009 (17.95 per 100,000) is the fifth highest in the world after Central America (29.03), Southern Africa (27.37), the Caribbean (22.37), and Middle Africa (19.16) (Geneva Declaration on Armed Violence and Development, 2011).

[6] There are some exceptions to it. Sometimes the scope and scale of illegal activities are so far beyond local authorities' capabilities that the armed forces

must assist. That assistance may take the form of logistics support to police who have no way to get to distant sites, intelligence support, training and other types of collaborative efforts (Hayes, 2003:47).

[7] In the aftermath of the Second World War, it was arguably E.H.Carr who pioneered this idea. He argued for a "shift in emphasis from the rights and well-being of the national group to the rights and well-being of the individual man and woman" with "security for the individual" (1945: 71, 58).

[8] Defined as actions that convey a conditional commitment to punish unless one's demands are met (see Baldwin, 1997:15).

[9] Violence is regarded broadly, as any action, performed as a link in a method of struggle, which involves the intentional infliction of death, physical injury, or other type of harm, upon an unwilling victim. For a monumental study of "violence" see Pontara (1978).

[10] Secretary-General's message to Ministerial Council of the Organization for Security and Cooperation in Europe (7 December 2011).

[11] In second place comes Africa with fifteen organizations (Tavares and Tang, 2011: 223).

2

South American Security: An Overview

"A number of (South American) cities have a level of violence that may be compared to an epidemic." —José Miguel Insulza, Secretary General of the OAS, 2010

In the late 1980s, when the spotlights were on Berlin, Moscow, and Washington, South America was also waking up to a new political phase that brought about significant change in its security profile. No longer magnetically drawn to either side of a global confrontation, South American states were free to pursue their own interests as they relate to neighboring states. With the Cold War over, "the big power master narrative would no longer overlay the newly liberated regional mini-narratives" (Pion-Berlin, 2005:221). This new chapter was thus marked by five waves of transformation.

The End of the Cold War

The first is related to the end of military regimes. The late twentieth century witnessed the birth of an impressive number of new democracies in South America. This wave of democratization starting in 1979[1] has been by far the broadest and most durable in the history of the region (see Table 2.1.). It is true that presidentialism and a disregard for checks and balances, low institutional trust and corruption, authoritarian enclaves, a lack of accountability, and neoclientelism, all remain instruments used by politicians in a framework of growing socioeconomic gaps and lasting widespread poverty (Sznajder and Roniger, 2003:338). But the current political situation is a major advancement from the previous military regimes. Sharing new common political values and, above all, bearing similar economic challenges helped downgrade previous rivalries and disputes and constrained the political prominence of the military in most South American countries. There is no political alternative to democracy in South America – no other viable alternative capable of generating confidence, obedience, and governability with local support and international recognition. To consolidate the new democratic parameters, South American states have quickly adopted new constitutions or reformed their basic charters. New constitutions were enacted in Brazil (1988, reformed in the 1990s), Colombia (1991), Paraguay (1992), Peru (1993), Uruguay (1997), and Venezuela (1999). Chile adopted a new constitution in 1980, under military rule, only slightly reforming it after democratization. Ecuador adopted a new constitution in 1998, after reforming its 1979 constitution in 1984 and 1996. Argentina reformed its 1853 constitution in 1994 (Sznajder and Roniger, 2003:334).

With the terminus of the Cold War, the "communist threat" no longer justified the concentration of power in the hands of the South American military. The fall of the generals brought about a new mindset with what security and the role of the armed forces are concerned (see Table 2.1.). Accordingly, the OAS adopted the Declaration of Managua in 1993, which stresses that "the strengthening of representative democracy in the Hemisphere" needs the armed forces to be "subordinate to the legitimately constituted civilian authority" and to "act within the bounds of the constitution and respect for human rights" (art.18). Indeed, the new context expected to generate a peace dividend that would permit countries to divert resources from defense to development. Demands for getting economies on a competitive footing precluded the excessive allocation of resources to a sector that by its very nature is unproductive. Politicians saw their political fortunes tied to providing for impoverished societies more than to building up military. Over the period 1984-1994, Latin America as a whole cut military expenditures and the size of armed forces by 2.8 percent and 3.3 percent, respectively; arms imports declined by 23.4 percent, while arms exports from the region fell 23.1 percent (Franko, 1999:114). Ministries of Foreign Affairs overtook Ministries of Defense in importance.

Civilian leadership in the security arena is thus evolving. The exercise of developing defense white papers has begun to clarify the roles and responsibilities of civilian leaders, legislatures, and public opinion in defining security and defense policy (Hayes, 2003:56). Proof of this was demonstrated when Brazil faced a serious institutional crisis in the wake of President Collor de Mello's 1992 impeachment but the military stayed in the barracks. As Hunter argues, "the unfolding of the rules and norms of democracy" confer on civil-military relations a dynamic character, one whose principal tendency is the erosion of military influence (Hunter, 1997:23; also Filho and Zirker, 2000). In Argentina, civilian control, although stable, has come at the cost of the military's accountability for its activities during the previous regime (Trinkunas, 2000:86). The Carlos Menem government (1989-1999) managed to wipe the military out of the domestic political science through a pragmatic mixture of symbolic concessions and budget cuts. And somehow it worked. During the political, economic, and social crisis of 2001, the military played no significant role.

At the hemispheric level, the downgrading of military participation in the designing of security practices in the region is also reflected in the weight of the Inter-American Defense Board. Created in 1942 in the middle of the Second World War, the Board is an international committee of nationally appointed defense officials who develop collaborative approaches on common defense and security issues. Since the end of the Cold War, however, the board has seen a decrease in staff, budget and competence, which led to its formal absorption by the OAS in 2006. In the changed security environment "of a region seeking to deepen democracy, in which countries have declared peaceful relations with their neighbors and see no global enemy, the Board's purpose was no longer clear" (Hayes, 2007:80).

Despite all this, the transition from military to civilian rule can sometimes be knotty. First, because the ghosts of the past have not yet been put to rest, despite considerable progress and general acceptance on the part of the military of subordination to civilian leadership. As argued by Martín, in spite of some reductions of its political autonomy and influence, the military institution still remains an important and overwhelmingly preponderant political actor in most of the South American polities. More importantly, he adds, it appears that the militaries plan to keep it that way even at the expense of domestic political stability and fiscal responsibilities (Martín, 2006). Paraguay[2] and Chile[3] are cases in point. And second, because there is a mismatch between perception and capacity. On the one hand, the wounds left behind by the dictatorships may still bring about some distrust of the military (Tulchin and Golding, 2002:3). On the other hand, the perception of inefficiency and corruption generally associated with the police and judicial systems, and the pressure of the populations for quick and resolute solutions, has often encouraged political leaders to resort to the military to deal with increasingly violent urban crime. Because of their organizational strength, numbers, and discipline, South American armed forces are called on to deal with a growing number of causes of insecurity in the region. This can be done by deploying the military in high criminality areas or by nominating military staff to police institutions (Dammert, 2007). The drug war has also enhanced the role of the region's militaries. As noted by Youngers, "precisely as civilian elected governments were seeking to limit the military's role in domestic politics and policing, the U.S. government was advocating, via the drug war, a military role in domestic law enforcement, including intelligence gathering" (Youngers, 2006:83). However, the policy of enlarging military activities to civil areas is a contradiction in itself. It is grounded in the fact that carrying out these activities by the armed forces is necessary because there are no civil institutions competent to perform them. Yet, developing this policy prevents those institutions that should engage in these activities from doing so (Varas, 1998:26).

In spite of that, the present economic ambience in South American countries is not conducive for militaries to reoccupy posts in power as it happened in the past when hyperinflation and economic distress were the distinctive feature of South American economies. Argentina, Bolivia, Brazil, Chile, Peru, and Uruguay together experienced an average annual inflation rate of 121 percent between 1970 and 1987. In Bolivia, prices increased by 12,000 percent in 1985 (other sources say 23,000 percent). In Peru, a near hyperinflation occurred in 1988 as prices rose by about 2,000 percent for the year, or by 30 percent per month. This scenario belongs to the past; controlled inflation is the insignia of post-Cold War South American economies.

The second transformation is related to the degree of U.S. involvement in the region. Although it has been argued that the region was considered of low strategic importance in the global scenario of the Cold War (Hirst, 1996:158; 1998:103) (unlike the Middle East or Europe, for instance), and was prioritized by neither the United States nor the Soviet Union, U.S. interference in South American domestic politics was long and salient. The dawn of the Cold War saw the rise of a type of military intimately linked to what began to be called "Pan-Americanism," which was not merely the expression of a transformation in international economic relations, but also a political and ideological program whose principal goals were "the defense of democracy" and "the struggle against communism." It was in the context of those goals that the 1947 Inter-American Treaty of Reciprocal Assistance (Rio Treaty), the Mutual Security Act of 1951, and the Alliance for Progress of 1961 were signed. These documents and programs laid the groundwork for U.S. cooperation with Latin American armies, which began seeing themselves as a fundamental sector of society: the only ones capable of guaranteeing "national survival" that was threatened by the "communist threat." Because of a "growing awareness of Soviet

Russia's aggressive police," wrote the State Department's Division of the American Republics, the United States now "swung back toward a policy of general cooperation [with military dictators] that gives only secondary importance to the degree of democracy manifested by [Latin America's] respective governments" (cited in Grandin, 2007:41). Out of the twelve countries in the region, ten were governed at some point by U.S.-supported military regimes. The level of support ranged from country to country and encompassed military, material or economic support. For instance, between 1950 and 1979, Argentina, despite its official independence from the Cold War, received U.S.$247 million in grants, credits, and other forms of military aid, and more than 4,000 Argentinean military personnel were trained by the United States (Gordon, 1984:94). On the other hand, in those countries whose policies were not aligned with the U.S., for instance in Velasco Alvarado's Peru, its relations with the U.S. were negatively affected.

Table 2.1: Transition to Democracy in South America

Countries	Period of Military Rule (post-Second World War)
Argentina	1943-1946, 1955-1958, 1962-1963, 1966-1973, 1976-1983
Bolivia	1951-1952, 1964-1966, 1969-1978, 1978-1979, 1980-1982
Brazil	1964-1985
Chile	1973-1990
Colombia	1953-1958
Ecuador	1963-1968, 1972-1978
Guyana	---
Paraguay	1954-1989
Peru	1948-1950, 1962-1963, 1968-1975, 1975-1980
Suriname	1980-1988
Uruguay	1973-1985
Venezuela	1948-1958

With the end of the Cold War, U.S. dominance over the region has taken a dramatic turn "changing the terms of the debate about regionalism from interdependence to the chances of preserving autonomy vis-à-vis the hegemon" (Pion-Berlin, 2005:222). Despite episodic controversies, it may be argued that there is now more identity of interests between the United States and South American countries than in decades. Public surveys mirror this view. In 2011, the U.S. was the country most South Americans wished their own country to be modeled after (with 28 percent of responses, after Spain with 19 percent and Brazil with 11 percent) (Corporácion Latinobarómetro, 2011:105), and President Barack Obama was the most valued world leader (after the king of Spain and the President of Brazil) (Corporácion Latinobarómetro, 2011:106).

The new common ground between the region and the U.S. is no longer the need to confront communism but the need to withstand the escalating drug trade. This was cemented after September 11, 2001 when the Bush administration linked counterdrug to counterguerrilla operations and both to the war on terror. Rapidly, guerrilla and paramilitary groups in Colombia such as the Revolutionary Armed Forces of Colombia (FARC), National Liberation Army (ELN), and the United Self-Defense Forces of Colombia (AUC) – and in Peru, the Shining Path – were coined as terrorist organizations. As put by Arceneaux and Pion-Berlin,

> "The fight against the narcos was the fight against terror; the United States believed it could not hope to stem drug trafficking unless it undercut those who gave it protections and, conversely, could not stem terrorism unless it cut off its financial lifelines" (2005:199).

Hence, the third major transformation concerns the war on drugs. Until the 1980s this was regarded as a domestic concern, to be handled by the police. But as the Cold War came to an end the incentives for the military to combat drug trade increased dramatically. As observed by Carpenter, "using the military to combat drug trafficking both in the United States and in other countries created a justification (or more accurately a pretext) for maintaining bloated military spending and personnel levels" (Carpenter, 2003:43). With the collapse of the Soviet adversary, the Pentagon faced the prospect of sizable losses in personnel and cherished weapons systems, as well as prestige and power, unless it had an alternative mission. The Andes quickly replaced Central America as the primary recipient of U.S. security assistance. At the same time, the U.S. Congress designated the U.S. Department of Defense as the "single lead agency" for the detection and monitoring of illicit drugs (Youngers, 2006:74). Hence, the U.S. Southern Command (SouthCom) – the Unified Combatant Command of the Department of Defense responsible for providing contingency planning and operations in Central and South America – embraced the war on drugs as a means of not only maintaining but expanding its role, influence, and presence in the region. With September 11 and the consequent political integration of the concepts of drug trafficking and terrorism, the role of SouthCom was consolidated. Not long after September 11, the U.S. attorney general, John Ashcroft, declared, "terrorism and drugs go together like rats and the bubonic plague. They thrive in the same conditions, support each other and feed off each other" (cited in Youngers, 2006:76).

In fact, it was President Nixon who proclaimed in March 1968 the initial war on drugs and since that time the United States has repeatedly pressured the drug-source countries of South America to stem the flow of illegal drugs. But it was President Reagan in the late 1980s who proclaimed drug trafficking to be a threat to the national security of the U.S. and escalated the pressure on America's hemispheric neighbors.[4] Reagan's appointment of Lewis A. Tambs – former Arizona State University professor and consultant to the National Security Council at the White House – as ambassador to Colombia was one of the first signs that the United States was looking to get tough on the drug issue in Latin America, if necessary by deploying the military in antinarcotic activities. This tendency was cemented with President Bush (first) and signaled in December 1989 with the invasion of Panama (codenamed Operation Just Cause). One of the official justifications for the operation was the need to combat drug trafficking since Panama (under Manuel Noriega) had become a center for drug-money laundering and a transit point for drug trafficking to the United States. Also in December 1989, the White House decided to station an aircraft carrier battle group in the waters off Colombia to help track and intercept drug shipments. This was preceded by the assassination of Colombian Liberal Party presidential candidate Luis Carlos Galán in August 1989 and the subsequent offensive against the Medellín cartel lunched by the Colombian government. These events indicated that drug trafficking and security were interconnected at an unprecedented level. Thus, in September 1989 President Bush announced his five-year U.S.$2.2 billion Andean Initiative, a broad-based counter-narcotics strategy, which resulted in making the Andes, rather than Central America, the leading recipient of U.S. military aid in the hemisphere. In Colombia alone, military aid rose from U.S.$8.6 million in 1989 to U.S.$40.3 in 1990 and U.S.$60.5 in 1991 (Crandall, 2008b:31). The Andean Initiative was thus a clear message to Andean states that the war on drugs needed to become a top priority in their countries. It also gave the U.S. an ongoing military presence in a region where low-intensity conflicts were occurring and were likely to occur. In an attempt to show that the U.S. was committed to multilateralism and concerted efforts, in February 1990 the U.S. and several Latin American states issued the Declaration of Cartagena that announced that the drug problem was both a supply and a demand problem. Tellingly, a CBS News/New York Times poll published in March 1988 showed that 48 percent of the U.S. public considered drugs to be the principal foreign policy challenge facing the United States, and that 63 percent thought drugs should take precedence over the anticommunist struggle (cited in Crandall, 2008b:28). As Johnson noted, the only thing that changed with the end of the Cold War was the varying performance and the different objectives of the hegemonic role of the United States, not the dominance itself (Johnson, 2001:43).

The fourth transformation is related to the new role played by regional organizations. In the past, mostly in the context of the Cold War, regional institutions and regional conflicts were subordinated to the particular interest of the superpowers. As former UN Secretary-General Boutros-Ghali stated in the 1992 Agenda for Peace, "The Cold War impaired the proper use of Chapter VIII and indeed, in that era, regional arrangements worked on occasion against resolving disputes in the manner foreseen in the Charter." This judgment seems justified as long as it was based on action by the OAS with regard to Cuba (1962) and the Dominican Republic (1965), the League of Arab States in Lebanon (1976-83), or the Organization of African Unity's (OAU) action in Chad (1981). For very different reasons, both North and Latin Americans arrived at the conclusion that the OAS served very little purpose, and for many years they tended to ignore it (Muñoz, 1994:191). The major factor behind the stagnation was the perception that the hemispheric organization was an instrument of one of the superpowers in the East-West conflict.

After the Cold War, however, a renewed interest in the global level and in the possibility of a new approach in terms of international peace was generated. Yet, the weak financial conditions of the United Nations, the poor record of its peacekeeping missions in the 1990s (e.g., UNPROFOR in the former Yugoslavia and UNOSOM in Somalia), and political pressure from Western powers for reform served as stumbling blocks on the UN's road toward complete self-sufficiency in peace and security. This has been acknowledged even by the UN itself; on numerous occasions the secretary-general has recognized that the organization "lacks the capacity, resources and expertise" to address all the problems; and therefore the support of regional organizations is "both necessary and desirable."[5] In 1994, the issuing of Presidential Decision Directive 25 (PDD-25) by President Bill Clinton was another blow to the universal aspirations of the UN. In the wake of the disastrous mission in Somalia, the directive prevented the United States from using peacekeeping operations as the centerpiece of its foreign policy. Interestingly, as a complement to America's unilateral actions, it foresaw supporting the improvement of regional organizations' peacekeeping capabilities. In 2000, this point was reinforced in PDD 71 of February 2000, which identified the strengthening of the capacity of regional organizations as a major objective. It is clear today that the UN has neither enough resources nor political will to engage with all security problems. These impediments have, hence, paved the way for greater regional involvement. The beginning of this renewed trend toward the regionalization of security mechanisms arrived with the Economic Community of West African Countries' (ECOWAS) armed intervention in Liberia in 1990.

In addition to the aloofness of the UN, an additional factor sparked the emergence of regional projects in South America. At the same time as U.S. influence has diminished, South America's own capabilities have grown. The region has entered into an era of unprecedented economic, political, and diplomatic success. South American countries started looking for solutions among themselves, forming their own regional organizations that exclude the United States and seeking friends and opportunities outside of Washington's orbit. The establishment of Mercosur and the Ibero-American Summit in 1991, the overhaul of CAN in 1996, and the creation of ALBA in 2004, UNASUR in 2008, CELAC in 2011, and the Pacific Alliance in 2012 were enabled by the new post-hegemonic context. Even the OAS was forced to adjust. Although it still carries the negative historical image of alignment with the United States, the OAS has been able to confront new challenges free of the ideological straitjacket of the Cold War period. The passing of that conflict sharply reduced "the risk that resolutions endorsing hemispheric action on behalf of democracy would be treated as licenses for the pursuit of political ends related loosely, if at all, to the consolidation and preservation of representative government" (Muñoz, 1994:195).

Finally, as pointed out earlier, the end of the Cold War also paved the way for a reconceptualization of the meaning and practice of security. Discussions about traditional and new threats to regional security began at the 1991 meeting of the OAS to consider the region's commitment to democracy, but it was by the end of the 1980s that regional leaders started to recognize that the inter-American security system required profound reform and revision (Hayes, 2007:73). At that meeting in 1991, OAS foreign ministers adopted the Santiago Commitment to Democracy and the Renewal of the Inter-American System, which expressed their commitment to the "adoption and execution of appropriate measures to prevent and combat the illicit use and production of narcotic drugs and psychotropic substances, and traffic therein, chemical precursors and money laundering, and related clandestine traffic in arms, ammunitions, and explosives" (art.f). The Santiago Commitment also called for increased cooperation on hemispheric security among member states "in light of the new conditions in the region and the world" that would lead towards an *"updated and comprehensive perspective of security* and disarmament" (art.i, italics added). Within this new context the regional security agenda has expanded dramatically. Starting from discord and with a focus almost entirely on disarmament, demilitarization, and avoidance of state-on-state conflict, the security agenda now encompasses a full range of traditional and new threats, concerns, and other security considerations. It has taken a clear turn in the direction of democratic and human security (Hayes, 2007:88). Beyond the OAS, other South American organizations have enlarged their concepts of security, gradually expanding from traditional to human security. For instance, one of the objectives of UNASUR, as defined in its Constitutive Treaty is to foster "Cooperation for the strengthening of citizen security" (Art. 3-uu), whereas CAN adopted the Guidelines of the Andean Policy on External Security, which listed as its objective "to prevent, combat and eradicate the new threats to security . . ." (Art. 3).

The Rationale Behind Conflicts

Most conflicts in the region involve borders and territory. Land is a unique, valuable, and immovable resource of limited quantity. It is not only the most basic aspect of subsistence for many people in South America, but it can also contain valuable structures and natural resources on (or beneath) it. Land is therefore a very strategic socioeconomic asset, particularly in poor societies where wealth and survival are measured by control of, and access to, land. Resource extraction in the contemporary era spurs extremes of violence and war. Jeffrey Sachs and Andrew Warner examined the economic performance of ninety five countries between 1970 and 1990 to find out that the higher a country's dependence on natural resource exports the slower their economic growth rate (Sachs and Andrew Warner, 1997). Paul

Collier analyzed fifty-four large-scale civil wars that occurred between 1965 and 1999 and found that a higher ratio of primary commodity exports to GDP significantly and substantially increases the risk of conflict (Collier, 2003). Given the growing importance ascribed to economic vigor in the security policy of states, the rising worldwide demand for resources, the likelihood of significant shortages, and the existence of numerous ownership disputes, "the incidence of conflict over vital materials is sure to grow" (Klare, 2001:25, also Homer-Dixon, 1994). Several examples in South America vindicate this view. For example, the Chaco War between Bolivia and Paraguay was, to a large extent, driven by the belief that the northern part of the Gran Chaco region (the Chaco Boreal) could be a rich source of petroleum. In another example, Bolivian long-standing concerns about access to the Pacific Ocean became exacerbated following the discovery of oil in the Santa Cruz region of the country in 1966. And Chile and Peru bickered over their maritime borders for decades – at stake is a large area of sea that is rich in fish, representing an important source of commercial income. Beyond resource-rich land, agricultural land is also a source of conflict in some countries. In South America, in fact, popular discontent with land-related institutions has been one of the most common factors in provoking revolutionary movements and other social upheavals. In Bolivia, for instance, despite the implementation of Bolivia's land reform in 1953, the agrarian structure continues to have an extreme concentration of land and is bult on on centuries of exploitation and corruption.

Boundary conflicts have also lingered due to the physical complexity and the cost of demarcating some terrains – some of them covered by rainforests or snow-capped mountains. The numerous *gobernaciones, audiencias*, captaincies, and viceroyalties of the Spanish and Portuguese administrations were governed on vague boundary lines (Caviedes, 1988:13; Heredia, 2006:310-311; Baud, 2004:43). It is ironic that up until the 1980s, the Tordesillas Line (1494), the Treaty of Madrid (1750), the Treaty of Saint Ildefonso (1777), and the decrees, regulations, and maps of the Spanish empire were still being cited to solve disputes (Pittman, 1988:31; Parodi, 2002). The negative burdens of the colonial legacy of the nineteenth century in the region have yet to be overcome. Inexact maps have for instance fueled the protracted conflict between Ecuador and Peru.

Although most of the territorial disputes in the region are legacies of the nineteenth century, others are the product of new advances in law and technology. The change in international maritime law leading to the 1982 United Nations Convention on the Law of the Seas, extending zones of economic and environmental jurisdiction out to two hundred miles, created the need to draw these boundaries and provoked fresh disputes (Domínguez, 2003a:26). Also, the development of new technologies for the exploitation of marine and seabed resources raised the salience and accorded urgency to the new need to delimit maritime boundaries. The maritime conflict between Venezuela and Colombia over the limits of the Venezuelan Gulf would not have persisted if were not for the measurement instruments. New technologies are also helping states in mapping out underground reservoirs such as the Guaraní Aquifer, located beneath the surface of Argentina, Brazil, Paraguay, and Uruguay. As it may be the largest single body of groundwater in the world (although the overall volume of the constituent parts of the Great Artesian Basin, in Australia, is much larger), and due to expected shortage of fresh water on a regional scale, the control of this resource is likely to become controversial.

Other factors ignite conflicts. Some of these contentious boundary issues have been exploited by policy makers to drive away attention from ineffective governance. For nationalists of all shades there is nothing more comforting than to believe that pressing priorities to improve the social and political conditions can be replaced by the mobilization of a nation behind nationalistic causes (Caviedes, 1988:28). Right or wrong, historical interpretations and myths permeate the perceptions of foreign policy-makers and enjoy tremendous popularity with the general public (van Klaveren, 1996:47. See also Pittman, 1981:175). As Calvert observed, "given the widespread practice in Latin America of military interventions in politics, all governments, military and civilian, have a high degree of sensitivity to questions of national dignity." He added that "the government that incurs the odium of giving up even a square meter of the historic soil of the fatherland, may find its term of office abruptly curtailed" (Calvert, 1983:6). When colonial powers withdrew in the nineteenth century, they left a heritage of poor border demarcation and therefore drawing lines and populating border areas became an important pillar in the process of state building (Baud, 2004).

It has been demonstrated through extensive research that South American states created inaccurate historical accounts of their territorial evolution and losses that in time allowed them to feed on nationalistic and revisionist theories. Escudé calls this "a self-perpetuating process of indoctrination through the educational system and the mass media" (Escudé, 1988: 156). In Peru and Bolivia, and to some extent also in Argentina, there is, for example, an internalized conception of Chile as an expansionist state. Public officials in these countries have expressed the view that Chilean territorial expansion at the expense of its neighbors has been the cornerstone of Chilean economic growth (Sicker, 2002:150). Also the border controversy between Ecuador and Peru goes back in time to the very beginning of both states as republics. The myths and historical accounts referring to the border have provided the bases for creation of national images, state institutions, and communities' understanding of the very essence of the nations (Bonilla, 1999:67). President Fujimori of Peru, for instance, sought to build national unity based on the 1995 border conflict with Ecuador. A few months after the conflict he was reelected with 60 percent of the votes, even though three years earlier he had closed the national Congress and subjected the judiciary to the executive power (Oliveira, 1999:141-142).

Although they do not constitute a direct reason for conflicts to erupt, arms races may also accentuate existing disagreements. This is what is traditionally known as a "security dilemma:" it may arise where a state has the opportunity to develop a game-changing new weapons system, even if for purely defensive purposes. For fear of strategic disadvantage other powers may elect to develop the weapon – an arms race – resulting in none gaining a strategic advantage and all bearing a significant cost. From 2008 to 2013, some events sharpened concerns about South American arms acquisitions: Venezuela announced the acquisition of air defense systems and battle tanks, supported by a U.S.$2.2 billion loan from Russia. Banned by the United States from receiving most Western sources of supply since 2006, Venezuela has looked to Russia, China, and Iran for arms during the past years. Moreover, Brazil's agreement with France, worth U.S. $3.9 billion for a nuclear-powered submarine development program and the purchase of 36 Saab Gripen fighter jets worth U.S. $4.5 billion were considered the largest military contracts in South America. Also, the Chilean Air Force is preparing for another very large purchase as it is set to retire, by 2015, its 16 Northrop F-5 Tiger IIs.

Rather than being seen as the implementation of a careful long-run strategy for the region, understanding patterns of arms transfers as tied to an arms race can misrepresent the important political and military changes in the region (Franko, 1999:114). Although neighbors constantly watch each other, and further transparency is needed in the reporting of off-budget funding for arms acquisitions, military spending in South America has actually remained stable in recent years: from U.S. $66.4 billion in 2009 to U.S. $67.7 billion in 2012 (Table 2.2.). The military announcements mentioned above are more related to the modernization or replacement of old arsenals.[6] Much of the existing military equipment in the region is twenty or more years old and obsolete. Although we could extrapolate, for example, that Venezuela's recent acquisitions were related to the fierce disagreements that surfaced with Colombia in 2008-2009, in practice there was a 25 percent decrease in Venezuela's military spending in that period (Table 2.2.).

The Rationale Behind Peace

The first major deterrent of conflict in the region is the effective balance of power that has sustained South America's peace after the 1880s. In South America, warfare was frequent and at times devastating from the 1830s to the early 1880s. South America's last war of the nineteenth century, the War of the Pacific (Chile versus Bolivia and Peru), ended in 1883. Thereafter, no war broke out until the 1930s. A balance of power system anchored in successful deterrence developed in South America during the second half of the nineteenth century and the first third of the twentieth. It was actively pursued by Brazil, which placed particular emphasis upon maintaining Chilean independence against threats from Peru and Argentina. This balance of power policy sought to prevent Spanish encirclement, and to assure the independence of the buffer states (Bolivia, Uruguay, and Paraguay) (Kelly and Child, 1988:6). In this light, states assessed their relative capabilities effectively and interacted continuously with, and deterred, one another (Dominguez, 2003:20). In 1898 and again in 1901 Argentina and Chile were on the verge of war over their unresolved boundary dispute along the Andes, but in May 1902 they reached a comprehensive understanding in their famous Pacts of May (Kacowicz, 1998:73). This balance of power is still palpable today. The practical reason why peace still holds between Peru an Ecuador, despite the repeated minor flare-ups and one major outbreak of fighting in 1995, is because of the relative balance in military power between both countries.[7] In a similar vein, Benjamin Miller has developed his explanation about peace in South America in terms of what he calls the state-nation balance in a region in particular. Simply put, this balance has to do with the level of congruency that exists between the division of the region into territorial states and the national aspirations of their respective populations (Miller 2007: 2). He claims that, "South America was better disposed than Europe to enjoy peace relatively early because it entered the twentieth century with a higher level of state-to-nation balance than Europe did" (Miller 2007: 328). Balances of power may have a negative side, however (Snyder, 1984), as they may sometimes be prone to war, buck passing, chain-ganging or arms races, as we saw above. But the balance of power that

Table 2.2: Military Expenditures in South America (selected years)

Countries	1990		2009		2010		2011		2012	
	In constant (2011) U.S.$ m.	As % of GDP	In constant (2011) U.S.$ m.	As % of GDP	In constant (2011) U.S.$ m.	As % of GDP	In constant (2011) U.S.$ m.	As % of GDP	In constant (2011) U.S.$ m.	As % of GDP
Argentina	[2,520]	[1.4]	3,264	1	3,607	0.9	4,052	0.9	4,356	0.9
Bolivia	[62]	[2.8]	394	2	364	1.7	351	1.5	377	1.5
Brazil	[52,182]	[6.3]	34,334	1.6	38,127	1.6	36,932	1.5	36,751	1.5
Chile	2,266	3.4	4,569	2.2	5,131	2.2	5,440	2.2	5,357	2.1
Colombia	2,661	1.6	11,158	3.9	11,072	3.6	10,307	3.1	11,446	3.3
Ecuador	497	1.9	2,109	3.7	2,188	3.6	2,454	3.7	2,263	3.4
Guyana	6.1	0.9	30.5	2.3	30.2	2.1	30.2	1.9	30.1	1.8
Paraguay	[212]	[1.7]	238	1.2	264	1.2	302	1.3	430	1.8
Peru	(53.7)	(0.1)	1,965	1.4	2,076	1.3	2,029	1.1	2,363	1.3
Uruguay	[1,007]	[3.5]	877	2.1	885	2	902	1.9	944	1.9
Venezuela	[3,395]*	[1.8]*	3,302	1.2	2,574	0.9	2,385	0.8	3,316	1.0

Sources: SIPRI Military Expenditure Database

Notes: [ ] = SIPRI estimate; ( ) = Uncertain figure; *1991 data, 1990 data not available; Suriname data not available.

started to be formed in South America 150 years ago is clearly one of the sources of regional stability.

The second major impediment is geography. In South America, problems posed by distance, mountains, rivers and climatic extremes can severely limit military capabilities. The Amazon jungle makes sustained large-scale action difficult among Peru, Ecuador, Colombia, Venezuela, Brazil, and Guyana; ice fields and narrow sea passages separate Argentina and Chile in the south. Hence, geography produces an environment where foreign policy can primarily be crafted for a domestic audience alone, with little regard to international reverberations. As pointed out by Child, "this situation is compounded by the fact that the South American military establishments have only limited logistical means with which to overcome these formidable obstacles, and have not focused their attention on efforts to solve their basic logistical problems of transportation, communications, and supply" (Child, 1985:8). Although this situation changed in the 1960s with progress in communications and transportation, the search for economic prosperity and technological advancement and the need to develop and control borderlands (Kacowicz, 1998:97), interactions are still difficult in some Amazon or Andean areas. For instance Brazil's densely forested interior, with the exception of the pampas to the south, effectively buffers the country from most of its neighbors, permitting it to focus on the challenge of developing the Brazilian interior.

The third major deterrent is the United States. The U.S. has periodically acted as a formal guarantor of peace settlements between South American countries (such as the Rio Protocol between Ecuador and Peru) and is sometimes perceived as an informal guarantor of settlements and balances in the region (Domínguez, 1998:4). Its preponderance in South America dates back from the end of the First World War. The British withdrew their South American fleet and the United States began to consolidate the significant advances in economic penetration gained at the expense of Europe during the war. Bryce Wood noted that the increased level of intrastate violence in South America in the 1930s was largely a result of the U.S. reticence to discipline those who would "misbehave" in the Hemisphere (Wood, 1966). Although Mares challenge those who would overemphasize the United States' influence in these matters, he acknowledges the importance of that period to South America's stability:

> "For a time the U.S. was willing to provide diplomatic leadership, economic incentives and military interventions to maintain peace, but the costs proved too great and the U.S. retreated behind the Good

Neighbor Policy after 1933. In the 1932-1954 period of the Good
Neighbor Policy the U.S. ceased military intervention and diplomatic
interference in Latin American affairs" (Mares, 2001b: 68)

Other studies are more emphatic. Kacowicz's qualitative work finds
that the presence of the U.S. as a regional hegemon was important in
keeping the negative peace (1998: 193–194). As a result, Kurth labeled
the U.S. the "Colossus of the North," which constructed a "hegemonic
international system" in Latin America. This system has four features: a
military alliance (Rio Treaty), Latin American economic dependence on
the U.S., ideological commonality with the U.S., and (in)direct
intervention by the U.S. (Kurth, 1986). By the same token, Thies'
equation modeling suggests that "U.S. intervention [in Latin America]
appears to reduce the likelihood of the formation of specific rival role
relationships while simultaneously maintaining the negative peace of the
region" (Thies, 2008:251).

Military intervention is perhaps the most obvious example of the
exercise of imperial power. And according to the statistical analysis
conducted by David R. Mares and Steven A. Bernstein, the United
States has overtly used or threatened to use military force against Latin
American countries thirty-four times in the twentieth century (Mares and
Bernstein, 1998:31). Between 1898 and 1933 alone, the United States
conducted more than thirty interventions in Latin America, often
involving the U.S. Marines (Smith, 1996:52). In fact, a pioneering study
on motivations of U.S. interventions in domestic political disputes
abroad suggests that geographic proximity significantly influences the
decisions of the U.S. to intervene in intrastate disputes (Mullenbach and
Matthews, 2008). Other views, however, contest that the theory of
hegemonic stability cannot singly justify regional peace. For instance,
once the U.S. started its hegemonic decline after the mid-1960s we did
not witness a period of heightened tensions in South America, as
expected from the theory (Kacowicz, 1998:90). We have therefore to
take additional variables into account.

The fourth factor is cultural and is related to common norms, rules
and identities. Domínguez, for instance, expounds that since
independence the majority of Hispanic elites accepted the norm that they
were part of a cultural, and possibly political, larger identity, and
therefore conflict between them should be prevented (Domínguez,
2003b: 22. See also van Klaveren, 2000:132). He later added that state
elites constructed new interests and identities and internalized norms to
ban the likelihood of war in a subregion where not so long ago it still
seemed likely (Domínguez, 2007:112). Norms are intimately linked to

the values of a society because they express the shared values among its members and are sustained by the members' approval or disapproval. In his analysis of security norms in Latin America, Kacowicz considers eleven case studies beginning chronologically with the Misiones arbitration (Argentina-Brazil, 1858-1898) and the Tacna-Arica settlement (Chile-Peru, 1883-1929), and finishing with the Argentina-Brazil nuclear cooperation agreement (post-1979) and the Contadora/Esquipulas accord (Central American states, post-1984). He concludes that the "core of Latin American international society has been its common values, norms and institutions" (2005:70). In a previous book Kacowicz also noted that the South American countries, through a gradual historical and learning process, have managed to establish a unique Latin "diplomatic culture" that has helped their governments to resolve their international conflicts short of war (Kacowicz, 1998:102). Martín has also advanced the notion of "Militarist Peace." It posits that over time, members of the armed forces develop similar socioeconomic values, beliefs and principles. Facing a similar political landscape at both the national and international levels, the regional military sectors have increasingly harmonized their interests and have come to view themselves as "friends" whose "enemies" are not the other intraregional national armies, but rather, the civilian sectors within their own state's boundaries. He concludes that the evolution of this spontaneous and informal socioeconomic and political association has reduced and softened the number and nature of conflicts of interest among them; and it has decreased the possibility of crisis and war (Martín, 2006). In another interesting study, Santa Cruz argues that it was the region's common normative structure that contributed to the emergence of election-monitoring practices in the early 1960s, mainly through the OAS. Election monitoring, he adds, has redefined sovereignty in the region (Santa Cruz, 2005).

The bloody wars of the nineteenth century prove that this common background has not always prevailed but it can nonetheless be argued that South Americans have a tendency to cooperate and even integrate when they sense that their interests are being challenged by outside actors, namely the United States. The book *Ariel* published by the Uruguayan José Enrique Rodó in 1900 is a good example of the expression of a common culture in the region and the rejection of the utilitarian materialism emanating from the U.S. Yet, this idea is not universally accepted. Other authors argue that the regional identity is weakened by the diversity among the countries in terms of domestic politics, size, location, economic scale, resources, and capabilities, as well as among their different strategic preferences. As da Costa notes,

"This desired (by some) integration of identity may someday be possible, but as yet there is too little substance behind the concept to define any unity for practical analytical purposes." (da Costa, 2001:93). Aravena walks on the same line when he argues that the very idea of Latin America, which conveys a sense of unity and common destiny, is in crisis as regional cooperation is still an unfulfilled objective (Aravena, 1998b:82).

The fifth factor is the transformation in diplomatic and economic interstate relations that occurred in the region in the late 1970s and early 1980s (Domínguez, 1998:9; Resende-Santos, 2002). The case of Argentina and Brazil is symptomatic (see Table 2.3.). Marked by the inheritance of unresolved territorial disputes and numerous periods of muted hostility, the Argentine-Brazilian relationship reached an important breakthrough in 1979. Although one of the most acrimonious bilateral disputes concerned the control of water resources along the Alto Paraná basin, they managed to conclude the Itaipú-Corpus Multilateral Treaty on Technical Cooperation, resolving the dispute over water resources. As Gardini notes, the water dispute was not only about water but also about distribution of power and competition for dominance in the region (Gardini, 2010:31). Pion-Berlin adds that, "through the process of diplomatic negotiation, Argentina and Brazil began to break down the political and psychological barriers which had separated them for so long" (Pion-Berlin, 2000: 45). Thus, the treaty opened the way for a dramatic improvement in relations. Resende-Santos argues that these first institutional bilateral structures created "one of the world's most durable security regimes" (Resende-Santos, 2002: 89).

João Figueiredo, the last president of the military rulers who had governed Brazil for twenty-one years, visited Buenos Aires in May 1980 and signed, among other agreements, a series of accords to collaborate on nuclear issues. Reflecting their shared opposition to the nuclear nonproliferation regime, Argentina and Brazil agreed to cooperate and exchange technical information, materials, and products on all aspects of the nuclear fuel cycle. It is widely acknowledged that domestic and regional security motivations were behind the integration initiative that started in 1985 and resulted in the signature of the Treaty of Asunción (1991) and the formation of Mercosur (Oelsner, 2009: 198). But the drive towards cooperation was also economic with both countries attempting to capitalize on the opportunities emerging from increased trade. Following the South American debt crisis, the 1980s became the region's "lost decade," during which efforts aimed at industrialization via import substitution were reversed, and poverty and high inflation grew to epidemic levels. Far from being considered low politics, development reached the top of the security agenda (Oelsner, 2009: 199-200).

Table 2.3: Milestones of Brazil-Argentina Rapprochement, 1979–2011

1979
• Itaipú-Corpus Multilateral Treaty on Technical Cooperation
1980
• Brazilian President Figueiredo visits Argentina and Argentinean President Jorge Vileda visits Brazil
1985
• Joint Declaration on Nuclear Policy of Foz de Iguaçu
1986
• Declaration of Brasilia Program for Economic Integration and Cooperation (PICE)
1987
• Brazilian President José Sarney visits Argentina • Declaration of Viedma
1988
• Argentinean President Alfonsín visits Brazil • Treaty on Integration, Cooperation and Development • Declaration of Ipero
1990
• Declaration of Buenos Aires • Bilateral Declaration on Common Nuclear Policy of Iguazu Falls
1991
• Treaty of Asunción (establishment of Mercosur) • Bilateral Agreement for the Exclusively Peaceful Use of Nuclear Energy • Creation of the Brazilian–Argentine Agency for Accounting and Control of Nuclear Materials (ABACC) • Quadripartite Agreement between Argentina, Brazil, ABACC and the International Atomic Energy Agency • Mendoza Commitment

1994
• Full adhesion of Argentina (in January) and of Brazil (in May) to the Treaty of Tlatelolco
1996
• First joint military operation (Southern Cross)
2005
• Puerto Iguazu Commitment
2008
• Declaration to jointly develop nuclear power reactors
2010
• Joint Presidential Declaration on Nuclear Policy
2011
• Cooperation Agreement between Argentina's Atomic Energy Commission (CNEA) and Brazil's National Nuclear Energy Commission (CNEN) on the New Multipurpose Reactor Project

In the same period, Chile and Argentina also improved their bilateral relationship. In 1978 they were an inch away from facing each other militarily, but in 1984 they signed the Treaty of Peace and Friendship. Politically, these accords broke down the psychological barriers to cooperation that had separated these countries for so long (Pion-Berlin, 2005:212). In an unprecedented move, the Southern Cone states realized that long-term prospects of collaboration were a more viable route to pursue their security interests. Isolationism was replaced by collective security. A collective, multinational security approach was also thought to provide economic benefits by reducing public expenditure on defense and removing some impediments to regional trade. Some countries are, however, more devoted to this idea and, as we saw above, conflicts are still persistent.

The rationale of peace or the understanding and avoidance of military confrontations is a complex issue, thus. Mares contends that various factors must be considered, including: political-military strategy, strategic balance, the nature of the force to be used, the constituent willingness to accept the costs of war, and political accountability. These five factors constitute part of a "militarized bargaining model," and they exist to a greater or lesser extent in all countries. The manner in which they coexist determines when and how a government may respond to international exigencies. Peaceful negotiations occur between South American states when the costs of militarized confrontation exceed its benefits. Conversely, Mares concludes that relations among countries turn violent when constituencies (civilian or military) determine that the benefits of war outweigh its costs (Mares, 2001b: 201-205).

The theory of democratic peace is another illustration of this complexity. By stating that liberal democracies never go to war with each other, the theory could provide an additional explanatory factor for South American countries to eschew military violence. However, statistical research has demonstrated that it is not the case in South America. As Mares and Bernstein have shown, countries in the region are unaffected in their decision to use force in their foreign policy by whether or not the country with each they have a dispute is democratic (Mares and Bernstein, 1998:34-37; also Mares, 2001b:103). For instance, when Ecuador and Peru fought in 1995 they were led by democratically elected and constitutional governments. The disputes between Venezuela and Guyana and Venezuela and Colombia also follow the same pattern (Domínguez, 2003b:31). And the above-mentioned cooperation agreements between Argentina-Brazil and Argentina-Chile, which recalibrated the strategic interests and the territorial disputes in the region, were all concluded during periods of military rule. Similarly, meaningful negotiations to resolve the Bolivia-Chile-Peru dispute took place during 1975 to 1978, when all three countries were under authoritarian regimes. In fact, the military regimes were successful in maintaining cooperation links, namely through the exchange of intelligence, which was considered fundamental to curb the rise of communism. Democratization emerged as a trend within South American in the early 1980s, long before any new regional consensus developed around security issues (Grugel, 1996:157), and therefore democratization is an important but insufficient condition to intensity security cooperation in the region (Hirst, 1998, 116).

Notes

[1] In 1977 the military leaders in Ecuador announced their desire to withdraw from politics; a new constitution was drafted in 1978; and elections in 1979 produced a civilian government (see Huntington, 1991:22).

[2] With the end of the military rule, civil-military relations remained tense and uncertain since democratic values were notoriously limited.

[3] Overall, the Chilean military managed to preserve considerable political autonomy due to two critical factors: first, the economic autonomy granted to

the armed forces by the Copper Law, and second, the explicit support given by powerful segments of civil society (Hirst, 1998:107). Unlike Argentina, the Chilean military were not defeated at war, were relatively successful in their economic administration of the country, and thus retained an enormous amount of power when they handed the government to democratically elected civilian authorities. The military still retain a virtual veto power against any action of the civilian government that affects their interests.

[4] On 8 April 1986 President Reagan issued a national security decision directive (no. 221) to the effect that drug production and trafficking constituted a grave threat to the security of the hemisphere. Hence those nations under attack by the drug lords, especially in the Andes, ought to defend themselves individually or in concert. In practice this meant a greater emphasis on control at the source and a relentless effort in source countries to interdict illegal drugs. The United States would provide advice, training, and equipment, although the drug war would be waged first in South America and second in its surrounding international waters. This directive is also thought to have authorized the CIA's involvement in international drug interdiction efforts.

[5] The Causes of Conflict and the Promotion of Durable Peace and Sustainable Development in Africa, Report of the Secretary General, (General Assembly Security Council document A/52/871-S/1998/318), para. 41, 13 April 1998.

[6] See "Há Risco de Guerra na América do Sul," interview with James Lockhart-Smith (*O Estado de São Paulo*, 7 February 2010).

[7] The balance in military power is also reflected in the balance in military expenditures, which have been constant and similar over the last years (Table 2.2). In 2007, the spending were virtually the same ($1,420 million for Ecuador and $1,417 for Peru).

PART 1

REGIONAL SECURITY ISSUES

3

Traditional Security Threats

"We are seeing the end of an era of senseless confrontations that only benefited others, and which more precisely did not belong to South America." —Cristina Kirchner, president of Argentina, speaking at the ceremony that put an end to the Chaco War in 2009

In South America there are still orthodox beliefs about the primary object of security, namely that it is to ensure the survival of the nation-state (or ruling regime) from external attack and subjugation or internal subversion and overthrow. In both cases, the threat and use of countervailing force to deter and defend against the enemies of the state are the primary means by which security is sought and maintained. This way of conceiving security is still dominant amongst policy makers in the region. States can indeed actively promote or repress rights to personal security, social services, and economic opportunities. They can exercise their sovereign rights to mediate between global flows in ways that enhance or undermine all or certain groups' livelihoods. So the state is a critical institution for livelihoods. Although this state-centric vision does not comprehend the full spectrum of security, traditional visions still occupy an important place in decision making.

In fact, reality on the ground demonstrates that South American countries are still impacted by classical threats – be they interstate or intrastate – that need to be tackled by conventional military means. Since the end of the Cold War, nine armed conflicts have occurred in the region. Armed conflict is defined by the Uppsala Conflict Database as "a contested incompatibility that concerns government and/or territory where the use of armed force between two parties, of which at least one is the government of a state, results in at least twenty-five battle-related deaths in one calendar year." Armed conflicts may be considered "minor" – when there are at least twenty-five but less than 1,000 battle-related deaths in one calendar year, or a "war" – when there are at least 1,000 battle-related deaths in one calendar year.[1]

Within these nine armed conflicts, only once a war was fought between two states (Ecuador-Peru), which inspired some authors to endorse the idea that South America has turned the page on war and embarked on an era of multilateral peace. This assertion, however, is hardly able to portray the security environment in South America. Interstate peace is an important factor, but utterly insufficient in the definition of peace. Worldwide, most conflicts are in fact internal and not between states. In 2012 alone, there were thirty-two armed conflicts worldwide, twenty-three of which (72 percent) were intrastate (Themnér and Wallensteen, 2013). Hence this trend is reproducible in South America, too. Since the end of the Cold War, eight out of the nine armed conflicts were intrastate. Inter-state warfare has indeed declined, but armed conflicts and violence are still widespread.

Most of the intrastate conflicts in the region are caused by violent coups or by civil unrest. This is indicative of the quality of governance in the region. Some states have not yet been able to create a system of checks and balances among the presidency, the legislature, and the courts. Others have weak parliaments, which are not able to practice their constitutional responsibilities of managing budgets and formulating efficient policies. Personality cult and political authoritarianism is also widespread.

Other intrastate conflicts (armed and nonarmed) still involve left-wing guerilla groups. In the 1960s, 1970s, and 1980s, South America guerilla movements chose a violent path (through long and low-intensity confrontation) when military dictatorships or authoritarian governments squelched dissidents and freedom, often in the name of stamping out communists. Although guerilla warfare is centuries old (the term was first coined to describe the informal groups that fought Napoleon's occupation of Spain in the early nineteenth century), it was first experimented in contemporary Latin America with Augusto Calderón Sandino in Nicaragua in the 1920s (Prieto, 2007:274). Yet, it was the overthrow of the regime of Fulgencio Batista in Cuba (1959) by the 26th of July Movement, the revolutionary group of Fidel Castro, which sparked a wave of guerilla groups all over South America (Correa-Lugo, 2007:39). They remained active for more than three decades, until the end of the military regimes in the region in the 1980s and 1990s, paving the way for former guerilla members to join the democratic political process and be voted to power. In recent examples, José Mujica, who spent fourteen years in prison for waging war against the state as a Tupamaro guerrilla, was elected president of Uruguay in November

2009. Álvaro García Linera, Bolivia's vice-President, was a leader in the Tupac Katari Guerrilla Army. In spite of this trend toward the democratization of guerilla groups, guerilla warfare is still discernible in South America, with groups operating in Colombia, Peru and Paraguay.

In total, forty-one disputes have been registered in South America since the end of the Cold War (including armed and nonarmed conflicts). This calculation does not include disputes between South American countries and nations outside the region (such as between Colombia and Nicaragua), with the exception of the Argentinean-British conflict over the Falklands/Malvinas, as the archipelago is unquestionably located in South America.

Armed Conflicts

Colombia (since 1964). The conflict, one of the oldest and more intricate in the planet, erupted in the mid-1960s when the first guerilla movements were formed – the Revolutionary Armed Forces of Colombia (FARC), the National Liberation Army (ELN), and, later, the April 19 Revolutionary Movement (M-19). At the beginning these movements had a popular agenda that aimed at empowering poor *campesinos*. In addition to these movements there were substantial paramilitary forces, known as *autodefensas* or self-defense forces (AUC). The FARC, the largest group, finances its operations through kidnapping and ransom, extortion, and narcotics trafficking. Initially, it rejected any involvement in the emerging phenomenon of drug production and trafficking, but during the 1980s the group gradually came to accept it as it became a burgeoning business. Taxes on drug producers and traffickers were introduced as a source of funding, in the form of the compulsory so-called *gramaje* tax. At least 50,000, and possibly as many as 200,000, people have died in the conflict since 1964, including some 17,000 since 1990 alone. The battle has oscillated between a minor armed conflict (1989-1993, 1995, 1997-1999, 2003, 2006-2012) and war (1994, 1996, 2000-2002, 2004-2005).[2]

Ecuador-Peru (1995). A longstanding territorial dispute between Ecuador and Peru erupted in fighting in January 1995, in the remote and rugged jungle mountains of the Cordillera del Condor, where a stretch of border had never been clearly marked and where deposits of gold, uranium, and oil supposedly lay. Peru claimed that the approximately 1,000-mile border between the two countries had been set by the 1942 Rio de Janeiro Protocol, which had confirmed its victory over Ecuador in a ten-day war in 1941. But Ecuador declared the protocol null in

1960, before the last forty-eight miles of the border had been marked. Vowing to enforce Peru's claim to the forty-eight-mile stretch, President Alberto Fujimori sent troops and warplanes into the region. A cease-fire and truce took effect in February 1995, after tense peace talks, calling for demilitarization of the disputed jungle border and the deployment of a military observer mission provided by the guarantor nations (Argentina, Brazil, Chile, and the United States), which was to be called Military Observer Mission Ecuador-Peru – MOMEP. In October 1998, the two countries signed a peace treaty defining the forty-eight-mile stretch of border. The dispute was considered a minor armed conflict.[3]

Paraguay (1989). The harsh regime of General Alfredo Stroessner, who had ruled Paraguay since 1954 and been criticized for violations of human rights, was toppled in a revolt led by General Andres Rodriguez, Stroessner's second-in-command. Military forces loyal to Rodriguez violently seized control of the government in Asunción, the capital, where an estimated 150-300 people, both civilian and military, were killed. Stroessner was placed under house arrest and allowed to go into exile abroad, whereas Rodriguez became president, vowing to restore democracy and respect human rights. In 1993, he was succeeded by Juan Carlos Wasmosy, Paraguay's first-ever democratically elected civilian president. The dispute was considered a minor armed conflict.[4]

Peru (1981-1999, 2007-2010). The Peruvian government has been engaged in a conflict since the 1980s with the Maoist group Shining Path (*Sendero Luminoso*) and the Cuban-inspired Tupac Amaru Revolutionary Movement (*Movimiento Revolucionario Tupac Amaru*). The main goal of these organizations was to overthrow the Peruvian government and other political institutions and replace them with a communist revolutionary command. In the space of the first six years of operations, the Shining Path may have carried out as many as 12,000 violent attacks, resulting in a possible death toll as high as 10,000 (McCormick, 2001:109). As of 1999, the conflict was terminated due to low activity. However, in 2007 renewed Shining Path activity led to the conflict again being active, along with the Peruvian cocaine trade. Indeed, similar to other revolutionary uprisings, the Shining Path funds many of its operations through narco-trafficking and forced taxes on small business and individuals in the areas they predominately operated within. In December 2011 Shining Path's leader Comrade Artemio announced that the armed struggle was over, but that the political struggle would continue. In 2012 Artemio was captured. The dispute qualified as a war (1989-1991) or as a minor armed conflict (1992-2010). [5]

Suriname (1986-1992). Since gaining independence from the Netherlands in 1975, Suriname has endured coups and a civil war. In 1986-1988 an insurgent group called Surinamese Liberation Army (SLA) or Jungle Commando, led by Ronnie Brunswijk, began attacking economic targets alongside the porous eastern border with French Guiana. Their aim was to restore democracy by overthrowing the regime of Dési Bouterse, the nation's de facto military ruler. The group consisted mainly of Maroons (an ethnic group of African descent), and in an attempt to suppress the rebellion, the government army indiscriminately targeted the Maroon people and thousands of Maroons fled to neighboring French Guiana. The conflict came to an end only in August 1992 when a peace accord was signed. Although there are many unconfirmed accounts of battle-related deaths, the armed conflict was not likely to have caused more than 1,000 battle-related deaths in a single year, and therefore it should be considered a minor conflict. [6]

Venezuela (1989). The "El Caracazo" riots of 1989 – the worst in Venezuelan history – mobilized more than one million people around the country. The riots were brutally repressed by the military at the time, leaving thousands of Venezuelans dead, according to human rights groups. The main reason for the protests was the neoliberal, promarket reforms imposed by the government of Carlos Andrés Pérez. Although the government of Perez claimed the death toll to be around 400 people, independent investigators have claimed that the death toll could have reached as many as 10,000. Venezuelans still do not know the exact death toll of that day. Depending on the sources it could be considered either a minor armed conflict or a war.

Venezuela (1992). Against a backdrop of protests over economic policies, a coup attempt against President Carlos Andrés Pérez was launched in February 1992 by a regiment of paratroopers under the command of Lt. Col. Hugo Chávez. The rebels, backed by tanks, launched coordinated attacks at key strategic locations in the capital city. As army troops loyal to President Pérez moved in to counter the revolt, intense fighting erupted in the capital, and the following morning Chavéz ordered the rebel soldiers to surrender. Chávez identified his faction as MBR-200 (*Movimiento Bolivariano Revolucionario 200*). A second coup attempt was initiated in November the same year, staged by a faction of junior officers associated with MBR-200. This coup also failed in its aim to overthrow the government. Pérez escaped in disguise using a secret underground tunnel connected to the presidential palace (Baburkin et al., 1999:148). But the coup triggered a state-of-emergency declaration, curfew, and suspension of constitutional rights and restrictions on the free press. Institutionalized civilian control of the military is what allowed the democratic regime to survive in Venezuela in 1992 (Trinkunas, 2000: 77). The disputes were considered a minor armed conflict. [7]

Bolivia (2008). At the center of the political turmoil were the demands by the wealthy eastern states of Santa Cruz, Tarija, Beni, and Pando (where Bolivia's vast natural gas reserves are located) for greater autonomy. The demand was a response to President Evo Morale's proposed new constitution that would see more land being transferred to the Bolivia's poor indigenous majority. Demonstrators in the eastern states escalated the protests by seizing natural gas infrastructure and government buildings. Clashes erupted between the army and opponents of the government resulting in at least thirty deaths. In Pando alone, twenty pro-Morales farmers were killed. Following negotiation, the autonomy proposals by the Eastern provinces were rejected but President Evo Morales, and the opposition agreed to hold a referendum on the new constitution (which was approved with 61 percent). The dispute was considered a minor armed conflict.

Brazil (2010). In November a military and police campaign saw the security forces take control of two of the city's most violent *favelas* (shanty towns), Complexo de Alemão and Vila Cruzeiro, marking the biggest security operation in Brazil's history, with more than 17,500 police and members of the military taking part (using tanks and armored vehicles). Rio's *favelas* have for years been controlled by heavily armed drug-trafficking gangs. The operation left about 100 people killed. The dispute was considered a minor armed conflict.

Nonarmed Conflicts

Conflicts do not inevitably escalate into open violence and do not always entail military warfare. Nonarmed conflicts are contested incompatibilities between or within states that have not resulted in at least twenty-five battle-related deaths in one calendar year. In South America (and elsewhere) there is no correlation between the low or inexistent number of battle-related deaths and the level of complexity or significance of a conflict. In fact, the most intricate and long-standing conflicts in the region are nonarmed. These include, firstly, territorial disputes, defined as disagreement over the possession, control or demarcation of land between two or more states. They also encompass domestic political crises, which correspond to any direct threat to the governing bodies of a state which has the potential to disrupt or suspend the exercise of executive or legislative powers. Crises include military uprisings, government's deposition or resignation, or coup d'états; this latter is defined as the sudden, forcible overthrow (or attempted overthrow) of a government by a group of people already having some political or military authority. Other nonarmed conflicts include intrastate disputes, such as guerilla operations (which do not cause more than twenty-five battle-related deaths in one calendar year) or nonterritorial interstate conflicts.

Territorial Disputes

Border disputes die hard. State territorial boundaries are complex political phenomena whose current relevance in a globalized world should not be easily discounted. In South America, boundary disputes seem to operate in a domain of their own. As David Mares has shown, the existence of such disputes is unrelated to many other significant issues. No clear pattern associates the existence of a boundary dispute in South America with a decreasing level of economic cooperation or human development or with democratic instability. Boundary-related conflict occurs even between partners with preferential trade agreements and between democracies (Mares, 2001a; 2003; also Domínguez, 2003b:31). In the region, Brazil is the only country with no active territorial disputes (Table 3.1). This accomplishment can be traced back to Barão do Rio Branco, Brazil's foreign minister in the early twentieth century, who designed a policy to address and, where possible, resolve Brazil's boundary and territorial disputes with its neighbors. Between 1850 and 1910, Brazil signed final boundary treaties with all its ten neighbors, gaining territory in all of them. All the other countries have had at least one active territorial dispute since the end of the Cold War (Chile tops the list with three active disputes). In total, eleven territorial disputes are recorded.

Venezuela has contested boundaries with Guyana and Colombia. The history of the dispute with Guyana dates back to a contested 1899 treaty that established the current international border between the two countries. Venezuela refuses to accept the legitimacy of this agreement, claiming a 56,000-square-mile area of mineral rich territory around the Essequibo River in western Guyana. The claim includes roughly five-eights of Guyana's national territory, and is rich in natural resources like uranium, gold, diamonds, copper, and hardwood forests, as well as being home to approximately 160,000 Guyanese citizens. With Colombia, on the other hand, the territorial dispute is centered on control over the entrance to the Golfo de Venezuela and the ownership of the Islas Los Monjes. By gaining recognition of its claim to the islands, Colombia could expand national territory into the Caribbean by declaring the extension of its 200-nautical-mile Exclusive Economic Zone around the islands.

Also in the northwestern part of the region, Suriname's borders with Guyana and French Guiana remain disputed. Since the 1960s, the Government of Suriname has made claims to New River triangle, an area of about 6,000 square miles (about 15,600 square kilometers) of Guyana's territory located on the south-eastern corner of the country. Suriname has also claimed the entire Corentyne River as its territory, and a section of Guyana's territorial sea. In 2004, Guyana took the dispute to the UN law of the sea tribunal which ruled that the two countries will have access to the area – called the Guyana-Suriname Basin – which is believed to rich in oil and gas deposits. With French Guiana the dispute is over the Marouini River Tract, which covers approximately 5,000 square miles of inland Amazon forest and apparently contains significant bauxite, gold, and diamond resources and potential hydroelectric production. The area has remained undeveloped and subject to dispute for more than 300 years.

In the Andean region, Chile is involved in a border dispute with Bolivia and Peru over the demarcation of their common border. The longest-running disagreement is over Bolivia's access to the ocean. To put an end to the War of the Pacific (1879-1883), Bolivia signed a truce in 1884 that gave control to Chile of the entire Bolivian coast, the province of Antofagasta, and its valuable nitrate, copper, and other mineral deposits. A treaty in 1904 made this arrangement permanent. Chile built a railroad connecting the Bolivian capital of La Paz with the port of Arica and guaranteed freedom of transit for Bolivian commerce through Chilean ports and territory. However, successive Bolivian governments have challenged this outcome and condemned Chile in international forums. La Paz has, for instance, supported Argentina in the Beagle Channel and the Falklands/Malvinas disputes in return for Argentine backing for their claims (Pittman, 1988:33). It may even be argued that the conflict is part of the Bolivian ethos. As observed by Child, "the national obsession with the sea outlet unifies Bolivia, gives it a national purpose, and in this sense can be interpreted as serving some of the functions of a political ideology (1985:90). Numerous Bolivian presidents have promised to regain the lost territory, and schools teach that this land should be returned to its rightful owner – Bolivia. In April 2013, as the latest move in the longstanding territorial dispute, Bolivia intensified pressure on Chile in order to secure for itself "sovereign access to the Pacific Ocean," in the words of Bolivian Foreign Minister David Choquehuanca.[8] It did so by filing a lawsuit against Chile at the International Court of Justice (ICJ) in The Hague.

The dispute between Chile and Peru also dates back to the War of the Pacific, in which Peru lost substantial territory to Chile. Central to the row is 38,000 square kilometers, or about 14,500 square miles, of fishing-rich sea that Chile currently controls. Peru and Chile are the world's top producers of fish meal, a cattle feed, and fishing is one of the engines of Peru's economy. Lima filed a claim at the International Court of Justice in The Hague in 2008, alleging that marine boundaries had never formally been set by the two countries. Chile's position was that the line had been defined in agreements signed in 1952 and 1954, which Peru argued were strictly fishing accords. In a 15-1 vote in January 2014, the court ordered that the common marine border be redrawn giving Peru about 21,000 square kilometers of the disputed 38,000 square kilometers.

Peru, additionally, has endured a long-standing dispute with Ecuador. As we saw earlier, the bilateral dispute has episodically resulted in armed violence and caused more than twenty-five battle-related deaths in one calendar year (such as in 1995). But the conflict should also be regarded as a historical and nonarmed claim over territory. If examined retrospectively, the conflict is primarily a dispute that has not led to any outburst of violence or to any battle-related deaths.

This conflict is a consequence of the imprecise geographical definitions used in colonial times to define the limits of the Royal Audiences (Spanish appellate courts). After Peru and neighboring Gran Colombia proclaimed independence from the Spanish crown in 1821 and 1819, respectively, they ended up fighting a war in 1828 over the demarcation of the common border. In the aftermath, the belligerent parties agreed to proclaim their limits on the basis of the principle *uti possidetis juris* and the border became the one that existed between the Spanish viceroyalties of Peru and New Granada. When the Republic of Ecuador proclaimed its secession from Gran Colombia in 1830 its government negotiated a swap of territories in the Amazon basin for debt with the British creditors, and the dispute over the territories reignited in 1857. Ever since the bilateral dispute has oscillated between an armed conflict and a nonarmed one. Tension has been always high, but often the conflict has scaled down to a nonviolent bilateral disagreement. For instance, an armed conflict was avoided in 1991 after representatives of both countries established a common security zone in the disputed region. Ecuador and Peru are aware of the economic value of the land they dispute as it is believed to have deposits of gold, uranium, and oil. Ecuador also considers this area of strategic importance since control of the Amazon is one of the country's primary objectives (Child, 1985:93).

Besides the dispute with Chile, Bolivia also had a long-standing conflict with Paraguay. The boundary dispute arose over the Chaco Boreal, a low region to the north of the Pilcomayo River, to the west of the Paraguay River. As both countries claimed the entire territory, which was believed to contain large reserves of oil, a war was waged between 1932 and 1938 (Chaco War), leaving more than 100,000 dead. The war was stoked up by U.S. company Standard Oil and Dutch company Shell. Both backed opposing sides in the hope of gaining control over assumed hydrocarbon deposits in the Chaco region. While Paraguay gained control of a majority of the Chaco, both countries came out of the war politically and economically weakened. The conflict only came to an end when Bolivian President Evo Morales and his Paraguayan counterpart, Fernando Lugo, inked an accord in April 2009. Morales lauded that day as "transcendental and historical."[9]

Although Argentina served as the mediator in the Bolivian-Paraguayan dispute, in 2010 it saw no reservations to revive a long-time border dispute with Chile over a piece of territory in Patagonia. The dispute is over 2,200 square kms of contested land known as the Southern Ice fields (called "Campos de Hielo Sur" in Chile and "Hielo continental patagónico" in Argentina), which contain the second largest reserve of potable water in the world. The area was only one of two left with undetermined status during the demarcation of twenty-four disputed borders in 1990 (along with Laguna del Desierto), but it ended up being resolved in 1998, when a treaty was signed that instructed a mixed commission to demarcate the border. The country has also made several efforts to keep the Falklands/Malvinas conflict animated. Fought in 1982, the Falklands War was the result of the Argentine invasion of the British-owned Falkland Islands. Located in the South Atlantic, Argentina had long claimed these islands as part of its territory. The settlement that ended the conflict called for a return to status quo antebellum. But despite its defeat, Argentina still claims the territory.

Domestic Political Crises

South America is the region where coup d'états are more frequent. Unlike revolutionary or guerrilla threats, which albeit frequent, are rarely successful, the armed forces "have been the principal threat to the stability of constitutional government" in South America (Domínguez, 1998:5). In the 1960s-1980s domestic political instability was the single most visible attribute of the region. Repeatedly, military regimes seized and remained in power in Argentina (1962-1963, 1966-1973, and 1976-1983), Bolivia (1964-1966, 1969-1978, 1978-1979, and 1980-1982), Brazil (1964-1985), Chile (1973-1990), Ecuador (1963-1968 and 1972-1978), Paraguay (1954-1989), Peru (1962-1963, 1968-1975, and 1975-1980), and Uruguay (1973-1985) (Oelsner, 2005:9) (see Table 2.1.). As late as the mid-1970s, seventeen of the twenty Latin American countries were under one form or another of authoritarian rule (Wiarda, 2005: xiv). The fall of the military regimes is an epitome of what Huntington called the "third wave" of democratization. South America was pushed towards democracy by a set of factors, including deepening legitimacy problems of authoritarian governments which were unable to cope with military defeat and economic failure, and the burgeoning economies of many countries, which raised living standards, levels of education, and urbanization, and consequently have also amplified civic expectations and the ability to express them (Huntington, 1991).

Yet, although the end of the Cold War has unfolded new opportunities for democracy and political stability, the region is still far from reaching a stage where unconstitutional changes of government (or attempts to do so) have become history (see Table 3.1). In fact, some scholars have argued that many of the democratic transitions "have not worked out as well as expected" (Wiarda, 2005: xv) since democratic political parties, civil society, or parliamentary or government institutions did not develop or become institutionalized as much as was hoped earlier. The economic and social base of South America is low, underdeveloped, and too weak in many countries to be supportive of strong and stable democracies (Millett, 2009:2). It has not been uncommon for elected presidents to use their popularity as a weapon to intimidate opponents and manipulate elections under cover of a political mandate. As Peeler notes, "the formal presence of a liberal democracy is not assurance of its vitality" (Peeler, 2009:188). Back in the 1970s, Robert Dahl coined the term "polyarchy" to refer to contemporary regimes that are usually called democracies even though they fall short of the ideal (Dahl, 1971: chap.1). Public surveys mirror this discontent: in 2011, only 58 percent of Latin Americans were satisfied with how democracy worked in their countries (against 61 percent in 2009) (Corporación Latinobarómetro, 2011). Not surprisingly thus, the region has seen nineteen domestic political crises in eight countries since the end of the Cold War:

Table 3.1: South American Territorial Disputes and Domestic Crises

Countries	Number of Territorial Disputes (since 1990)	Number of Domestic Political Crises (since 1990)
Argentina	3[10]	2
Bolivia	2	2
Brazil	0	1
Chile	4	0
Colombia	1	0
Ecuador	1	5
French Guiana	1	0
Guyana	2	0
Paraguay	1	4
Peru	2	2
Suriname	2	1
Uruguay	0	0
Venezuela	2	2

In Suriname, on the Christmas Eve of 1990 the Army overthrew the elected Government of President Ramsewak Shankar and Vice-President Henck Arron in a bloodless coup d'état. The coup was engineered by former leader Dési Bouterse who had stepped down under international pressure in 1987 (in July 2010 Bouterse was again elected president). In Brazil, in 1992, Collor de Mello resigned as president immediately following the beginning of his impeachment trial in the Brazilian Senate for corruption. In September that year the Brazilian Chamber of Deputies suspended his presidential powers pending the outcome of the trial. The obscure actions included receiving a car and an estimated U.S.$ 1.3 million worth of work on personal property from the man identified as the main operator of the influence-trafficking ring, his former campaign manager, Paulo Cesar Farias.

In the same year, in Peru, President Alberto Fujimori with the support of the military carried out a presidential coup d'état, also known as the *autogolpe* (auto-coup or self-coup). He shut down Congress, suspended the constitution, and purged the judiciary. Although Fujimori had been elected president in 1990, it was the opposition who remained in control of both chambers of Congress. According to Fujimori, this hampered the government's ability to enact economic reforms. The *autogolpe*, backed by 80 percent of the population, did succeed in reestablishing a sense of order and security, but at the price of bringing authoritarianism back to Peru after twelve years of electoral democracy (Calderón, 2001:48). A controversial figure, Fujimori has been credited with restoring macroeconomic stability, though his methods are described as autocratic, and his human rights abuses led to his conviction and prison sentence. In 2000, he formally resigned (while in Japan) following a tortuous political crisis sparked by corruption allegations against his former spy chief and top aide Vladimiro Montesinos. But after a marathon debate that became an outpouring of accumulated rage and political grudges, Peru's Congress rejected the resignation and instead ousted him on the grounds that he is morally unfit to hold office. The ouster was the political equivalent of an indictment and conviction. It was approved by sixty-two of the 111 legislators present and opposed by nine.

Since emerging from dictatorship in 1989, Paraguay has lurched from one political crisis to the next. In 1996, Paraguayan General Lino Oviedo, who ironically played a prominent part in the uprising that overthrew the regime of General Alfredo Stroessner and set the country on the path back to civilian government, threatened a coup d'état against then President Juan Carlos Wasmosy after the president ordered him to step down as commander of the army. A key element in stopping it was the international support for the president coming from Argentina, Brazil, the United States, and Uruguay (along with OAS Secretary General César Gaviria acting on his own authority). As underlined by Valenzuela, the rapid, decisive, and overwhelming international support for the constitutional order in the country was critical in providing President Wasmosy with the resolve to stand firm in the face of military insubordination while dissuading General Oviedo from hasty action

(Valenzuela, 1997:53). Another important factor was President Wasmosy's promise to General Oviedo that he would get the defense ministry post if he resigned his command. Yet, when Oviedo went to the presidential palace to take the oath, the president, backed by popular demonstrations, withdrew the offer. In 1998, one month before the national elections, and while leading the polls, Oviedo was finally condemned to a ten-year prison term for his 1996's military mutiny. His running mate Raúl Cubas continued the campaign and eventually won the elections, largely based on the promise to free Oviedo, which in fact he did days after taking office, over the protest of the Paraguayan Supreme Court and opposition leaders.

In 1999 Congress voted to begin impeachment proceedings against President Raúl Cubas for freeing Lino Oviedo. In the same year, Vice President Luis Maria Argana, a bitter rival of President Cubas, was shot dead. Oviedo is believed to have masterminded the assassination. One year later, President Luis Gonzalez Macchi (who succeeded Cubas after his resignation in 1999) announced that an attempted coup by soldiers and police was stopped. Lino Oviedo was again behind, the failed coup. In 2012, the country was back on the spotlight. In June Paraguay's Senate voted to remove President Fernando Lugo from office in an impeachment trial. The Senate tried him on five charges of malfeasance in office, including an alleged role in a police operation to evict about 150 farmers from a remote, 4,900-acre (2,000-hectare) forest reserve that left seventeen dead. Conflicts also developed as leftist groups of landless farmers began to invade large soybean and cattle farms, trying to force the government to expropriate them. Lugo's government didn't have enough funds to pay compensation to farm owners, and the land seizures upset politicians who previously supported the president. The impeachment trial was legally sound although politically undexterous. The Senate rejected a request by his lawyers for a period of eighteen days to prepare their arguments, which was one of the arguments used by Mercosur and UNASUR to suspend Paraguay's membership for 14 months. In August 2013, when the new President Horacio Cartes took office, after a fair electoral process, the suspension was lifted.

In Ecuador, millionaire Abdalá Bucaram won the presidency in 1996 based on an unorthodox platform, known as the "Convertibility plan," that he vowed would curb inflation and correct macroeconomic imbalances. The unconventional plan that helped Bucaram ascend to the office of the president, in combination with his own intrigues, ultimately lead to a heated conflict with Congress and a national protest in February 1997 that demanded the ousting of his regime. Empowered by the president's unpopularity with organized labor, business, and professional organizations, Congress unseated Bucaram on grounds of mental incompetence. He was replaced by Fabián Alarcón who ran the country for only a short period before Jamil Mahuad took power in August 1998. He was, nonetheless, forced to resign in 2000 after a week of demonstrations by indigenous Ecuadorians (who make up nearly half the population of Ecuador) against Mahuad's policies to turn around the country's worst recession in decades. The demonstrations paved the way to a military revolt led by Col. Lucio Gutiérrez[11] and an interim government led by the head of the armed forces General Carlos Mendoza, indigenous Indian leader Antonio Vargas, and former supreme court judge Carlos Solorzano briefly assumed power before turning over the government to Vice President Álvaro Gustavo Noboa, whose position was quickly ratified by Congress. It was the first military coup in Latin America since 1991. Noboa attempted to revive the Ecuadorian economy and injected some stability to the country.

But that was short-lived. In April 2005, amid a growing political crisis and protests in the city of Quito against the Government, President Gutiérrez (who won the elections of 2002) declared a state of emergency. He was removed in the same year by a vote in Congress and replaced by Vice President Alfredo Palacio. Some months after these incidents, Gutiérrez was arrested on charges of attempting to subvert Ecuador's internal security by repeatedly proclaiming to the international media that he continued to be the legitimate president (the charges were dismissed in 2006). Rafael Correa was elected president in November 2006 and replaced Palacio as president in January 2007 but the country still undergoes political instability. In March 2007, the decision of Ecuador's President Rafael Correa to settle a Constituent Assembly with or without Congressional approval has plunged all three branches of government into legal chaos. Fifty-seven legislators (out of 100) were dismissed by the Electoral Tribunal on the grounds that the congressmen had illegally interfered with a referendum pushed by President Correa on whether to draft a new constitution. And in September 2010 it was once again plunged into a political crisis as troops seized Quito's international airport and stormed the Congress. In response, Rafael Correa declared a state of emergency and denounced what he termed a coup attempt orchestrated by the opposition and some members of the military and police. Correa was hospitalized when a tear gas canister exploded near him when he went to talk to the protesting police officers. Ten hours later, loyal troops stormed the hospital, where police had continued to hold the president hostage. Correa blamed Lucio Gutiérrez for the rebellion that left eight dead and 274 wounded but the former president denied the charge.[12] Between 1997 and 2010 Ecuador had eight presidents.

In Argentina, although no change of government has been achieved by force of arms since Bartolomé Mitre's winning of power in 1861, a military uprising led by Mohamed Alí Seineldín in December 1990 did not reach its goals only because a majority of the senior commanders remained loyal to the elected government. An ardent nationalist, Seineldín became a member of the *Carapintadas*, or "painted faces," group within the Argentine Army, which demanded that the Argentine government halt legal proceedings against army officers accused of human rights abuses during the Dirty War during Argentina's military dictatorship from 1978-1983. Seineldín had also participated in a failed uprising against the elected government of President Raúl Alfonsín in 1988. Known for its political and institutional stability, Argentina, however, faced another major crisis in 2001 when President Fernando de la Rua resigned after violent nationwide protests in which at least twenty people died. Discontent with de La Rua was stoked by four years of bitter recession that exhausted the country and left it lurching close to default on its massive public debt.

In Venezuela, in May 1993, Carlos Andrés Pérez became the first Venezuelan president to be forced out of the office by the Supreme Court for the misappropriation of 250 million bolívars belonging to a presidential discretionary fund. After more than two years of house arrest, Pérez was released in September 1996. Nine years later the country plunged into crisis again. President Chávez, who had been elected president in 1999, was ousted by military officers in April 2002, following the deaths of seventeen people in anti-government protests. They have detained him, and installed pro-opposition businessman Pedro Carmona as interim president. But the coup quickly faltered and ultimately crumbled amid massive protests and bloody confrontations between Chávez-backers and security forces. Less than forty-eight hours after his ouster, a triumphant Hugo Chávez returned to power and Carmona went into exile. He was reinstated two days later. Ever since, President Chávez has accused the United States of orchestrating the coup, whereas U.S. officials have repeatedly denied the charge.

In Bolivia, President Gonzalo Sánchez de Losada was forced to resign in October 2003 in midst of violent protests and an acute economic crisis affecting the urban workers and the farming/indigenous population. In order to avoid bloodshed, Sánchez de Losada handed out power to his Vice-President Carlos Mesa. But the latter ran into similar problems. With escalating protests paralyzing the country, President Mesa resigned in March 2005. His retirement was sparked by a social confrontation centered on the exploitation of the country's vast natural gas reserve. Three years later, the issue was again in the spotlight, as we saw above.

Other Nonarmed Conflicts

Conflicts that do not cause more than twenty-five battle deaths in one year do not encompass only territorial disputes or domestic political crises. Other disputes – interstate and intrastate – have also surfaced signalizing the existence of heated incompatibilities. In a region brimful of leaders with intense characters and strong egos, verbal clashes and diplomatic pouting happens recurrently. These other nonarmed conflicts are of a more dangerous nature. More than an episodic clash of leaders, they represent real incompatibilities that could lead, or have already led, to a violent confrontation.

The dispute between Argentina and Uruguay over the pulp mill is a case in point. Although the demarcation of the border between them was not a contested issue since the Uruguay River forms a natural division, a conflict was triggered in 2003 when Uruguay authorized the construction of a riverside pulp mill, which Argentina claimed was contaminating. The Uruguay River is protected by a treaty, which requires both parties to inform the other of any project that might affect the river. Besides the issue of pollution, Argentina claimed that the Uruguayan government had not asked for permission to build the mills. Uruguayan authorities countered that the Treaty did not require that permission be obtained, but merely that the other part be appropriately informed. After Argentina lodged a complaint before the International Court of Justice (ICJ) in 2006, the ICJ issued a ruling in April 2010 declaring that Uruguay had breached its procedural obligations to inform Argentina of its plans but had not violated its environmental obligations under the treaty and therefore the mill could continue operations. Despite the ruling, fresh political storms still rise frequently as both the Argentine and Uruguayan governments release combative statements couched in diplomatic prose and often highlight regular reports by local NGOs and citizen's assemblies, which are often produced to ignite tensions rather than to offer cooperative solutions.

When the problem is not centered on the pulp mill, then it is about the dredging of the Martín García Canal, a 106-kilometer waterway, beginning near the city of Colonia del Sacramento, Uruguay, and leading to Nueva Palmira, which has become the country's leading commodities-export terminal. President Mujica has repeatedly stated that dredging the Martin Garcia canal is a priority for his administration and has gone to lengths to reach an understanding with the administration of Argentine President Kirchner. Kirchner resists the dredging because it would overshadow the economic importance of the Mitre Canal, which leads directly to Buenos Aires and is kept in reasonably good condition to accommodate maritime traffic in the port of the Argentine capital. The port of Buenos Aires is not interested in having an efficient effective port on the other side of the River Plate and supports any excuse to delay the deep dredging process. Both situations – the pulp mill and the Martín García Canal – are actually two faces of the same conflict, born out of the need to control a vital and strategic economic site for both countries.

Paraguay's small guerrilla force is the second case. The country has struggled with small guerrilla operations conducted by the Paraguayan People's Army (*Ejército Paraguayo del Pueblo-EPP*), which operates in the northeastern part of the country. The Marxist-Leninist group has deep roots in the landless peasants in the states of Concepción and San Pedro, where there are frequent conflicts between landless peasants and large landowners, with the landowners regularly hiring death squads to kill peasants. The group, formed by young and poor *campesinos*, is said to have about 100 members. The Paraguayan government says that they were trained by the Colombian FARC and are supported by Venezuela's and Cuba's armed forces.[13]

Notes

[1] See www.pcr.uu.se/gpdatabase/search.php. Visited 23 February 2012.
[2] See www.pcr.uu.se/gpdatabase/search.php. Visited 23 February 2012.
[3] See www.pcr.uu.se/gpdatabase/search.php. Visited 23 February 2012.
[4] See www.pcr.uu.se/gpdatabase/search.php. Visited 23 February 2012.
[5] See www.pcr.uu.se/gpdatabase/search.php. Visited 23 February 2012.
[6] See www.pcr.uu.se/gpdatabase/search.php. Visited 23 February 2012.
[7] See www.pcr.uu.se/gpdatabase/search.php. Visited 23 February 2012.
[8] "Bolivia Takes Chile Sea Dispute to International Court" (*BBC News*, 24 April 2013).
[9] "Lugo y Morales Firman Histórico Acuerdo Limítrofe" (*El Heraldo*, 27 April 2009).
[10] As twenty-two of the twenty-four border disputes between Argentina and Chile were settled in 1990, they are not counted in this table. The table only lists disputes on Southern Icefields and Laguna del Desierto and over the Falkands/Malvinas.
[11] Gutierrez claims however, that he only supported the popular rebellion, not the coup. See "Não Dei Golpe Nenhum. É Tudo Mentira" (*O Estado de São Paulo*, 3 October 2010).

[12] Gutierrez claims however, that he only supported the popular rebellion, not the coup. See "Não Dei Golpe Nenhum. É Tudo Mentira" (*O Estado de São Paulo*, 3 October 2010).

[13] There have also been allegations that President Lugo of Paraguay, a former radical bishop, used to have some sympathy over EPP's actions. The EPP was formed in the 1980s by trainee priests who were thrown out of the seminary for their radical views. See "A Ligação de Lugo com a Guerrilha Paraguaia" by Alfredo Boccia Paz (*O Estado de São Paulo*, 2 May 2009).

4

Human Security Threats

"I believe that the biggest problems to our security in the 21st century and to this whole modern form of governance will probably come not from rogue states or people with competing views of the world in governments but from the enemies of the nation-state, from terrorists and drug runners, and organized criminals who, I predict, will increasingly work together and increasingly use the same things that are fueling our prosperity: open borders, the Internet, the miniaturization of all sophisticated technology, which will manifest itself in smaller and more dangerous weapons. And we have to find a way to cooperate, to deal with enemies of the nation-states, if we expect progressive governments to succeed." —Bill Clinton, U.S. president, 1999

In a narrow sense, human security is about a new central reference point for security – the individual. This approach can be traced back to the 1993 Human Development Report, which triggered debate over the need to challenge crystallized views of security: from an exclusive stress on national security to a focus on the security of the individual and of people; from security through armaments to security through human development; and from territorial security to food, environmental and employment security. The old edifice was shaken. It became evident that the traditional conception of security – based upon military defense of territory – was a necessary but indeed not a sufficient condition for people's security and welfare. The 1994 edition of the Human Development Report elevated the discussion to a level of doctrine. The intent of human security was to bridge freedom from fear – indicating freedom from violence, and freedom from want – related to poverty alleviation. It thus included economic security, food security, health security, environmental security, personal security, community security, and political security. Human security is therefore:

"An underlying condition for sustainable human development. It results from the social, psychological, economic, and political aspects of human life that in times of acute crisis or chronic deprivation protect the survival of individuals, support individual and group capacities to attain minimally adequate standards of living, and promote constructive group attachment and continuity through time" (Leaning and Arie, 2000).

Human security threats are not bound by geographical restraints. Indeed, we may still be living in a world of borders, but it is ultimately a world of borderless threats. In the past, threats were external and controllable within the confines of a state, but that is seldom the case now, as no country can insulate itself from the broader security environment in which it is living.

The classical definition of the modern state was penned by Max Weber and essentially points out that a state is a compulsory political association with continuous organization whose administrative staff successfully upholds a claim to the monopoly of the legitimate use of force in enforcement of its order within a given territorial unit (Gerth and Mills, 1946). But modern states are currently undergoing a process of erosion of sovereignty. Susan Strange was one of the first to disclose this reality. She observed that the need for a political authority of some kind, legitimized either by coercive force or by popular consent – or more often by a combination of the two – is the fundamental reason for the state's existence. But "many states are coming to be deficient in these fundamentals" (Strange, 1996:5). The most basic cause is their increasing interconnectedness. Globalization is "the process whereby state-centric agencies and terms of reference are dissolved in favor of a structure of relations between different actors operating in a context which is truly global rather than merely inter-national" (Evans, 1998). Globalization is about mobility: mobility of labor, ideas, capital, technology, and profits – but also threats – can move across borders with minimal governmental interference. This is reflective of the postmodern world, where the lines between domestic and international affairs are diffuse, national borders are disappearing, and security has evolved beyond nationalist concerns to mutual interdependence.

This new security agenda evolved in several different but mutually supportive tracks. At the hemispheric level, there have been the OAS and its Committee on Hemispheric Security, the Summits of the Americas, and the meetings of the defense ministers of the Americas. The first landmark was the Santiago Commitment of 1991 where delegates called for a process of consultation "on hemispheric security in light of the new conditions in the region and the world, for an updated and comprehensive perspective of security and disarmament, including the subject of all forms of proliferation of weapons and instruments of mass destruction, so that the largest possible volume of resources may be devoted to the economic and social development of the member states." This set off a discussion that had important milestones in the Summit of the Americas of 1994 (which dealt with drug trafficking and related crimes, and national and international terrorism), the OAS 1998 Santiago Summit, the 1999 Guatemala General Assembly, and the 2002 Bridgetown General Assembly. This latter meeting declared that, "the security of the Hemisphere encompasses political, economic, social, health, and environmental factors."[1]

In the same year, the Conference of Defense Ministers of the Americas, held in Santiago, adopted a final declaration stating that the region faces a "diverse and complex set of threats and challenges to states, societies and peoples" (Art. 9). The proclivity towards a comprehensive concept of security became more salient one year later when the OAS adopted the landmark Declaration on Security in the Americas which proposed a "new concept of security in the Hemisphere . . . multidimensional in scope," and includes "traditional and new threats" to the security of the states of the Hemisphere (Art. 2). A year later, at the Special Summit of the Americas in Monterrey, Mexico, they adopted the Declaration of Nuevo León reiterating that "the basis and purpose of security is the protection of human beings" (para.68).

Inspired by the same objectives, parallel talks have also been held subregionally, championed by UNASUR, the Andean Community or CELAC. The Constitutive Treaty of UNASUR of 2008 called for "cooperation for the strengthening of *citizen* security" (Article 3-t, italics added), thus putting the stress on the security of individuals and not of the state, and exhorts countries to cooperate in the fields of drug trafficking, terrorism, transnational organized crime, or trafficking in small and light weapons (Article 3-q). CELAC was even more emphatic. The Cancún Declaration adopted in 2010, stated that heads of state,

> Consider that the new security threats, such as terrorism in all its forms and manifestations, the world drug problem and related crimes, transnational organized crime, illicit trafficking in arms, petty crime that affects citizen's security, threats to international public health, particularly HIV/AIDS and H1N1, natural disasters, the transit of toxic waste and radioactive material through our waters, among others, and particularly its effect on Latin America and the Caribbean should be addressed comprehensively through effective international cooperation. . . . " (Art. 78).

This new security agenda is consistent with the human-security focus promoted by the United Nations since 1994. In practice, however, South American policy-makers are still mostly preoccupied with traditional military threats, such as interstate and intrastate violence. For instance, the Argentine National Defense White Paper (*Libro Blanco de la Defensa Nacional*), stipulates that "the principal or primary mission of the Military Instrument is to act in a dissuasive manner by using its resources in an effective way such as to permanently protect and guarantee the vital interests of the nation from externally originated aggression" (cited in Hayes, 2003:52). Nevertheless, most threats are transnational and not necessarily external, and are so volatile and intangible that they cannot be tackled by military instruments and doctrines. As José Miguel Insulza alerted in 1990, long before becoming OAS Secretary General, "the concept of national security cannot be mistaken by defense or military security, as unfortunately it has occurred in South America" (Insulza, 1990:104). Nontraditional and borderless threats are thus of paramount importance in the context of South America and deserve careful attention.

Drug Trafficking

Transnational organized crime is considered one of the major threats to human security, impeding the social, economic, political, and cultural development of societies worldwide. It is a multifaceted phenomenon and has manifested itself in different activities, among others, drug trafficking. The illegal drug trade directly threatens the security interests of all South American states. As no other criminal activity can match the profits generated from illegal narcotics trafficking this translates into an unrivaled ability for drug criminals to corrupt public officials, undermine democratic governments, and sabotage sustainable economic development. Globally, the United Nations Office on Drugs and Crime (UNODC) estimates that, in 2011 between 167 million and 315 million people aged fifteen to sixty-four (3.6-6.9 percent of the world's population in that age group) had used an illicit substance at least once in the previous year (UNODC, 2013a:1). North America is still the subregion with the largest number of cocaine users worldwide, accounting for more than a third of all cocaine users worldwide (UNODC, 2013a:2).

South America is the largest producer of cocaine in the world. Multiple aspects of the drug supply chain take place in the region, including drug crop cultivation, drug production, drug trafficking, and, ultimately, drug consumption. Coca-leaf production increased considerably in the 1980s, when it was concentrated mainly in Peru, followed by Bolivia. That changed during the mid-1990s, and the two key producing countries were Colombia and Peru. Coca-bush cultivation — and thus coca-leaf production — declined, in particular in Peru, in the late 1990s, whereas coca-leaf production in Colombia increased markedly. The total area under coca-bush cultivation thus stabilized, at a high level, in the 1990s. In the 2000s, the area under coca-bush cultivation declined by almost a third. Massive eradication programs undertaken by the authorities in Colombia over the past few decades have offset the increases reported in the Bolivia and Peru. In 2011, Colombia and Peru each accounted for some 40 percent of the total area under coca-bush cultivation worldwide, and Bolivia accounted for the remaining 20 percent (UNODC, 2013a:xiii).

While Colombian traffickers have produced most of the world's cocaine in recent years, between 2000 and 2011, the area under coca cultivation in Colombia decreased from 144,800 hectares to 64,000, mainly due to eradication. At the same time, coca cultivation increased by in Peru (from 46,200 to 64,400) and in Bolivia (19,900 to 27,200), while traffickers in both countries increased their own capacity to produce cocaine (UNODC, 2013a:xiii). In UNODC's view there is evidence that the United States market continued to be almost exclusively supplied by cocaine produced in Colombia, and that the European markets have compensated, at least partially, for the shortage of cocaine produced in Colombia with cocaine produced in Bolivia and Peru (UNODC, 2013a).

But why does South America have this prominent position in the drug trade? The illicit drug market stems largely from the Andean region's unique position as the world's only source region for coca and cocaine. The monopoly over the production of cocaine puts the region in a key position to dictate the terms of trade. Another contributing factor is its proximity to the United States, a major drug-consumption market. Other underlying factors that have allowed drug trafficking to flourish include social and political indicators such as poverty and a lack of viable alternative livelihoods for farmers, corruption and other weaknesses in law enforcement, the presence of insurgent groups involved in drug production and trafficking in some countries (such as in Peru and Colombia), and the geographical impediments to interdiction, including difficult-to-monitor political borders and maritime terrain.

How did it all start? In the 1950s illegal cocaine laboratories were reported in all Andean countries: Peru, Bolivia, Chile, Ecuador, Colombia, and even Argentina (Guizado and Restrepo, 2007:65). Personnel, means of transportation and routes were available as Latin

America had a long tradition in smuggling (liquor, cigarettes, and fabric). In Colombia, the main laboratories were established in Medellín and soon Colombian and Cuban criminals established strong ties in order to introduce marijuana and cocaine into the U.S. market. They faced little competition "since the long-established U.S. mafias, mostly Italian, had enough on their hands with the heroin trade, which had a much more extended market than cocaine" (Guizado and Restrepo, 2007:65). Coca grown in Peru and Bolivia was moved through Colombia and Mexico, where traffickers built powerful local organizations with the complicity of corrupt government officials. In order to diversify their operations, the Colombian cartels also built smuggling routes through Central America and the Caribbean. Nowadays, one thing that has become obvious during the fight against the drug cartels has been the weakness of the judicial and legal systems. As pointed out by Ulloa, "neither the penal code with its categorization of offences, nor the system of evidence, nor the procedures for mutual legal assistance between countries, nor common jurisdiction, nor the traditional protection afforded lawyers and witnesses, have been sufficient to combat criminal organizations linked to the drug trade" (Ulloa, 1998:3).

There are two main ways for drug trafficking to pose a threat to political stability. The first involves countries where insurgents and illegal armed groups draw funds from taxing, or even managing, drug production and trafficking. The two main left-wing insurgent groups in Colombia – the FARC and the ELN – are primarily funded through drug production and trafficking operations. While the two groups differ in terms of size and territorial reach, both have increased their involvement in the drug trade from levying "taxes" on coca harvesters and midlevel buyers to directly controlling multiple aspects of the drug supply chain.[2] The FARC derives somewhere between U.S.$1 and 2 billion a year from the drug trade.[3] In contrast to the smaller ELN, the FARC is also particularly known for its international contacts and relationships with foreign terrorist groups and transnational organized crime groups, such as the Basque group ETA and the Irish IRA. Similarly, in Peru, the previously dormant *Sendero Luminoso* (Shining Path) appears to be reviving its involvement in both terrorist and drug activity, launching small-scale attacks on Peruvian police and military forces. It appears that *Sendero Luminoso* has begun to re-establish its relationship with Peruvian coca growers, taxing the coca industry in its area of operation in exchange for providing coca growers protection from drug-trafficker violence and ensuring fair prices for their coca crops (Seelke, Wyler and Beittel, 2010). In the 1980s, when the *Sendero Luminoso* reached its peak, coca production was a significant factor in Peru's economy. It earned between U.S.$800 million and 1.2 billion annually, a third or more of the value of Peru's legal exports and more than the combined value of copper and petroleum, its two biggest exports. Besides protecting growers, *Sendero* performed an intermediary role, acting as a kind of armed union for the growers, forcing traffickers to pay higher prices for coca than farmers could negotiate for themselves (Kay, 1999:101 and 103).

The connection between drug trafficking and armed conflict was the basic rationale for President Pastrana of Colombia to propose the creation of Plan Colombia (see below). As he pointed out in 1999, "[Drug crops are] a social problem whose solution must pass through the solution to the armed conflict" (Pastrana and Gómez, 2005:48). Ivelaw L. Griffith coined the term "geonarcotics" to stress the idea that the multidimensional nature of drugs (including production, trafficking, consumption, and money laundering) gives rise to actual and potential threats to the security of states (Griffith, 1993-1994). Other authors have used the term "narco-terrorism" to describe "the use of drug trafficking to advance the objectives of certain governments and terrorist organizations" (Ehrenfeld, 1990: ix) or to depict the "systematic use of violence to confront the state, to weaken and destabilize it with the objective of obstructing its action against the drug trade" (Ulloa, 1998:12-13).

The second way for drug trafficking to pose a threat to democracy and stability concerns countries that do not face guerilla problems, but where drug traffickers become powerful enough to take on the state through violent confrontation or high-level corruption. The cartels in Colombia have grown so powerful that they challenge the power of the state and undermine the country's democracy. This was particularly salient in the 1980s, when the Medellin Cartel waged war on the Colombian government, killing hundreds of judges, police investigators, journalists, and public figures. In other countries the authority of the state is also put in jeopardy. For instance in Brazil the *favelas* located in the largest urban centers such as in Recife, Sao Paulo, and Rio de Janeiro offer fertile ground for drug traffickers. The conflict between gangs and other gangs, and gangs and police is deadlier than the war in Afghanistan and claims tens of thousands of lives every year. In the state of Rio de Janeiro alone the homicide rate in 2011 reached 28.3 per 100,000 habitants, the best score for a decade, but very high nonetheless (Waiselfisz, 2013:25). In the city, drug traffickers effectively control and administer hundreds of neighborhoods (*morros*). The narcotics trade threatens democracy, assaults the integrity of the state, corrupts, creates problems of territorial control, and affects national sovereignty, the electoral process, and human rights.

Since drug trafficking is a regional problem, transnational solutions are preferable to confront it. As stated by Ban Ki-moon, "The transnational nature of the threat means that no country can face it alone. This fight requires a comprehensive international approach based on a strong sense of shared responsibility. States must share intelligence, carry out joint operations, build capacity, and provide mutual legal assistance."[4] In a 2012 address, he reinforced that "transnational organized crime, including drug-trafficking, affects peace, security and stability wherever it occurs. It undermines the authority and effectiveness of State institutions, erodes the rule of law and weakens law enforcement structures."[5]

The United States has put in practice two main programs to cope with drug production and trafficking in South America. The first is the Andean Trade Promotion and Drug Eradication Act, a trade agreement enacted under the George Bush administration in 1991 in which the United States gives preferential tariffs on products from Bolivia, Ecuador, Colombia, and Peru in exchange for participation in drug eradication and trafficking-prevention efforts. Not only does the Act allow the United States to expand its trade links in the Andean region, it also seeks to enhance regional efforts to combat drug trafficking through these countries. Bolivia, however, saw its agreement suspended in 2008 because of its unwillingness to fulfill its part of the bargain. As soon as the U.S. suspended the Act, Morales decided to expel the Drug Enforcement Administration (DEA) from the country. The DEA's presence in Bolivia was dependent on the Act's maintenance.

The second main strategy is the Andean Counterdrug Initiative (ACI), a program within the State Department, responsible for supporting antidrug initiatives in Colombia, Peru, Bolivia, Ecuador, Venezuela, Panama, and Brazil. ACI's policies are designed to strengthen democracy, increase stability in the region, help restore the faltering economies of Andean countries and eradicate coca crops by working with local farmers. The ACI is the primary U.S. program that supports Plan Colombia (the other being the Foreign Military Financing Program). The Plan was developed by former President Andrés Pastrana (1998-2002) with strong inputs by the Bill Clinton administration as a blueprint to end Colombia's long armed conflict, eliminate drug trafficking, and promote economic and social development. ACI funding for Plan Colombia from 2000 through 2012 totaled approximately U.S.$ 8 billion. Although the Plan includes components which address social aid and institutional reform, the initiative is fundamentally a program of counternarcotics and military aid for the Colombian government. Overall, results are mixed. On the positive side there was an increase in the eradication of drug crops and a very significant reduction in Colombia's illicit cultivation of coca bush (from 160,100 hectares in 1999 to 64,000 in 2011) (UNODC, 2013a: xiii). On the other hand, U.S. government agencies responsible for tracking drug trends report that the availability, price, and purity of cocaine and heroin in the United States have remained stable. Most critics condemn Plan Colombia's focus as being far too "militaristic" and in turn diminishing the importance of the social development aspects that are increasingly significant in a poverty-stricken country like Colombia. As pointed out by Youngers, "the war on drugs strengthens military forces at the expense of civilian authorities, exacerbates human rights problems and undermines civil liberties, further impoverishes poor farmers, harms the environment, and generates social conflict, violence, and political instability (Youngers, 2006:73. See also Hoskin and Murillo-Castaño, 2001:38).

Urban Criminality

The popular image of urban crime in South America is normally sensational. The slums of the major metropolis have set the scenario for innumerable action movies, consumed avidly by an interested audience. But despite the image portrayed by the entertainment industry, it is a fact that crime spreads across varied urban settings and has become a part of the daily rhythm of urban living.[6]

But what causes urban criminality? All research undertaken showed that there is no single cause of delinquency, but rather a combination of causes. In the first half of the twentieth century, eminent European sociologists such as Émile Durkheim, Max Weber or Ferdinand Tönnies pointed out that urban crime may be explained in part by the transition of societies from agrarian and village-based forms to industrial and urban-based ones. According to UN-DESA (Department of Economic and Social Affairs), the urban population in South America increased from 42.7 percent in 1950 to 83.1 percent in 2011.[7] Other social reasons also hold. Social exclusion due to long periods of unemployment or marginalization, dropping out of school or illiteracy, and the lack of socialization within the family seem to be recurring factors amongst the social causes of delinquency. Several countries report that unemployed persons are more likely to be involved in drug trafficking than those in formal employment. In Argentina, 54 percent of all arrested drug traffickers with known employment status were unemployed in 2009 (UNODC, 2012: 88).

In addition, in many South American countries the judiciary is not capable of facing the increase in the overall number of minor offences, which damages the quality of life and perpetuates a general perception of insecurity. Justice is slow, ill-suited to developing urban conflicts, overloaded, and uses an outdated working methodology. Bureaucracy and political favoritism have trapped judges, prosecutors, public defenders, and other criminal justice officials in a cycle of inefficiency. Fewer than 2 percent of homicides are resolved by Latin America's notoriously slow and biased criminal-justice systems (Ungar, 2006:182). Prisons, with the exception of some modern and experimental prisons, constitute technical schools for the training and development of criminal networks. In Brazil, for instance, Fernandinho Beira-Mar, one of the leading drug traffickers in South America has not stopped his criminal activities although he was put in jail in 2002. Reaching a similar conclusion when looking at world trends, UNODC has inferred that in all countries where there has been a strengthening of the rule of law in the last fifteen years there has also been a decline in the homicide rate, while most countries where homicide has increased have a relatively weak rule of law (UNODC, 2011a:10).

In addition to these, another fundamental variable is inequality. A widely cited study by Fajnzylber, Lederman, and Loayza (2002) shows that increases in income inequality and reductions in the level of economic activity are significantly related to increases in crime rates. This point is corroborated by the United Nations Office on Drugs and Crime (UNODC) which alerts that "countries with high levels of income inequality are afflicted by homicide rates almost four times higher than more equal societies" (UNODC, 2011a:10). South America is one of the most socially unequal regions in the world. The region's average Gini Coefficient – which measures inequality of income distribution within a country on a scale in which zero is perfect equality and 100 implies perfect inequality – is traditionally around 50, the highest in the world, with some countries reaching 56.3 (Bolivia), 55.9 (Colombia), and 54.7 (Brazil).[8]

The detrimental effects of these causes are heightened by drug trafficking (Bodemer, Kurtenbach and Steinhauf, 2001:12). In countries where trafficking in drugs is significant, crime rates are higher. In Colombia, as the cocaine economy expanded, the number of homicides rose from around 5,000 per year in the late 1970s to some 30,000 in the early 1990. Similar trends can also be observed in Peru. In line with a massive decline of coca cultivation in the 1990s, terrorist incidents, mostly related to the activities of the *Sendero Luminoso* operating out of the main coca cultivation areas of the country, declined drastically

(UNODC, 2010a:9). Ecuador also saw a steady increase in its homicide rate up to over eighteen per 100.000 people in 2010 (as compared to 16.4 in 2007), as the country became an alternative route for drug trafficking to North America (UNODC, 2013).

In brief, as an interesting study pointed out, factors related to violence in South America include social inequalities, lack of employment opportunities, urban segregation, a culture of masculinity, local drug markets, and the availability of firearms and widespread use of alcohol (Briceno-Leon, Villaveces, and Concha-Eastman, 2008). The very high mortality rate associated to this multiplicity of sources is thus responsible for the development of a generalized and not often objective feeling of insecurity, common in many urban populations. This perception crystallizes all the fears of the population (insecurity with respect to employment, health, the future of children, domestic violence, and the risk of impoverishment). It arises from an impression of abandonment, powerlessness, and incomprehension in the face of shocking crime and the multiplication of minor acts of delinquency or vandalism. (Vanderschueren, 2000).

The human and economic consequences of urban criminality in South America are devastating. The OAS Secretary-General José Miguel Insulza calls it an "epidemic, a plague on our continent that kills more people than AIDS or any other known epidemic . . . the integrity of the democratic institutions in our region is seriously at risk."[9] While the global average in 2011 was a homicide rate of 6.9 per 100,000 inhabitants, the estimated average for South America was twenty, the fifth highest regional rate in the world (UNODC, 2013). The occurrence of deaths is roughly five times higher than in Europe, more than three times that in North America, and more than twice the world's average. According to UNODC, the South American countries with highest homicide rates are: Venezuela (45.1 per 100,000 people), Colombia (33.2), Brazil (21.8), and Ecuador (18.2) (UNDOC, 2013) (Figure 4.1.).

The material cost of crime is equally drastic. The Inter-American Development Bank reported that violence against goods and people represents the destruction or transfer of resources equal to nearly 14.2 percent of the Latin American GDP (Londoño and Guerrero, 1999:3).[10] Other authors, however, conclude that the costs are lower: 5.1 percent (Bourguignon, 1999). Opinion polls invariably reflect the empirical scenario. In 2011, public security was considered by South Americans to be the most important problem in their countries (Corporación Latinobarómetro, 2011:65).

Figure 4.1: Homicide Rate, Selected Countries in South America, 1995–2010

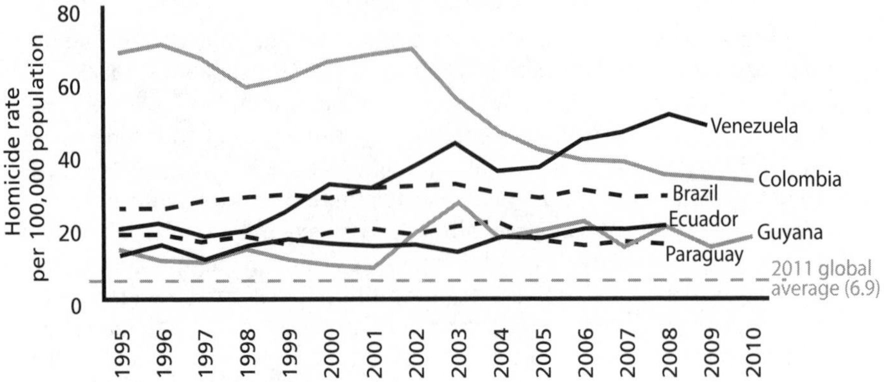

Source: UNODC, 2011a, p.54.

Illegal Small-Arms Trade

The annual value of authorized international transfers of small arms, light weapons, their parts, accessories, and ammunition is at least U.S.$ 8.5 billion. The top exporters are the United States, Italy, Germany, and Brazil (Graduate Institute of International and Development Studies, 2012).

In South America, between 45 million to 80 million small arms and light weapons – that is, weapons operated by an individual or small group, including handguns, assault rifles, grenades, grenade launchers, and even man portable surface-to-air missiles – are circulating throughout the region. Small arms flooded South America during the Cold War, most significantly during the Central American civil wars of the 1980s. Both the United States and the Soviet Union supplied their Latin American allies with mass quantities of weapons through proxy arms dealers (Stohl and Tuttle, 2008). And they continue to do so. According to data provided by the Norwegian Initiative on Small Arms Transfers,[11] in 2005 Latin America legally imported at least U.S.$ 175 million worth of small arms and light weapons, as well as ammunition and spare parts. The United States was the main supplier to the region, exporting almost U.S.$ 50 million worth of these weapons.

In addition to international legal-arms sales, diversion of domestic production and privately owned stocks contribute further to illicit ownership in South America. Brazil is the second-largest producer of small arms in the Western Hemisphere. Production has grown steadily over the past three decades, reaching some U.S.$ 100 million per year. The firearms used in the country's crime are mainly these domestically produced weapons, particularly handguns. There are 17.6 million small arms in Brazilian hands, of which 57 percent represent illicit holdings (Graduate Institute of International and Development Studies, 2010). As observed by the Small Arms Survey, the leading annual publication in the field:

> "Research suggests that the extent to which perpetrators possess and use firearms varies according to the general availability of and obstacles to buying an illicit gun, as influenced by the presence of black markets or the ease of firearm smuggling. Possible factors of armed violence discussed in the chapter include the availability of firearms, the prevalence of youth gangs, the drug trade, and weak security systems" (Graduate Institute of International and Development Studies, 2012).

Other additional factors instigate the problem, namely lack of proper domestic institutional and legal capacity: epitomized in lax firearms regulations (such as in Bolivia or Paraguay), failure to implement existing legal instruments, or weak border controls. There is also a lack of a shared global agreement on standards and methodology to consistently and objectively guide South American states (and others) to avoid arms transfers in instances where there is a substantial risk of serious violations or abuses of human rights or serious violations of human rights. After seven years of negotiations, the UN adopted in 2013 an Arms Trade Treaty. It was signed by 86 states (in South America it was only signed by Argentina, Brazil, Chile, Guyana, Paraguay, Suriname and Uruguay) but has not yet entered into force. CELAC rejected the treaty on the grounds that it was an unbalanced document in favor of the interests of arms exporting states.

The consequences of the high level of small-arms use and holding are severe. According to the Small Arms Survey, armed violence is a defining problem for contemporary Latin America and the Caribbean. Not only do countries in the region show significantly higher homicide rates than countries elsewhere in the world, but many of them also have significantly higher proportions of firearm homicides than the global average of 42 percent. Firearms were used in an average of 60 percent of homicides in South America (Graduate Institute of International and Development Studies, 2012). Also, irresponsible arms transfers can undermine the Millennium Development Goals (MDGs) through the substantial opportunity costs of the resources used. While developing countries may need to import arms to meet legitimate self-defense and security needs, spending beyond those legitimate needs represents a waste of resources that are often crucially needed for social development (Oxfam, 2008).

Islamic Terrorism

With only a residual Muslim population (approximately six million inhabitants), South America has been secluded from the spotlight of Islamic insurgency and terrorism. However, it would be far-fetched to claim that Islamic terrorist groups do not operate in South America. Ungoverned areas primarily in the Amazon regions of Suriname, Guyana, Venezuela, Colombia, Ecuador, Peru, Bolivia, and Brazil, and regions with unregulated businesses with Arab presence such as Iquique (Chile), Maicao (Colombia) or Isla Margarita (Venezuela) present easily exploitable terrain over which to move people and material (Abbott, 2004:4). It is, however, in the Tri-Border Area (TBA) – where Paraguay, Argentina and Brazil converge – that Islamist presence has been speculated (Figure 4.2.). In the early 1970s, when Brazil and Paraguay were seeking to exploit the energy-generating and tourist potential of Iguazu Falls and to promote regional trade, government planners established a free-trade zone in the rapidly growing boomtown city of Ciudad del Este (in Paraguay), thereby allowing Argentines and Brazilians to purchase cheap electronic products there. The TBA, with already more than half a million inhabitants, soon became a risky corner of Argentina, Brazil, and Paraguay. Cross-border transit is easy. Ciudad del Este is connected to Foz do Iguazu by the east-west Bridge of Friendship, while Puerto Iguazu is connected to Foz do Iguazu by the north-south Tancredo Neves International Bridge.

The TBA has one of the most important Arab communities in South America, consisting of a Shi'a majority and a Sunni minority, whose members emigrated from Lebanon, Syria, Egypt, and the Palestinian territories about fifty years ago. Estimates of the size of the Arab community of immigrants in the TBA (mainly in Ciudad del Este and Foz do Iguazu) range from 10,000 to 30,000 (Amaral, 2008:15). It is also in the Brazilian city that is located the Omar Ibn Al-Khattab mosque, the largest outside the Middle East.

In addition to a substantial Arab community with links to their home countries, the TBA has natural advantageous conditions for criminal organizations. It has fluvial communications by way of the Paraná River to the River Plate, Buenos Aires, and Montevideo, as well as the

Atlantic Ocean. In an irony with echoes in NAFTA, Mercosur's success in breaking down economic barriers between neighboring states and multiplying the movement of people and goods across the TBA had also stimulated illicit transborder activities (Pion-Berlin, 2005:217). Apart from the border with Mexico and Colombia, U.S. counterterrorism officials see the TBA as the most potentially threatening area for U.S. interests in the Western Hemisphere (Crandall, 2008:48).

Figure 4.2: The Tri-Border Area

Some U.S. sources claim that Islamic terrorist groups in the area may include Egypt's Al-Gama'a al-Islamiyya (Islamic Group) and Al-Jihad (Islamic Jihad), al-Qaeda, Hamas, Hezbollah, and al-Muqawamah (the Resistance; also spelled al-Moqawama), which is a pro-Iran wing of the Lebanon-based Hezbollah (Hudson, 2003:1,5). This was publicly stated by Francis Taylor, then Coordinator for Counter-Terrorism of the U.S. State Department, when he visited Paraguay at the end of 2001 (Montenegro and Béliveau, 2006:52-53). The same sources indicate that al-Qaeda may have begun to establish a network in the TBA when Osama bin Laden and Khalid Sheikh Mohammed reportedly visited the area in 1995 (Hudson, 2003:2). Hezbollah, on the other hand, reportedly began planting agents and recruiting sympathizers amongst Arab and Muslim immigrants in Latin America much earlier, in the mid-1980s, at the height of the Lebanese civil war. Its cells allegedly began to form in the TBA as a result of Hezbollah proselytizing in the Lebanese communities. It is believed that these terrorist groups have used the TBA for fundraising, drug trafficking, money laundering, plotting, and other criminal activities. Roger Noriega, a former assistant secretary of state for Western Hemisphere affairs (which includes Latin America) and a former U.S. ambassador to the OAS, has also claimed that "Iran is working through its terror proxy Hezbollah to cultivate a network of radicalized operatives in a dozen countries in the region, centered in Venezuela but making significant progress in Brazil and Colombia, among others" (Noriega, 2011).

In 2003, U.S. sources estimated that Islamic fundamentalist groups in the TBA and similar areas in Latin America were sending between U.S.$ 300 and 500 million a year in profits from drug trafficking, arms dealing, and other illegal activities, including money laundering, contraband, and product piracy, to radical Islamic groups in the Middle East (Hudson, 2003:4). In 2010, a cable by the U.S. Consulate in Sao Paulo leaked to the press, claimed that there were about 20.000 Shiite immigrants in the TBA with connections to Hezbollah, some of which received around U.S.$ 50 thousand by the Lebanese organization to set up businesses in the TBA and send back the profits.[12] RAND scholars claim that the TBA is the most important center for financing Islamic terrorism outside the Middle East (Rabasa et. al., 2006:153), and a number of high-profile arrests have vindicated this view. Lebanese nationals Khaled Hussein Ali and Moussa Ali Hamdan were arrested in 2009 and 2010, respectively. The first was regarded by the Brazilian Federal Police's intelligence division as "the global head of the Jihad Media Battalion [who] performed duties for the terrorist group, ranging from propaganda, to logistics, recruitment, and other activities."[13] The latter was accused of manufacturing counterfeit money and documents and trading stolen vehicles and video games in the U.S. He allegedly sent the proceeds of his criminal enterprises back to Lebanon to finance operations for Hezbollah.

Other views, however, contend that the presence of Islamic insurgents in the region is speculative at best. Amaral, one of the leading Brazilian experts on this topic, claims that there is no concrete evidence that would allow us to affirm that terrorist groups are active in the region (Amaral, 2010. See also Aravena, 2005:210). Argentinean researchers have also monitored in detail the news coverage of the TBA and concluded that associations between the triangle and terrorism and between Arabs and terrorism (which populates most of the news about the TBA) is repetitive, it has seldom been questioned, and is embedded in the mainstream narrative about the war on terror (Montenegro and

Béliveau, 2006). Even if the Group 3+1 on Security in the Tri-Border Area, composed of Argentina, Brazil, Paraguay, and the U.S., formed in the early 1990s (the U.S joined in 2002), has acknowledged that the TBA is a sensitive area that needs to be regularly monitored, terrorist presence in the region has not been traced in a way that would leave no doubt. No clear presence does not necessarily mean no presence at all. In fact, a 2009 cable from the U.S. Embassy in Brasilia to the U.S. State Department revealed by WikiLeaks stated that although the Brazilian government publicly denies "the possibility that terrorist groups or individuals connected to such groups operate or transit through Brazilian soil and vigorously protest any claims made by US authorities to that effect," in private it is concerned about terrorist activities in its territory and it cooperates with the United States on antiterrorism.[14] In fact, in 2012, a disclosed 1999 report produced by the Presidency of the Republic revealed that the country suspected of the existence of terrorist activities in the TBA and feared that Osama bin Laden could strike in Brazilian territory.[15] At the official level, however, the discourse is quite different. In December 2002, Argentina, Brazil, Paraguay, and the United States agreed that, "no concrete, detailed tactical information . . . support[s] the theory that there are terrorist sleeper cells or al-Qaeda operatives in the TBA"[16] and in 2006 the governments of Argentina, Brazil, and Paraguay officially declared that "there is no evidence of occurrence in that region [TBA] of activities linked to terrorism or its funding" (Ministério das Relações Exteriores, 2007:309). For that reason, several International Relations scholars have shied away from employing resolute words to describe terrorist activities in the triangle, preferring terms such as "strong suspicion" (Harmon, 2000:90), or "allegedly" (DeRouen Jr. and Heo, 2005:81).

Although there is no good intelligence confirming that al-Qaeda or any other terrorist organization maintains permanent cells in the region, Argentinean intelligence believes that Islamic terrorists have used the TBA as a temporary base for carrying out two major terrorist attacks in Buenos Aires in the early 1990s – one against the Israeli Embassy in March 1992, and the other against the Argentine-Jewish Mutual Association (AMIA) in July 1994. These attacks killed some 117 people and injured hundreds more. Presently, criminal activities should be confined to the presence of facilitators that participate in fundraising and logistical support activities such as money laundering, document forgery, and illicit trafficking. But even if TBA groups have no terrorist operational capacity, criminal activities in the region are likely to continue as long as the social and political context remains the same. Corruption is endemic within the police and criminal justice systems, and the training, equipment, funding, and law-enforcement techniques are poor. These organizations also feed on the limited supervisory capabilities of the countries in the area and the difficulty in coordinating activities between them (Shai, 2004:56).

Environmental Threats

As the Brundtland Commission Report alerted, "Few threats to peace and survival of the human community are greater than those posed by the prospects of cumulative and irreversible degradation of the biosphere on which human life depends" (Bruntland, 1987). This applies to the South American context where environmental threats, defined as unsustainable environmental problems caused either by human activities or by natural disasters, affect the security and welfare of individuals. In the Mercosur foundational treaty of 1991, for instance, member states declared that regional integration "must be achieved by making optimum use of available resources, preserving the environment . . . " (Preamble), whereas through CELAC's Cancún Declaration of 2010, member states pledged to "act jointly in the construction of a international cooperation strategy to strengthen the relationship between the environment and development . . . stimulating actions that protect and enhance the natural heritage of the region" (Art. 54).

Although both documents have been treated as declaratory remarks, it is indeed a fact that the people of South America are heavily dependent on the continent's natural resources – from the rangelands at the foothills of the Andes, to the plants and animals of the Amazon rainforest, to the fisheries off the coast of Peru. Hence, the region's ecosystems are particularly vulnerable to the changes in water availability expected with a changing climate. Indeed, the most severe man-made threat to the environment is related to climate change. Higher global temperatures along with more frequent El Niños may bring increased drought, and melting glaciers in the Andes threaten the future water supply of mountain communities. In the region, the impact of climate change is seen for instance in changes in rainfall patterns, increased water levels in rivers in Argentina and Brazil, and the shrinking of glaciers in the extreme southern region of Patagonia and the Andes mountains.

Climate change is associated with deforestation. South America – the land of the five-and-a-half-million-square-kilometer Amazon rainforest – is often iconized as the "lung of the world." For this reason, human activities that may have an impact on the environmental ecosystem are constantly under the attention of the international community. Tropical forests are a unique environmental resource that provide numerous global benefits. Of the world's biomes, they provide the greatest biological diversity of plants and animals. It is estimated that these forests contain at least 50 percent of the world's animal species and almost 75 percent of the world's plant species. Increased deforestation reduces this biodiversity and results in many other negative impacts such as soil erosion, nutrient depletion, flooding, increased levels of greenhouse gases, disturbances in the carbon cycle, and loss of forest products such as pharmaceuticals, timber, and fuel. In regions like the Brazilian Amazon, where the largest portion of the world's tropical forests is located, concern regarding deforestation has arisen because the current rate stays high at approximately 5,000 square kilometers each year. The Atlantic Forest in Brazil is also in peril. It is a unique rainforest that once covered more than a million square kilometers, extending from Recife southward through Rio de Janeiro to Florianópolis and westward into Paraguay. Today, the forest is reduced to less than 5 percent of its original size, and is located mostly in steep mountainous regions. Deforestation comes from coastal development, as well as uncontrolled logging and agriculture and charcoal production. But the highest deforestation rates are seen in Ecuador, which faces strong population pressure, and Argentina, where the expanding agricultural frontier continues to encroach on the country's forests. South American leaders have frequently pledged to protect the environment.

Other human interventions in the South American environment may also have detrimental effects, including the Hidrovía Paraná-Paraguay project that calls for the transformation of the Paraguay-Paraná-Uruguay-La Plata river system into a 3,400-kilometer-long shipping canal. Experts have been warning of the environmental costs of the project since the first drawings were made in the 1980s. Other interventions are also noteworthy. The spiraling foreign demand for soya beans could mean the loss of millions of hectares of forest and savannah in South America, conservationists warn. The area cultivated for soya in countries like Argentina, Bolivia, Brazil, and Paraguay has more than doubled since 1994, contributing to the near disappearance of the Atlantic Forest.

Human threats to the environment can also cause conflict. Environmental deficiencies create conditions that render conflict all the more likely. They can serve to determine the source of conflict, they can act as multipliers that aggravate core causes of conflict, and they can help to shape the nature of conflict. The conflict between Argentina and Uruguay about the construction of pulp mills on the Uruguay River

(Chapter 3) could be viewed through this lens. Argentina was opposed to the construction of the pulp mills primarily on the grounds that they polluted the river, interfering thereby with the ecosystem and the welfare of the local population. In addition, the Guarani Aquifer, a huge underground reservoir that lies under Paraguay, Uruguay, Argentina, and Brazil, covering an area the size of Texas and California combined, is also sparking political bickering between the four countries that share it. The aquifer contains enough fresh water to sustain the world's population for 200 years, and as water shortages are likely to affect us all in the future, the Guarani Aquifer could be a lifeline for millions (Reboratti, 2007:173).

Other threats are caused by natural disasters.[17] Historically, natural hazardous occurrences have had an important impact in the development of the region. Historians now believe that an unusually long and severe drought was a primary cause of the disappearance of the Maya civilization (Hodell, Curtis and Brenner, 1995). According to a study by the Inter-American Development Bank, published in 2000, in the period 1970-1999, there was an average of 32.4 natural disasters per year, which caused a total of 226,000 fatalities (or around 7,500 deaths a year) in Latin America. In addition to causing deaths, homelessness, and injuries, natural disasters have represented an enormous cost for the countries affected and the international community. It was estimated that the annual average cost between 1970 and 1999 ranged between U.S.$ 700 million and 3.3 billion (Charvériat, 2000). Some of the natural disasters are worth mentioning. For instance, in January 2005 between 441 million and 663 million trees were destroyed by a powerful storm in the Amazon, based on a study by Tulane University in New Orleans, which used satellite data, on-site observations and computer models. Earthquakes are also frequent phenomenon. South America is part of the circum-Pacific belt, one of the highest seismic-risk regions in the world, which encircles the Pacific Ocean, affecting the West coasts of North America and South America, Japan, and the Philippines. In February 2010, an earthquake of magnitude 8.8 hit Chile claiming 525 victims. Besides the tragic direct effects of natural disasters, one should also highlight their weight in increasing the risk of civil conflict. Using a comprehensive data set that covers 187 political units and the whole second half of the twentieth century, Nel and Righarts found robust evidence that rapid-onset natural disasters significantly increase the risk of violent civil conflict in the short to medium term (Nel and Righarts: 2008). These events have variously been attributed with halting colonial expansion, fuelling resistance to corrupt or incompetent regimes, the entrenchment of dictatorships, the instigation or escalation of ongoing conflicts and/or insurgencies (including resource-based conflicts), and creating an enabling environment for the cessation of long-running hostilities.

Notes

[1] Declaration of Bridgetown: the Multidimensional Approach to Hemispheric Security (adopted at the fourth plenary session held on 4 June 2002).

[2] In the 1980s, the U.S. government through Ambassador Lewis Tambs, played a role in conferring political status on the drug trade. Indeed, in April 1984, a police squad found an enormous cocaine laboratory in the southwestern jungle region of the country which was allegedly being protected by the FARC. Ambassador Tambs then coined the term *narco-guerrilla*, with the intention of slandering the gruerrilla group, ignoring its character as an insurgent political force (Guizado and Restrepo, 2007:80).

[3] "FARC's Cocaine Sales to Mexico Cartels Prove Too Rich to Subdue" (*Bloomberg*, 20 January 2010).

[4] Secretary General Ban Ki-moon Remarks to Security Council meeting on Drug Trafficking as a Threat to International Peace and Security (8 December 2009).

[5] Remarks to Security Council on impact of transnational organized crime on West Africa and the Sahel (21 February 2012).

[6] Urban criminality is a different phenomenon than urban guerrillas, which normally encompass armed groups that fight military dictatorships by attacking authorities and institutions of power in order to force the creation of a new and revolutionary social and political structure (Marighella, 1974:88-89).

[7] Available at http://esa.un.org/unpd/wup/CD-ROM/Urban-Rural-Population.htm. Visited 12 September, 2013.

[8] World Bank GINI index, accessed on 14 January, 2013.

[9] "Rampant Violence is Latin America's 'Worst Epidemic'" (*The Guardian*, 9 October 2008).

[10] "High Crime Stifles Latin Economies" (*The New York Times*, 17 October 2006).

[11] Online at http://www.prio.no/NISAT. Visited 13 July, 2010.

[12] "Consulado Americano Relaciona Imigrantes Libaneses a Hizbollah" (*Folha de São Paulo*, 30 November 2010).

[13] "Brazil won't acknowledge terrorists, raises global concerns as host of World Cup and Olympics" (*The Washington Post*, 2 September 2011), and "A Rede, o Terror Finca Bases no Brasil" (*Veja*, 3 April 2011). Ali was released after twenty-one days because Brazil does not have antiterror laws.

[14] "Brazil Denied Existence of Islamist Militants, WikiLeaks Cables Show" (*The Guardian*, 5 December 2010).

[15] "Governo FHC Temia Ação Terrorista no País" (*Folha de São Paulo*, 3 July 2012).

[16] J. Cofer Black (2003), Testimony to the Committee on International Relations, Subcommittee on International Terrorism, Nonproliferation, and

Human Rights, U.S. House of Representatives. Washington, D.C., 26 March (Black was the Department of State Coordinator for Counterterrorism). Available at wwwc.house.gov/international_relations/108/blac0326.htm. Visited 15 July 2010.

[17] Defined as temporary events triggered by natural hazards that overwhelm local response capacity and seriously affect the social and economic development of a region (Charvériat, 2000:9).

PART 2

STATE ACTORS

5

Argentina

"La inseguridad es la mayor preocupación" [Insecurity is the top concern] —Headline of Argentine newspaper *La Nacion*, August 2012[1]

The 1980s was a watershed decade for Argentina. The defeat at the Falklands/Malvinas war[2] in 1982 led to the widespread discredit of military adventurism and to a radical loss of political support for the military.[3] It accentuated preexisting divisions between the different services to such a degree that the air force and the navy temporarily abandoned the governing military junta (Trinkunas, 2000:87). Globally, Argentina's national image, already tarnished by human-rights violations during the military regime, suffered further by defeat against Britain. Moreover, the return to democratic rule in 1983 was not necessarily coincident with economic stability and development. Following years of expansion, Argentina faced chronic inflation (mainly in 1989 and 1990), endemic capital flight, persistent internal and external deficits,[4] a stagnating per-capita revenue, a formidable external debt, an oversized and corrupt state apparatus, and a market deformed by protectionism as well as an infinity of abusive regulations (Hufty, 1996:165).

This gloomy scenario was contrary to Argentina's track record since independence. The country's past prosperity (from approximately 1880 to 1942), which had generated expectations of future world-power status; and its geographical isolation, that made it possible to nurture inflated ideas of Argentine development and power, encouraged exaggerated perceptions of Argentina's future that ended up not materializing (Escudé and Fontana, 1998:52). The country possessed also a highly educated labor force, and its large middle class did represent significant potential. Until the 1970s several authors echoed the popular view that Argentina was destined to emerge as a significant middle-range power in global affairs (Milenky, 1978:7). But this detrimental context brought the country back to its senses, both economically and with respect to security and foreign policy. In the 1980s Argentina suffered one of its worst crises.

In December 1983, Raúl Alfonsín (1983-1989) took office as president of Argentina to end almost eight years of military rule. The perception of him as a modern and progressive politician surrounded by young, talented advisers with political experience gained during the recent resistance to the military dictatorship, gave Alfonsín a halo of heroism and boldness. The first step of the new democratic administration was to adjust the country's isolationist and nonaligned foreign policy as traditionally embodied by the nationalist and anti-imperialistic rhetoric of Juan Perón, who was president for three times in the 1940s, 1950s, and 1970s. The reinsertion of Argentina into world affairs was therefore a vital facet of the nation's transition to democracy and its redefinition of itself. Alfonsín advocated the economic integration of the Southern Cone, the consolidation of cooperative relations with Brazil, and the betterment of relations with Chile – solving a territorial dispute and setting the bases for future cooperation.

Moreover, Alfonsín supported a policy focused on strengthening peace and discouraging all types of arms races in the region and opposed any doctrine that subordinated the interests of South America to the strategic objectives of superpower conflicts. In this light he maintained an assertive policy against British interests in the South Atlantic and did not show any interest in forming part of any military Western bloc. Alfonsín also punctuated his government by the defense of democracy in South America as a way to seek external reassurances for support of the process of internal consolidation of democracy, and promoted policies for "regionalizing problems and their solutions" and pushed for Latin America integration (Russell, 1988:75). He was actively involved in the Rio Group, which sought to systematize political coordination among Latin American states. At the same time, he participated in the nonaligned movement – by establishing closer relations with India and Yugoslavia for instance – trying to gather support in its dispute against Great Britain.

Under the tenure of Carlos Saúl Menem (1989-1999), Argentina's foreign policies underwent an even more pronounced transformation. As the military's systematic influence over foreign policy contracted since the democratic process began, "President Menem probably had more freedom to independently form foreign policy than any elected Argentine president since the early 1900s" (Norden and Russell, 2002:50). The country explicitly aligned itself with the West, abandoned the nonaligned movement (in September 1991),[5] and completely changed its voting profile in international fora, adopting a clearly pro-Western policy. In a few years, he reestablished cooperative and indeed friendly relations with Britain, discontinued the Cóndor II medium-range missile project because of political pressure from the United States, ratified the Tlatelolco Treaty for the prohibition of nuclear weapons in Latin America, subscribed to the Non-Proliferation Treaty (NPT), and signed a separate nuclear safeguards agreement with Brazil and the International Atomic Energy Agency (IAEA). Additionally, and despite the doubts of then-Foreign Minister Domingo Cavallo, and Ambassador to the United States Guido Di Tella, Menem, achieved the first successful insertion in world military affairs, intervening in the Gulf War. He decided to send two naval vessels to join the blockade of Iraq – no other Latin American country did as much. Meném also began a struggle against drug trafficking when it was a top priority on the U.S. agenda. At a late stage of Menem's administration Argentine officials even sought tight links with NATO. The shift became even more salient in March 1991 when Argentina voted for a U.S. proposal before the Human Rights Commission to investigate human rights abuses in Cuba. At the regional level, his policies were not as divergent vis-à-vis Alfonsin's. He continued his predecessor's policy of political rapprochement with Chile further advancing in the demarcation of the boundary, and it deepened the process of economic integration with Brazil through the creation of Mercosur (Escudé and Fontana, 1998:54).

These policies were not an attribute of independent power politics; rather, they were a calculated assent to the political needs of the United States. This harmony is not surprising given that some of Menem's closest advisers had close links with the United States. Cavallo and Guido di Tella – perhaps the most influential members of the cabinet in terms of foreign-policy development – both studied in the United States: Cavallo at Harvard and di Tella at MIT (Hufty, 1996:174). Until President Menem took over the presidency in 1989 and ever since 1889 (when the first Pan American Conference was held in Washington[6]) Argentina and the United States had relations that, with few exceptions, were usually stiff. In the nineteenth century, Argentina's place in the world was defined without reference to the United States or even in spite of the United States (Tulchin, 1996:169). Menem, to the contrary, postulated that Argentina's traditional opposition to the U.S. was considered a useless strategy, as well as an undeniable obstacle to reaching economic objectives. The government had the view that the alliance with the nonaligned and developing nations sent out the wrong message to those who controlled international financial flows; and if

Argentina was serious in its desire to develop it would have to make itself more attractive (Mulins, 2006:63). This perspective inspired Minister of Foreign Relations Guido Di Tella to suggest a new kind of bond with the United States: "The new foreign policy is based on the need to end the traditional hostility towards Washington with respect to irrelevant problems which are neither here not there for us in making us shine. We want carnal relations (*relaciones carnales*) with the United States; it interests us because we can extract a benefit" (cited in Norden and Russell, 2002:71). Di Tella later regretted the hyperbole because it distracted attention from the serious purpose of its policy, but it was nonetheless indicative of new posture of Argentina vis-à-vis the United States. When in 1990 George Bush visited Buenos Aires, he was the first U.S. president to do so since 1960.

Menem was replaced by President Fernando de la Rua (1999-2001) but the new administration's foreign policy did not differ in any substantial aspect from the one implemented by his predecessor. The new administration stated its intention to maintain close ties with the United States, particularly advocating the establishment of a hemispheric free trade area and supporting the U.S. positions in relation to Cuba, while emphasizing the country's trustworthiness as a permanent ally of Western powers (Vacs, 2003:304). De la Rua inherited a severe economic crisis that he was not able to mitigate and was forced out of office in the midst of popular unrest and riots that left twenty-three dead.

After the caretaker governments of Adolfo Rodríguez Saá (2001) and Eduardo Duhalde (2002-2003), Argentina returned to political stability with the election of late President Néstor Kirchner (2003-2007) and of his wife Cristina Fernández de Kirchner (2007-2015). Both were to leave an important mark in Argentina's foreign and security policies. As it is often claimed that the 2001 financial crisis was brought about by the neoliberal policies of the Washington Consensus, Argentina's foreign policy was used to seek a more equitable international order. Equitability is often a rhetorical term but in the Argentinean case it specifically meant pursuing alternative partners and markets and striving for the strengthening international law, the promotion of values associated with international peace, democratic forms of government, respect for human rights, a more balanced system of commerce, a better distribution of the benefits of globalization, and a democratization of the decision-making system in international organizations (even if the regime's democratic record was contested at home). Kirchner's policies were, however, difficult to implement in practice and were often superseded by internal political conflict that inevitably spilled over into the foreign-policy realm. Argentina's foreign policy has often been criticized for being erratic. As underlined by Margheritis, "Apparently contradictory and inconsistent foreign policy behavior shaped Argentina's reputation as an erratic and relatively unpredictable international actor – the adjectives going, in fact, from pariah to wayward to unreliable partner" (cited in Malamud, 2011:90). Indeed, on several occasions it seemed that the Kirchner couple political team was primarily concerned with public opinion and with "recovering" Argentina's former status and influence in the region.

This is not a new phenomenon in Argentinean politics. Civilian and military governments alike have utilized issues such as the Beagle Channel dispute, Falkland/Malvinas, and even the soccer World Cup to build popular support and distract attention from internal difficulties (Gordon, 1984:88). Since his inauguration, relations between Britain and Argentina have come under strain as Kirchner has made a point of reasserting Argentina's claim to sovereignty over the islands. This position gained the spotlight in 2010 (under Cristina) when the decision of British oil explorer companies Desire Petroleum and Diamond Drilling to start drilling off the Falklands in February of that year led to a furious response from Argentina. The government stopped all charter flights between the island and the mainland, refused to send scientists to the binational commission that decides fishing licenses, sent fifteen letters of protest to the British Embassy, and used the OAS, the UN, UNASUR, the Ibero-American Summit, the Summit of South American-Arab Countries, and the Latin American and Caribbean Summit on Integration and Development as vehicles to attack Great Britain over its continued control of the islands. Although the Falklands/Malvinas is a hot spot for marine resources and oil reserves, the 2010 crisis was largely driven by Argentinean domestic situation (Malamud, 2011). In the same way that the military regime of Leopoldo Galtieri was undergoing serious economic difficulties when it decided to invade the Falklands/Malvinas in 1982, so was the government of Cristina Kirchner facing a weak economic situation and very low popularity rates in early 2010. In another good example, the audacious threat to disrupt the weekly flight between Chile and the Falklands made by Cristina Kirchner in a speech at the UN in September 2011 was done just one month before the key general election of October 2011 (she was reelected).

The foreign policy of the Kirchner couple also signaled a change in the relations with the United States. The restoration of diplomatic relations with Cuba and the warm relations between Kirchner and Presidents Chávez and Maduro of Venezuela are examples of a shift leftward in the foreign policy of the country. During the Néstor Kirchner administration, Argentina signed more international agreements with Venezuela (sixty-two) than with any other country. After Venezuela, came Chile (forty-one), Bolivia (thirty-nine) and Brazil (twenty-two) (Malamud, 2011:94). When Venezuela made its formal entry into Mercosur in 2006, the move was lauded as "a historic moment" by Argentina's president, Nestor Kirchner.[7] And when the integration was finally granted in 2012 (after Argentina took advantage of the political void generated by Paraguay's temporary suspension of Mercosur to advance Venezuela's interests) it was his wife Cristina who made the formal announcement. In his populist style, Chavez reacted saying that the integration of his country into Mercosur was "a defeat of imperialism and the bourgeoisie."[8]

Contribution to Traditional Security

Argentina has not been the victim of interstate aggression since at least 1865 and it faces no direct and immediate threat to its security from neighboring countries. This is a natural consequence of its rapprochement with Chile and Brazil. The long-standing rivalry with Chile came to an end in 1984 (war almost broke out in 1978[9]) with the issuing of a Joint Declaration of Peace and Friendship (23 January) and the adoption of the Treaty of Peace and Friendship (29 November) between Argentine President Raúl Alfonsín and Chilean President General Augusto Pinochet. The 1984 Treaty solved the historical differences around the Beagle Channel[10] and opened the path to increased levels of cooperation between the two nations in the 1990s. In fact the treaty goes beyond the Beagle dispute since both governments expressed their decision to solve, through strict peaceful means, any additional controversy that might arise between them. It also led to the official establishment in October 1985, of the Binational Commission for Economic Cooperation and Physical Integration between Chile and Argentina.

The search for a prompt solution to the territorial dispute with Chile had to do with Argentine domestic politics. Alfonsín and his Economic Minister Bernardo Grinspun knew that the government's capacity to effect domestic reforms would be conditioned or constrained to a significant degree by specific international problems, such as the Beagle Channel and the Falklands/Malvinas (Tulchin, 1996: 176). The fear that the military might utilize these pending problems of conflicts with neighboring countries to recoup lost areas of influence did factor in various foreign-policy decisions, especially during the first years of the

Raúl Alfonsín's administration (Norden and Russell, 2002:59-60). The stabilization of peace with Chile continued during Menem's regime. In August 1990, Carlos Menem and Patrick Aylwin signed a new protocol committing their governments to complete the task of border demarcation entrusted to the old Mixed Commission of 1941. As a result, within one year, twenty-two out of the twenty-four pending border issues were resolved by technical teams, and in August 1991 both presidents met again to sign the agreement confirming these resolutions. The last two disputes (Laguna del Desierto and Campos de Hielo Sur/Hielo continental patagónico) were resolved in 1994 and 1998.

Once the conflicts were mitigated cooperation between both countries escalated. Possessing one of the world's longest common borders, bilateral trade grew exponentially, and sizeable Chilean investments have been made in Argentina. Contracts were also signed on gas interconnection and natural gas supply, and cooperation improved in connection with mining, electric energy, and terrestrial, maritime, and air transport.

A similar process unfolded with Brazil. Until 1979 relations with Brazil, which included a nuclear race, were very tense. A concrete example of Argentine-Brazilian rivalry was their decision to reject the Non-Proliferation Treaty (NPT) on the grounds of its discriminatory nature as it ensured that the number of nuclear states did not increase. They also refused to fully adhere to the Treaty for the Prohibition of Nuclear Weapons in Latin America and the Caribbean (Tlatelolco Treaty), as it required them to renounce the right to carry out peaceful nuclear explosions and involved inspections of nondeclared facilities (Oelsner, 2005: 144–161). Another example was the competition to develop the hydroelectric potential of the Paraná River. Each nation sought to exploit the Paraná through a joint project with Paraguay: Brazil aimed at building a large hydroelectric installation at Itaipu and Argentina at Corpus. Revealing its growing diplomatic prowess and power, Brazil offered Paraguay numerous inducements and stalled Argentina with a technical debate on international law while bringing construction at Itaipu to the point of no return (Gordon, 1984:90). The dispute was resolved only with the adoption of the tripartite Treaty of Itaipú-Corpus in 1979 (see Table 2.3.). Two days after signing the Agreement, the Argentine foreign ministry released a communiqué describing the accord as "excellent, from the energy viewpoint as well as from the political. The excellence of the agreement stems from the normalization and improvement of Argentine relations with Brazil and Paraguay" (cited in Russell, 1988:74).

In the 1980s it began to appear in diplomatic and military circles in Argentina that continuous competition with Brazil would place the country in the irreversible situation of being losers (Russell, 1988:73-74), and thus Argentinean leaders sought greater accord with its northern neighbor. In 1980, the two countries exchanged presidential visits and signed a variety of agreements on trade and technical cooperation, including the sale of 240 tons of fuel for Brazil's nuclear power program. Brazilian exports to Argentina, encouraged by the military free trade policies, grew from U.S.$ 331 million in 1976 to U.S.$ 1,091 million in 1980. Brazil also provided correct, if not enthusiastic, support to Argentina during the Falklands/Malvinas war (Gordon, 1984:90). In the same decade, Argentina and Brazil implemented a number of agreements for the peaceful use of nuclear energy. These led to the creation of a bilateral system of accountability and control, to reciprocal inspections of their nuclear programs, and to the inception of a bilateral agency (ABACC) dedicated to the administration of this system. Alfonsín's Undersecretary of Foreign Relations Jorge Sabato also conducted secret negotiations in Brazil that led to President José Sarney's visit (accompanied by Alfonsín) to Argentina's nuclear facilities in July 1987, including the top-secret nuclear plant in Pilcaniyeu in Patagonia. The Argentine ministry of foreign affairs characterized the visit as a "maximum demonstration of mutual confidence between the two countries" (Russell, 1988:80) (see Table 2.3.).

Menem's administration was also centered on the implementation of a neoliberal economic program, which included privatization, currency convertibility, and economic stability. Building on Alfonsín's foundations and interest in boosting economic stability with its neighbor, Menem called on José Sarney to sign a joint declaration of their Common Nuclear Policy at Iguazu Falls in November 1990, in which both nations committed themselves to confine nuclear energy to peaceful uses, to adhere jointly to the Treaty of Tlatelolco, and to submit jointly to the International Atomic Energy Commission for verification of their peaceful use of atomic energy. The process of nuclear rapprochment and increased transparency reached its culmination with the signature of a quadrilateral-safeguards agreement with the IAEA, in force since March 1994. And in October 1996, for the first time in modern history, the armies of Argentina and Brazil undertook a joint exercise in the Argentine province of Corrientes ("Operação Cruzeiro do Sul"). Although Argentina's influence and prestige have been directly challenged by Brazil's often subtle but powerful effective economic and political expansion, the bilateral relations between both countries have never been better. As the Argentinean Ambassador to Brazil said in a talk to Brazilian diplomats in June 1997, "in one word: there is no chance of conflict [between Argentina and Brazil]."[11]

The resolution of the bilateral dispute does not mean, however, that psychological perceptions have been eradicated. Some argue in Brazil that Argentina still does not accept fully the economic growth of Brazil and is therefore not willing to wave on Brazil's growth for its own national advantage.[12] If in the 1960s Argentina's GDP was larger than Brazil's, nowadays the GDP of the state of São Paulo alone outshines Argentina's. Moreover, Argentina contests any claim by Brazil for a permanent Security Council seat proposing instead a system of rotation among medium-sized states to be selected according to specific criteria. Often, Argentinean leaders have coined Brazil's UN claim as "elitist and little democratic."[13] It is symptomatic that President Nestor Kirchner left abruptly the inaugural South American-Arab Summit, which was held in Brasília in May 2005, standing up President Lula for a scheduled dinner and leaving a trail of recriminations in his wake. Kirchner criticized the politicized nature of the Summit, complained off the record that the gathering had become a platform for Brazil to advance its own interests worldwide, and recriminated Brazil's decision not to assist Argentina in its negotiations with the IMF (Lula announced his decision during the Summit). Kirchner's reluctance with Brazil is well incorporated in his own words: "Hay un lugar en la OMC, Brasil lo quiere; hay un lugar en la ONU, Brasil lo quiere; hay un lugar en la FAO, Brasil lo quiere. Si hasta quisieron poner al Papa"[14] (if there is a vacancy at the WTO, Brazil wants it; if there is a vacancy at the UN, Brazil wants it; if there is a vacancy at the FAO, Brazil wants it. They have even wished to choose the Pope). In a similar fashion, Malamud argues that "any time Brazil hints at affirming itself as either a regional leader or a global power, Argentine foreign policy moves closer to the United States – or other more circumstantial allies such as, more recently, Venezuela – in order to restore the regional balance (Malamud, 2011:92). Despite these bumps, Argentina's government has recently acknowledged that the bilateral relation stands "at the highest point in our history"[15] and the country's foreign policy has given special emphasis in "deepening the strategic alliance with Brazil in all its aspects."[16]

The easing of tensions between Argentina and Brazil paved the way to key multilateral activities between the Southern Cone countries. The most obvious of which are the regular military exercises they conduct. They are designed to promote transparency, understanding, trust, and shared democratic values. They have been an important initial step in building security cooperation. Among the most important joint-aerial, combat-training exercises are Cruzex (since 1996), which is hosted by the Brazilian Air Force; Salitre (since 2004), hosted by the Chilean Air Force; and Ceibo (since 2005), hosted by the Argentine Air Force. As leaders started to believe that their countries' economic fates were inextricably intertwined, they insisted that their armed forces behave in ways that support peaceful coexistence. Moreover, since the early 1990s the three countries have jointly promoted a series of reforms to the Tlatelolco Treaty for the Prohibition of Nuclear Weapons in Latin America in order to update it and to put it in force in the entire region. These amendments were approved and signed by the member states in Mexico City in August 1992 and were later ratified by the legislatures of the three countries. In the field of chemical and bacteriological weapons, Argentina, Brazil, and Chile signed the Declaration of Mendoza in September 1991, which was subsequently implemented by Bolivia, Ecuador, Paraguay, and Uruguay.

Argentina has also tried to conciliate relations with Bolivia. The relationship reached a high point with the November 1987 signing of the Act of Buenos Aires, which established a permanent system of bilateral consultation, thus institutionalizing a high-level political dialogue do deal with bilateral, regional, or global matters. At the same time, after a long negotiating process, the countries signed a Memorandum of Understanding, which provided for an overall solution to the issue of Bolivian gas imported by Argentina and the refinancing of the bilateral debt (Russell, 1988:78). An additional agreement was signed in 2006 (updated in 2010) to build a new 1,465-kilometer (910-mile) pipeline (the Gas Pipeline of Northeastern Argentina) between the two countries to facilitate gas supplies. The pipeline will cost U.S.$ 6.1 billion and benefit approximately 3.4 million people. In 2011, the presidents of both countries inaugurated the Juana Azurduy Integration Gas Pipeline, at a cost of U.S.$ 43.2 million. The pipeline stretches 48 kilometers (30 miles) from the Margarita gas field in Bolivia to the Refinor refinery in Campo Duran, Argentina, where it will link up in the future with the Gas Pipeline of Northeastern Argentina. The pipeline was named for a heroine of South America's war of independence in the nineteenth century. For Bolivia, which has South America's second-largest gas reserves after Venezuela, the Argentine market provides a welcome alternative to dependence on Brazil.

As to Uruguay, in addition to the fluid bilateral policies implemented when democracy was reestablished in both countries, the so-called Colonia Agreements (May 1985), created an Argentine-Uruguayan ministerial council for coordination and consultation, with the goal of promoting economic and social integration between the two countries (Russell, 1988:78). But relations grew tense in 2005 between them over the construction of one of the world's largest pulp mills on the Uruguayan side of a border river, lying some 30 km from the Argentinean city of Gualeguaychú, a popular tourist resort.[17] As we saw in Chapter 3, Argentina lodged a complaint before the ICJ in 2006 on the grounds that the mill polluted the river.[18] The fact that the Kirchner administration had done nothing to treat the highly polluted river that surrounds Buenos Aires, on whose shores millions of people live, speaks to the authentic reasons behind the official position: not to alienate potential voters or provoke demonstrations (Malamud, 2011:93). In the ruling issued in April 2010, the ICJ said that Uruguay had breached its procedural obligations to inform Argentina of its plans, but had not violated its environmental obligations under the treaty, and therefore the mill could continue operations. In November that year the foreign ministers of both countries signed an accord setting out how the plant and the river would be environmentally monitored putting an end to the five-year dispute. Argentine Foreign Minister Hector Timerman tweeted that "both governments are very satisfied."[19] Uruguayan President José Mujica also underlined that one of the country's largest revenues comes from tourism, and 80 percent of the tourists in Uruguay are from Argentina.[20] Despite the handshake, some hawkish statements are still heard in both margins of the River Plate.

Starting with the Menem government, Argentina has also pursued the normalization of relations with the United Kingdom. For Menem, the dispute was seen as one of the main impediments for his project of putting in practice a liberal strategy of economic growth, as it hindered the establishment of closer relations with the United States and the European countries (Vacs, 2003:299). During his administration Argentina initiated a serious of unilateral concessions, lifting trade restrictions and special measures against British enterprises, disbanding the commission in charge of the surveillance of British property, offering consular exchange and diplomatic normalization, and seeking an agreement in fishing rights around the Falklands (Hufty, 1996:175). Moreover, a system of bilateral military consultations has been operating since 1993, which holds two yearly meetings and which includes not only military officers but also civilian officials from both the defense and foreign ministries (Escudé and Fontana, 1998:62). Despite the warm-up in bilateral relations, the Falklands/Malvinas is still a sensitive issue in Argentina. The enactment in 1994 of a constitutional clause whereby the recovery of Falklands/Malvinas (through "peaceful means") is a mandatory policy for any Argentine government has not made the solution of this problem any easier. And as we saw earlier,

Argentina hardly misses an opportunity to regionalize what has always been a bilateral dispute (using Mercosur, UNASUR, CELAC, and so on) and often puts pressure on the United Kingdom to negotiate sovereignty.

Despite the ups and downs of its relation with Britain, Argentina has shown over the last two decades a proclivity to adopt policies in the field of nonproliferation. First, as we saw, it deactivated the Cóndor II missile. And second, it became a member of the Missile Technology Control Regime (MTCR), the Group of Six for Peace and Disarmament (with India, Mexico, Tanzania, Greece, and Sweden), the Australian Group, and the Group of Nuclear Exporters. The sum of these commitments, plus Tlatelolco and NPT, subject Argentina to the strictest nonproliferation constraints accepted by members of the international community (Escudé and Fontana, 1998:57).

Beyond its activities at the bilateral level, Argentina has also intervened to mediate disputes between South America's states. In 2009, Bolivia and Paraguay formally sealed the end to the Chaco conflict, considered the bloodiest of the last century in South America with more than 100,000 killed. In its role as committee president of guarantor countries of the 1938 Peace, Friendship and Limits Treaty, Argentina hosted the meeting and presented the Final Memory with the definitive and accepted international limits between the neighboring countries. The other members of the committee were Brazil, Chile, the United States, Peru and Uruguay. "This is a historic day for Bolivia and Paraguay, a time of peace and friendship, of solidarity among peoples," said President Morales during the ceremony. "The war between Paraguay and Bolivia was not triggered by its peoples but by the transnational corporations after our natural resources," he added, thanking Argentina for its mediation and task with the experts from the limits' committee.[21]

But Argentina's contribution to security in the post-Cold War era does not stop at the bilateral and regional levels. One of the salient features of Argentina's foreign and security policy – and an element in the redefinition of the mission of its armed forces after the military regime – is an emphasis on participation in United Nations peacekeeping missions around the world. Argentina increased its peacekeeping contribution from thirty peacekeepers in 1989; to 969 in 1992; and to almost three thousand in 1995. This is a one- hundred-fold increase in less than six years (Velázquez, 2010:180-181). Indeed, with Menem, Argentina became a pioneer in intense Latin American presence and participation in peacekeeping operations. Peacekeeping engagement was an explicitly designed strategy by Argentine decision makers to "bring Argentina from a very low level of agreement with the United

States, superior only to Cuba in Latin America, to a very high level of correspondence." (Norden, 1995: 339).

Peacekeeping brings several benefits. First, it keeps large numbers of Argentinean officers employed in a constructive fashion, helping to consolidate democracy through the gradual transformation of the role of the Argentine armed forces, which ever since the collapse of the last military dictatorship have suffered from a sort of existential crisis (Escudé and Fontana, 1998:56-57). The democratization process left the military without a role to perform, and the government had few economic incentives to offer (Velazquez, 2010:179). And second it helps to build for Argentina, step by step, a new reputation as a team player committed to multilateral efforts to keep the peace. As of October 2013, Argentina was the third-largest troop contributor in the Americas with 877 police and troops at UN service in the Western Sahara, Liberia, Sudan, Côte d'Ivoire, the Middle East, and more expressively in Haiti and Cyprus (the first is Uruguay with 2,183 people, followed by Brazil with 1,706). In addition, in 1995 Argentina established the Argentine Peacekeeping Academy (CAECOPAZ) offering peacekeeping courses and training for both its own national troops and those of foreign countries. It is revealing to note, moreover, that Argentina is the third country worldwide elected more times to the UN Security Council, as a nonpermanent member (after Brazil and Japan).[22]

Argentina has also been a staunch advocate of a regional security system. The effort began in April 1997, when Presidents Carlos Menem of Argentina and Fernando Henrique Cardoso of Brazil signed an accord creating a Permanent Mechanism of Consultation and Coordination on Defense and Security Affairs, designed to discuss a common defense system for the Mercosur region. Boasting that these first steps constituted the "cornerstone in the construction of a cooperative defense mechanism" that would lead to a system stretching from the "Amazon to Antarctica," the Argentine ambassador to Brazil said that it would include joint strategies, doctrines, operations, and arms purchases. In August 1998, a top-ranking army official said that Argentina wanted a small NATO for Mercosur and was awaiting support for this idea, first from Brazil and then from other member states (Pion-Berlin, 2000:50).

This initiative never materialized, but Argentina has remained a strong supporter of the cooperation between the UN and regional organizations in the field of peace and security, as recognized in Chapter VIII of the UN Charter and numerous resolutions of the General Assembly and the Security Council. In many ways, the United Nations and regional organizations have unique and complementary capacities that, when properly coordinated, can contribute decisively to the prevention and management of armed conflict. Argentina supported the ressurrection of this cooperation brought about by the adoption of Boutros Boutros-Ghali Agenda for Peace[23] in 1992. Moreover, Argentina has had an active role in the initiatives tending to update the structure and functions of the OAS in everything pertaining to security. It has been one of the strongest proponents of making the OAS an effective organization, even despite the oscillations in the institutional performance of the organization. At the outset, making something out of the OAS was intended principally as part of the policy of pleasing the United States, "because it was in hemispheric affairs that the Cold War emphasis on democracy and human rights seemed to have its greatest possibilities" (Tulchin, 1996:188). But over time the OAS card began to take on a form and meaning of its own. The Menem government played a leading role in giving greater teeth to the OAS's charter commitment to democracy and has supported the use of coercion to restore democratic regimes. It has also semiofficially floated ideas for developing a doctrine of "cooperative security" in the region, involving more active conflict prevention and the creation of multinational forces for the maintenance and restoration of peace (Hurrell, 1995:276). That being so, when a cloud of suspicion fell over the 2000 presidential election in Peru, Argentina (along with Canada and the United States) felt eager to avert another crisis of credibility for the OAS and played an important role in mustering resources for the successful OAS mission (Cooper and Legler, 2001).

Contribution to Human Security

Over the last three decades, Argentina has been affected by leftist terrorism, state terrorism, and Islamic terrorism. In 1992, the country was the site of the single-most- destructive terrorist act in South America. As we saw in Chapter 4, a car bomb virtually destroyed the Israeli Embassy in Buenos Aires, killing twenty-nine people and injuring 242. The Islamic Jihad organization, an arm of the Lebanese Hezbollah, took responsibility for the attack, claiming it was in retaliation for the Israeli attack that killed Hezbollah leader Sheikh Musawi that year. The second attack in 1994 targeted the Jewish Community Center building (AMIA) in Buenos Aires, and killed eighty-seven people and injured 151. The bombing focused attention on Hezbollah activity in Latin America, where communities of recent Shiite Muslim emigrants in the remote border areas of Argentina, Brazil, and Paraguay could provide cover for international terrorists (see Chapter 4). In 2013, the Argentinean special prosecutor investigating the bombing issued an updated report showing further evidences that Iran had set up intelligence stations in different parts of Latin America with the aim of carrying out terrorist attacks.

Following these attacks, national, regional, and local institutions responsible for emergency response in Argentina sought to improve their planning and preparedness for terrorism-related events. In 1996, the national government enacted legislation, which launched the *Sistema Federal de Emergencias* (SIFEM) (Federal Emergency System) under the direction of the president. Since 1997, several of Argentina's major cities have developed emergency plans for terrorism-related events, including intentional biological and chemical releases (Muro et.al. 2003). Cooperation with the U.S. also intensified. In 2011, the U.S. State Department described the cooperation in this way:

> "Argentina and the United States cooperated well in analyzing possible terrorist threat information. Argentina continued to focus on the challenges of policing its remote northern and northeastern borders – including the Tri-Border Area (TBA), where Argentina, Brazil, and Paraguay meet – against threats including drug and human trafficking, contraband smuggling, and other international crime" (U.S. Department of State, 2011).

At the international level, Argentina cooperates closely in all significant international counterterrorism efforts within the United Nations and the Organization of American States, ,where it was vice-chair of the Inter-American Committee Against Terrorism (the United States was chair). The Argentine Government was instrumental in promoting improved coordination with its neighbors (Brazil, Paraguay, Uruguay, Bolivia, and Chile) in strengthening security and countering terrorist-support networks in the region. Argentina is member of the 3+1 Group on Tri-Border Area Security (other members are Brazil, Paraguay, and the United States) to improve the capabilities of the three to address cross-border crime and thwart money laundering and terrorist financing activities.

Beyond terrorism, another nontraditional threat is drug trafficking. Recent decades have seen an increase in the consumption of narcotic and psychotropic substances in the country, and in recent years laboratories for the production of cocaine, though not on the scale of those in Colombia, Peru, or Bolivia, have begun to appear (UNODC, 2010:264). The highest prevalence of cocaine use in South America was reported from Argentina (2.6 percent), followed by Chile (2.4 percent), and Uruguay (1.4 percent). The annual prevalence of cocaine use in

Argentina and Chile are comparable to the United States' use. Brazil and Argentina constitute the biggest cocaine markets in South America in terms of absolute numbers (more than 900,000 and 600,000 users, respectively) (UNODC, 2011:91).

Argentina's criminal laws in relation to these substances have been evolving since 1924, but since the 1970s their repressive aspects have been accentuated. The growing persecution that has resulted from this legislation has come down especially hard on users and small-scale players in the trafficking business, in particular women and foreigners – groups that are overrepresented in the population of persons imprisoned for such offenses Transnational Institute, 2010). Within the international drugs market, Argentina is a "trans-shipment" country for cocaine. Cocaine seizures in the country rose steadily from 1.6 mt in 2002 to 12.1 mt in 2008, and in 2009 increased to 12.6 mt. Trafficking of cocaine from Argentina to Chile was reported by both countries in 2009; Argentina also assessed that, in 2009, some of the cocaine trafficked on its territory was intended for Europe, apart from Argentina itself (UNODC, 2011:110).

Conclusions

Argentina's foreign policy is epitomized by its discontinuities and by its selected activism. Unlike the external affairs of neighboring Brazil and Chile, which are more prone to institutional and programmatic conservatism, Argentina foreign affairs have been more susceptible to regime directives and domestic priorities. A good case study of this is Menem's explicit commitment to accepting U.S. leadership. It was a move almost without precedent. The importance of Argentina's engagement in world affairs has also been amplified by a tradition of activism in world affairs and its desire to achieve a level of prestige that has been somehow out of line with its relative power (Mullins, 2006:47).

The consciousness of its limited power associated with the need to foster economic growth were the ingredients that led to the pacification of its relations with Brazil and Chile in the 1980s and 1990s. The reconciliation between Brazil and Argentina has been the most profound change in not only Argentine policy but also in the inter-tate relations in the Southern Cone. Although there remains some unease about the preponderance of power on the Brazilian side – for instance Argentina has consistently opposed one of Brazil's most cherished foreign policy goals: to obtain a permanent seat in the UN Security Council – it is fair to say that the relationship is cordial and stable. The stabilization of the relations with the Southern Cone neighbors was the most palpable contribution of Argentina to regional security since the end of the Cold War.

But as Argentina's recent governments have often employed the wild card to generate domestic gains and electoral support, the country has also engaged in strident conflicts with Uruguay (over a pulp mill) and the United Kingdom (over Falkland/Malvinas). During Menem's government, the Falkland/Malvinas question was subordinated to the policy of reestablishing the pro-Western credentials of Argentina; but since his inauguration, Néstor Kirchner has made a point of reasserting Argentina's claim to sovereignty over the islands. Other initiatives that grant quick prestige have also been favored by Argentina such as the mediation that put an end to the Chaco War, the contribution to UN peacekeeping, or the polite participation in counter-terrorism or anti-drug-trafficking efforts. But these positive inputs are neither durable nor sustainable as Argentina's foreign policy is generally personalist and pragmatic.

Notes

[1] "La inseguridad es la mayor preocupación" (*La Nacion*, 5 August 2012).

[2] The territorial dispute has its origins in the late eighteenth century when England, France, and Spain almost went to war over the islands. Spain occupied the area in 1774, and the newly independent government of Argentina formally claimed sovereignty in 1820. Argentina maintained control of the islands until 1831 when a warship from the United States removed the Argentineans and set the stage for England to take control in 1833. Since 1833, the dispute has been a constant theme in Argentina's foreign relations.

[3] In planning the invasion, the military had expected that Great Britain and its allies would react with diplomatic protests but ultimately accept the occupation of the islands as a fait accompli. However, it rapidly became apparent that this was a complete miscalculation.

[4] The international debt of Argentina rose from U.S.\$5.5 billion in 1971 to U.S.\$35 billion in 1981 to U.S.\$63.7 billion in 1991. It had to allocate as much as 50 percent of its export revenues to cover the interest of its international debt in 1985-1986. Argentina's GDP growth rate fell from a yearly average of 2.6 percent between 1970 and 1979 to −1.5 percent between 1980 and 1989 (Hufty, 1996:160-161).

[5] As it withdrew from the movement, Argentina denounced the fact that its proposals supporting freedom of the press, respect for human rights, and democratization had been rejected in the Ghana meeting.

[6] The position of defiance toward the United States that Roque Saenz Peña and Manuel Quintana took at the first Pan-American Conference in Washington in 1888-1889 was a coherent expression of the Argentine role in world affairs at the time.

⁷ Later, Venezuela's entry was approved by the parliaments of Argentina and Uruguay, and finally Brazil in 2009. But opposition from Paraguay, which controlled the Senate, prevented its acceptance.

⁸ "Sem o Paraguai, Mercosul Admite Venezuela como Membro Pleno" (*Estado de Sao Paulo*, 29 June 2012).

⁹ Argentina even finalized a war plan, which received the code name Operácion Soberanía (Operation Sovereignty) to be launched on 21 and 22 December 1978. It involved the military occupation of two islands, Nueva and Hornos.

¹⁰ The Beagle Channel dispute focused on three small islands, Picton, Nueva, and Lennox, which lie at the southern tip of the continent. Though the area has been occupied by Chile since the late 1800s, Argentina, citing international law and numerous treaties, claimed the territory as its own.

¹¹ Available online in http://www.embarg.org.br/DisRBgue.html. Visited 20 December, 2010.

¹² "Ser ou Não Ser" by Rubens Barbosa (*O Estado de São Paulo*, 22 December 2009).

¹³ "Nuevo Roce con Brasil por el Consejo de Seguridad de las Naciones Unidas" (*Diário los Andes*, 28 May 2005).

¹⁴ "Desde Washington: ¿Alguien quiere poner a pelear a Brasil y Argentina?" (*El Clarin*, 2 May 2005).

¹⁵ "No journalistic speculation can tarnish the strategic relation between Argentina and Brazil" (*Telam*, 24 November 2010).

¹⁶ See http://www.mrecic.gov.ar/portal/seree/home.html. Visited 14 January 2012.

¹⁷ The pulp mill, which opened in 2007, is located in the Uruguayan town of Fray Bentos on the banks of the River Uruguay, which forms the border between the two South American nations.

¹⁸ Environmentalists in both Argentina and Uruguay maintained that the mills would release dangerous substances like organochlorines, sulphur dioxide, nitrogen and phosphorous.

¹⁹ "Argentina and Uruguay Settle Seven-Year Pulp Mill Row" (*BBC News*, 16 November 2010).

²⁰ "Um Socialista Atípico" interview to José Mujica (*Veja*, 29 September, 2010).

²¹ "Bolivia and Paraguay seal peace and limits 74 years after the Chaco war" (*Mercopress*, 28 April, 2009).

²² Argentina was elected eight times: 1948 – 1949, 1959 – 1960, 1966 – 1967, 1971 – 1972, 1987 – 1988, 1994 – 1995, 1999 – 2000, and 2005 – 2006. See http://www.un.org/sc/list_eng5.asp. Visited 16 April 2011.

²³ It "[R]ecognizes that regional organizations, arrangements and agencies can, in their fields of competence and in accordance with the Charter of the United Nations, make important contributions to the maintenance of international peace and security, preventive diplomacy, peacemaking, peacekeeping, and postconflict peacebuilding (art.VI-1); and it "encourages regional organizations, arrangements and agencies to consider, as appropriate, in their fields of competence, ways and means for promoting closer cooperation and coordination with the United Nations with the objective of contributing to the fulfilment of the purposes and principles of" (art.VI-2)

6

Brazil

"We are a great country, with traditions of growth and a long history of participation, very often as a protagonist, in the construction of international and regional relations . . . We are a 'global trader' and a 'global player.'" —Luiz Felipe Lampreia, Minister of External Affairs of Brazil (1995-2001)

"Diplomacy is not advertising." —Antonia Patriota, Minister of External Affairs of Brazil (2011-2013)

Foreign policy analysts and policymakers have been fascinated by Brazil's potential for more than two decades, and the country is always included in any debate about "emerging markets" or "pivotal states" (Bond, 1981:153; Núñez, 2002:20). Once the problems that characterized the country in the 1980s – continued high inflation, shrinking in the GDP, inability to manage its foreign debt, underemployment, and a rise in the concentration of wealth – were tamed, it became conventional to argue that Brazilian power and central continental position could afford to influence, if not dictate, outcomes to most conflicts as well as to most integrationist attempts in South America. In fact, since colonial times Brazil has pursued *grandeza* (greatness), a quest for world power recognition (Kelly, 1988:116; van Klaveren, 1996:48; Saraiva, 2011:55), and its elite seems to nourish a belief that the country was fated to have its own independent destiny, although not in an impositional sense (de Lima, 1996:140; de Souza, 2002:19-21). As a top Brazilian diplomat recalled, "if we were to list the countries with the largest territories, countries with the largest population, and the top ten GDP countries, only three would be included in the three lists, United States, China and Brazil" (Guimarães, 2010:14). It is therefore not surprising that Brazil has systematically claimed a permanent seat in the Security Council and that its pretensions have been backed by other powers such as Russia, United Kingdom,[1] and France.[2]

Brazil leads other continental states in land and population size and in most areas of industry, technology, transportation, natural resources, and military power projections. It dominates South America as the largest country and it is more than twice as large as the second largest country – Argentina. It also leads South America demographically, with more than 200 million people, thus making it the second most populated country in the Americas, after the United States. It is also the regional powerhouse – it is the seventh largest economy in the world, far outpacing Argentina (ranked twenty-six), and larger than NAFTA member Mexico (ranked fourteenth).[3] Its dominance is also perceptible at the military level. It possesses the largest active duty military force in South America – second in the Americas behind the United States – with 300,000 personnel in uniform. Brazil's military has transformed from a strictly conventional force into a versatile force that has garnered much peacekeeping experience over the last decade, thus gaining even more respect from other militaries in the region (Núñez, 2002:21). Finally, it is important to note that it holds mastery over the Amazon basin and shares control over the La Plata watershed. As the strongest military and economic power in the area, Brazil is not only the primary designer and enforcer of continental "rules of the game," but also the guarantor of territorial integrity and opposer of serious conflict within or among the region's states. As the Foreign Minister of Uruguay, Luis Almagro, said once to a local newspaper, "el mundo a nosotros, sin Brasil, no se nos abre, se nos cierra" ("without Brazil the world closes off on us, it doesn't open up").[4] Hence Brazil has the ability to obtain what it wants through co-option and attraction – the basic definition of soft power.

The geographical location of Brazil, surrounded by ten non-Portuguese-speaking and historically hostile neighbors could lead to a perception of encirclement. Yet, Brazilian security never was seriously threatened by this enclosure, potential adversaries being "too weak, divided, or isolated" (Kelly, 1988:115). Today, whether because of its broad geographical features, its physical detachment from the major points of friction in international politics, or its traditionally peaceful relations with its neighbors, "there is no concrete evidence that Brazil suffers any clear or present foreign threat to its national security" (da Costa, 2001:98).

There is however a flip side of the coin. As noted by Roett, "it is difficult to imagine that a nation-state that fails to address the basic welfare needs of its population will be able to play a significant role on the world scene" (Roett, 2003:189). Brazil suffers from severe socioeconomic inequalities — a legacy inherited from the country's colonial past when the Portuguese created a tiny land-owning elite that relied heavily on the African slave trade for labor to compete with the Spanish powerhouses of Mexico and Peru. This socioeconomic divide manifests itself in a number of ugly ways, from deep corruption to violent crime. It can also be seen in the stark difference in political culture between the country's socialist-leaning north and capitalist-leaning south. Whereas the north needs the state to survive, the south largely views the state as a hindrance to its growth. In this vein, Brazil will always have difficulties in asserting itself globally as long as it's unable to stem the growing violence erupting in lawless urban protectorates in Rio de Janeiro, Vitória, or Recife. It is also argued that the country's low levels of education and extreme levels of inequality and income distribution have retarded the emergence of a strong and vibrant civil society with interest in the way its leaders conduct foreign policy. Indeed, international affairs do not preoccupy Brazilian elites, with the exception of the Ministry of External Relations (so called Itamaraty). The Brazilian Congress infrequently addresses international issues and routinely approves executive-branch nominees for foreign posts without debate. Brazilian public opinion is also oblivious of international events (de Lima, 2005:7). A former Mexican Foreign Minister called Brazil a giant that behaves as a dwarf, unlike Israel or Cuba who are dwarfs with a global reach proper of giants.[5] President Fernando Henrique, when interviewed in 2012, has also acknowledged that in recent years Brazil has lost its political relevance in the continent.[6]

The country does not have a geopolitically powerful position either. "Its global position is peripheral and not of major strategic importance to North America or Eurasian competitors" (Kelly, 1988:121). Some surveys also show reservations. For instance, the Chicago Council on Global Affairs published a report that tracks American attitudes toward U.S. foreign policy and concluded that:

"Despite stable relations and warm feelings towards Brazil, Americans do not think it is very important or influential. Only 10 percent of the public thinks Brazil is "very important" to the United States, which puts Brazil with Turkey and Nigeria at the bottom of the list of importance (44 percent say "somewhat important"). Brazil also receives low ratings of present influence (4.2 on a ten-point scale) and predicted influence in ten years (4.8), though is clearly seen as rising in influence" (Chicago Council on Global Affairs, 2010:74).

In a similar fashion, Stratfor, a strategic intelligence company, argues that "for Brazil to graduate from regional hegemon to global player and command the respect of its global peers, it's going to need to demonstrate the ability to project real power beyond its borders. Speeches can be made anywhere, any time, but real Brazilian power – that is, words backed up with action – will not come fast, cheap or easy."[7]

Either way, it is a fact that since the end of military rule in 1985, the country is gradually increasing its status in international relations. An international poll conducted by Brazil's leading magazine *Veja* in 2012 revealed that 57 percent of non-Brazilians and 78 percent of Brazilians consider that the country has increased its influence worldwide.[8]

The end of the Cold War also buried the traditional developmentalism foreign policy of Brazil – which placed economic development at the center of political endeavors and institutions – and paved the way for neoliberalism (Bernal-Meza, 2007:12). Indeed, the main goal of Collor de Mello's government (1990-1992) – the first democratically elected administration after the military regime – was to restore the country's external credibility in the industrialized world, severing Brazil's identification to the developing world by modernizing its agenda in accordance with such new international themes as intellectual property, human rights, environment, and sensitive technologies – and establishing a new profile and convergence with the tenets and principles of modern developed countries (Vigevani and Cepaluni, 2009:35; Hirst and Pinheiro, 1995:6). His foreign policy also attempted to project internationally the internal reforms and the opening of the economy that characterized the government's domestic agenda. International partnerships were dictated by economic imperatives. Relations with the U.S. were less precise. On the one hand, the United States was known to support the military regime; therefore, drawing a red line was politically necessary. On the other hand, it would be unfeasible for the Collor government to settle down in the Western community with no U.S. blessing. Practice has shown this contradiction. Brazil decided not to join in supporting the two Reagan administrations' strategy of containment and opted to not become directly involved in the Central American crisis, declaring its allegiance to the principle of nonintervention. But on the other hand, Brazil tried to build up a positive economic agenda with the U.S. namely by adopting "Washington Consensus" policies, oriented towards free-market liberalism (Vizentini, 2008:81).

Collor was impeached in December 1992 on corruption charges, and the country was engulfed in a political and economic crisis. Naturally,

Collor's successor, Itamar Franco (1992-1995) put his focus on restoring international credibility by participating with responsibility in international forums. Brazil was elected to the Security Council, participated in seven peace operations, and laid the groundwork for the establishment of the Community of Portuguese-Speaking Countries (CPLP). However, the top priorities for the domestic agenda was to restore confidence in the political institutions and the battle against inflation.

A major turn arrived during Fernando Henrique Cardoso's administration (1995-2002). An accomplished sociology scholar who had been associated with top French and U.S. universities, Cardoso sought to root Brazil in the international community by carving a responsible and stable foreign policy. The president showed a proclivity to side with the Western world, permanently abandoning the traditional Third-World posture of the 1970s and 1980s and adopting a liberal discourse in conducting foreign policy (da Costa, 2006:284). Its support of U.S. policies was not unconditional, however. If on the one hand the administration boosted trade and other ties with the United States and Europe, and in 1998 decided to sign the Nuclear Non-Proliferation Treaty (in 1968 it had opted not to), it frequently showed reservations over the Free Trade Area of the Americas (FTAA), first proposed in 1994. Even if Brazil's Foreign Ministry Lampreia peridiocally declared that the FTAA would be welcome if it represented a step toward providing access to more dynamic markets, Brazil has never been a staunch supporter of the idea. In his biography, President Fernando Henrique admits that Brazil "had a strategy of dragging our feet in negotiations for the creation of the FTAA" (Cardoso, 2006:222).

The foreign policy methodology of his administration reflected, moreover, the president's inclination towards presidential diplomacy (Danese, 2009:227-228; Vizentini, 2008:94). Leader-to-leader diplomacy is often the most efficient way to cut deals that are stymied by lower-level bureaucratic politics. Cardoso consulted directly with the White House on emerging political crises in South America such as Colombia's conflict and the Ecuador-Peru war of 1995 (Hirst, 2006:109). He nourished personal relations with Bill Clinton and George W. Bush who often showed their willingness to assist Brazil in dealing with its often-troubled economy. During his two consecutive presidencies, Cardoso has also played a leading role in strengthening the democratic foundations of the inter-American system, actively advocating for the introduction of democratic clauses in regional and international agreements. In fact, an interesting study assessing Brazil's response to threats to democracy between 1991 and 2002 in ten case studies suggests that presidential diplomacy has played a key role in furthering the democratic commitment of Brazilian foreign policy (Santiso, 2003).

In Cardoso's view, Brazil's search for international participation presupposed also the cultivation of relations with its regional partners. In fact, the new constitution of 1988 included a paragraph stating that the country "shall seek the economic, political, social and cultural integration of the peoples of Latin America, viewing the formation of a Latin-American community of nations" (article 4). But the president adopted a discrete approach in the way he conducted regional bilateral affairs. As he stated, "under my government, Brazil would never attempt to use a heavy hand to become a regional power. I have always believed in the concept of national self-determination, and we refused to meddle in other countries' affairs" (Cardoso, 2006:222).

Contrary to Fernando Henrique, President Lula da Silva's administration (2002-2010) opted for a more interventive, autonomous, and global foreign policy. As the Foreign Minister declared in his first speech, "[Brazil] will not run away from an engaged and leading role, whenever it becomes necessary to defend the national interests and the values that inspire us. . . . Our foreign policy cannot be confined to a single region nor can be restricted to a single dimension." (Ministério das Relações Exteriores, 2007:17). Besides maintaining commercial interests with countries in Asia, Africa, and the Middle East, President Lula reinforced cultural and political relations as well, trying to create a shared identity with those countries. In fact, South America is the region with the largest number of descendants of the African diaspora, and Brazil has the world's second-biggest black population, after Nigeria.

To fulfill these objectives, the Lula administration proposed the creation of the Summit of South American-Arab Countries (ASPA), a mechanism for biregional cooperation and a forum for political coordination amongst thirty-four countries (first Summit was held in Brasília in 2005; it was the largest event celebrated in Brasília since its foundation[9]); strongly supported the establishment of a regular Africa-South America Summit (ASA) (first summit was held in Abuja in 2006); doubled the number of its embassies in Africa, opening sixteen new ones; convened the Brazil-Africa Forum on Politics, Cooperation and Trade, held in Fortaleza in 2003 (Coelho and Saraiva, 2004); opened the doors for multiple Brazilian companies and agencies to invest in the continent, such as the Brazilian Agency for Industrial Development (ABDI), Oswaldo Cruz Foundation, and the Brazilian Agricultural Research Corporation (EMBRAPA);[10] and the president visited Africa eleven times (more than any other Brazilian President). It is also important to note that the Lula government approved Plan 2022 (*Plano 2022*), a list of national objectives to have fulfilled when Brazil celebrates 200 years of independence from Portugal. Tellingly, the chapter on foreign affairs includes eight goals, three of which encompass the objective to diversify and deepen political and economical relations with countries in Africa, Asia, and the Middle East. Inspired by these realizations, the Lula administration often spoke of the need to "to draw a new economical and commercial international geography"[11] (see also Ministério das Relações Exteriores, 2007:20). During the Lula administration, bilateral trade with Africa grew from U.S.$ 5 billion in 2002 to U.S.$ 20.6 billion in 2010; and with the Arab League countries from U.S.$ 4.9 billion in 2002 to U.S.$ 19.5 billion in 2010.

Brazil also put an emphasis on setting up a clutch of new clubs. These include IBSA, with India and South Africa and the BRIC, with Russia, India, and China. Since IBSA's creation (in 2003) to 2008, Brazil increased its trade with India by 380 percent, and with South Africa by 317 percent (Campbell, 2009:163). This course of action does not respond solely to the country's trade interests, in particular diversification of its export markets. It is regarded as a fundamental step to strengthen global multilateralism, another key objective of current Brazilian foreign policy. Its demand for a permanent seat on the Security Council follows the same pattern. As pointed out by Saraiva, "the increasingly accepted identification of Brazil as a bridge between developed and underdeveloped nations, a concept that had been talked about since the 1970s, would give the country a powerful position in international relations" (Saraiva, 2011:62). Symptomatically, a study that comprehended the views of approximately 200 Brazilian foreign policy-makers pointed that China (with 97 percent of answers) and India (94 percent) were expected to become "more important" than they are today. In contrast, only 15 percent answered that the United States would be "more important" (de Souza, 2009:18).

In fact, another Brazilian priority under Lula da Silva was checking the U.S. unilateralism in the region. The creation of the South American Security Council, proposed by the president in May 2008, purposefully excluded the presence of countries located outside the region, as would be the case of the United States. Three years before, the U.S. tried to participate as an observer in the First Summit of South American-Arab Countries (held in Brasília) as it was allegedly concerned that the forum would turn into a stage of accusations against President George W. Bush and Israel. But the U.S. saw its participation rejected and ended up pressuring its Arab allies not to take part. Saudi Arabia's Crown Prince

Abdullah and Morocco's King Mohammed VI, who had been welcomed with great pomp in Brasília the previous year, turned down the invitation.[12] In addition, Brazil has often shown its reservation over the presence of the U.S. military in South America (Colombia, Ecuador, and Paraguay), has criticized the militarization of the war on drugs (Hofmeister, 2007:75), and did not back the war on Iraq. In 2008, a cable sent to the State Department by the U.S. Ambassador to Brazil Clifford Sobel also signaled that top Brazilian diplomats were anti-U.S. In particular, Secretary General for External Relations Samuel Pinheiro Guimarães was regarded as an obstacle to the U.S. as the diplomat was "virulently anti-American, and anti-'first world' in general."[13]

Also on trade, Brazil and the U.S. got involved in several commercial disputes. For instance, the World Trade Organization, which ruled in June 2008 that subsidies to U.S. cotton producers were discriminatory, allowed Brazil to impose up to U.S.$ 829.3 million in retaliatory sanctions against U.S. products. Moreover, Brazil has also checked the U.S. by curbing the FTAA (in the same way Fernando Henrique had done). Despite the fact that the country has gone along with negotiations for an FTAA, it has been, and continues to be, at the forefront of those resisting U.S.-style trade liberalization. In fact, the country was one of the last countries in South America to accept neoliberalism during the most recent cycle of economic opening in the region (Schirm, 2007:51-52; Cason, 2007). Brazilian trade policy in the twenty-first century operates through reciprocal multilateralism: "We want free trade, but free trade characterized by reciprocity," said Lula in Davos in January 2003.

The growing maturity and economic strength of Brazil has been useful to occupy the empty space left by the United States post-September 11. For the U.S. the broader Middle East constitutes the ultimate priority, not South America. But the U.S. Obama administration has not quite opened the door to Brazil. In a subtle way, the 2010 National Security Strategy draws a line between "key centers of influence" (China, India, and Russia) and "increasingly influential nations" (Brazil, South Africa, and Indonesia) (The White House, 2010:3). In fact, despite recent protagonism, Brazilians continued to display a widespread preoccupation with the manner in which Brazil is perceived in North America and in Europe. There is an impatient ambivalence in the way in which they wish to be considered and judged (Penna, 1988:109).

The only major overlap between the Lula and Fernando Henrique administrations was the promotion of political stability in the region. But what region? During the military dictatorships, regional policies meant

Latin American policies, not South American (de Almeida, 2009:211; de Almeida, 2002:100). It was Fernando Henrique who inaugurated a new focus on South America as a way to assure that without Mexico, Brazil would be able to establish itself unanimously as a regional power. South American regionalism was the space in which Brazil reaffirmed its autonomy, in resistance to hemispheric participation (Campos Mello, 2000:112; Burges, 2009:3). As he wrote in his biography, "the concept of "South America" was still relatively new, and had yet to be properly reflected in our foreign policy" (Cardoso, 2006:220). Building on this new focus, Lula's administration was the mastermind behind the creation of the Union of South American Nations (UNASUR) in 2008, and of Venezuela's integration into Mercosur in 2006 (in 2009 the government strongly lobbied Brazil's Senate to ratify the acceptance of Venezuela).[14] At the end of Lula's tenure Brazil ended up resurrecting its earlier focus on Latin America, nonetheless, when it championed – along with Mexico – the establishment of the Community of Latin American and Caribbean States (CELAC) in 2010. Whether the focus is on South or Latin America, the promotion of regional integration will always be on the menu of Brazil's foreign policy. Tellingly, Brazil's National Defense Strategy, adopted in 2008, included regional integration as one of the priorities to the armed forces since enhanced cooperation would "put away the shadow of conflicts in the region" (Art.18). In the same line of thinking, Clodoaldo Hugueney, one of the most respected Brazilian diplomats, has affirmed that "the building of a politically, economically and culturally integrated area in South America, with projections in Latin America, the Caribbean and Africa, is certainly a top priority for Brazilian diplomacy in coming decades" (cited in Mullins, 2006:89).

If Brazil has been historically accepted as the political leader in South America, the leadership and charisma of President Lula took the country to an even larger leadership role. In fact, at the second Latin American and Caribbean Summit on Integration and Development, held in Cancún in 2010, the President of Mexico Felipe Calderón – the country that traditionally disputes with Brazil the spotlights in Latin America – even acknowledged that "President Lula is the unquestionable leader in the region, someone who provides Latin America with balance and strength."[15] On a wide range of important initiatives – nuclear proliferation, diplomatic negotiations, economic integration, and arms production – the Brazilian government has broken with its past isolation and became a strong advocate of multilateral regionalism. And leadership is to be exercised using the traditional tools of soft power – politics, culture, and economy – rather than by increasing its military credentials. During Lula's administration, the first sign that the country was ready for global projection emerged at the Fifth Ministerial WTO conference, held in Cancún in September 2003. In the meeting Brazil was instrumental in forming a bloc of developing nations – the Group of 20 – which was vocal against protectionist measures in developed countries (Fier, 2010:63; de Lima, 2005:20). Traditionally, developing countries were at the most spectators at negotiation tables, and would certainly abide by the rules imposed by the capitalism's center (Cervo, 2010:9). One year later, Brazil joined the Group of 5, a bloc that encompasses the five largest emerging economies (Brazil, China, India, Mexico, South Africa) and has operated as an important basis for the dialoque between developing and developed countries. Brazil has also been pivotal in renovating the Group of 20 of industrialized nations (not to be mistaken with the G-20 of developing nations) in the follow up of the economic crisis of 2008. Brazil proposed the G-20 to replace the G-8 as the main economic council of wealthy nations.[16]

During Lula's mandate Brazil's leadership was often equated with the personal style of the president and the foreign policy gained often a voluntaristic and personalist tone.[17] For example, in March 2010 he become entangled in a controversy for having compared Cuban political prisoners with Brazilian jailed criminals and was even severely criticized by members of his own party. Brazil's policy not to condemn human rights violations in Third-World countries has also been questioned. The country has been criticized for having abstained in past UN Human Rights Commission votes condemning North Korea, China, Sudan, Cuba, Myanmar, Iran, Sri Lanka, or the Congo.[18] In fact, to Brazil's embarrassment, it was forced to revert some of these positions later (such as on North Korea). And has been criticized for carving a foreign policy on party ideology rather than on national interest in order to appease the leftist segments of the Worker's Party, which were not content with the implementation of domestic economic liberal policies by the government (Ricupero, 2009:15).[19]

In 2010, President Dilma Rousseff (2011-2014) won the election due in large part to her ability to identify herself in the race with immensely popular President Lula. The change in political personalities did not make much of an impact on Brazil's current geopolitical trajectory, even if she has a less populist and effervescent style than Lula and has shown more sensibility towards human rights, which seems to be linked to her past as a political prisoner (under the dictatorship between 1970 and 1972).

In one of her first declarations on foreign policy after being elected, she condemned Iran for its treatment of Sakineh Mohammadi Ashtiani, convicted in 2006 of adultery, and criticized Brazil's decision to abstain in a UN voting to condemn human rights violations in Iran.[20] This path, however, has not been pursued with absolute coherence. In March 2011, Brazil abstained on UN Security Council Resolution 1973 that authorized member states to intervene in Libya to counter Muammar Gaddafi's savage crackdown on rebels (France, the UK, and the U.S. voted in favor). And three months later, when Iranian dissident and Nobel Peace Prize laureate Shirin Ebadi visited Brazil on an international tour to muster support for human-rights efforts in Iran, Rousseff declined to see her. Brazil's foreign policy on human rights, under Dilma, seems thus still to be searching for the right course.

Dilma has also avoided the ideological card in its relations with the U.S., and has favored a more institutional and less activist posture. In 2013 she postponed a planned state visit to Washington amid fallout over revelations that the U.S. has been spying on her government. Leaks from former-National Security Agency contractor Edward Snowden revealed, among other things, extensive spying by the U.S on the president and on state-run oil giant Petrobras. But the decision was more fueled by domestic than external concerns. It clearly intended to send a loud public rebuke to the United States and rally Rousseff's leftist domestic political base ahead of the following year's presidential election (Rousseff and her center-left party, Workers' Party, had seen their public approval ratings battered by a series of corruption scandals and the mass social protests that swept the country that year). Accordingly, her diplomatic affront to the colossus to the north has been splashed all over Brazilian media. But it did not affect the fairly cordial bilateral relation with the U.S.

Under Dilma, Brazil has also a mixed track record in the way it handled the democratic ruptures in neighboring countries. Traditionally, Brazil reacts by sponsoring the preservation of constitutionality and advocating noninterference in the evolution of domestic political institutions. This was Brazil's stance in Ecuador/2000, in Paraguay/2000 and in Venezuela/2002, for instance. Dilma's administration has attempted to cement this tradition. When the Paraguayan president was impeached in 2012, Brazil condemned the clumsy trial process, but let Mercosur and UNASUR head the fierce response. Yet Brazil was caught up in its own strategy. With the country watching on the stands, it was up to Argentina and Venezuela to maneuver on their own, leading to the ousting of Paraguay from both organization and to the formal acceptance of Venezuela into Mercosur. Paraguay's conservative senate had long opposed the integration of Venezuela into the block. Once the country was suspended, Venezuela forced itself into Mercosur, sponsored by ally Argentina. Brazil's tentativeness was criticized domestically, and its regional leadership was tainted. Dilma's passive posture was also evident in the way Brazil dealt with Bolivian senator Roger Pinto, a right-wing dissident who took refuge in the Brazilian embassy in La Paz after being accused of corruption by the Bolivian authorities. At the end of 2013, after fifteen months of confinement with no prospect of departure and no ongoing bilateral negotiations, a maverick chargé d'affaires in La Paz, Eduardo Sabóia, organized for the Senator to flee to Brazil. As the trip had no official permission by either country, Brazil's Minister of Foreign Affairs, Antonio Patriota, was forced by Dilma to resign. The incident also signaled Dilma's nod towards the leftist governments in Latin America, in tune with Lula's traditional posture. In an article published after the incident in a mainstream newspaper, former President Cardoso wrote that Brazil's diplomacy "is paralyzed by the unquestionable association of Lula and the Workers' Party to "bolivarism" and therefore it zigzags and stumbles"[21].

But although Dilma has opted for a more discreet posture internationally, she has not shied away from leaving her mark on Brazilian diplomacy. She has taken advantage of her trips abroad to strike agreements on science, technology, and innovation, namely through Science Without Borders, a large-scale, nationwide scholarship program that is primarily funded by the Brazilian federal government, whose goal is to qualify 100,000 Brazilian students and researchers in top universities worldwide through 2014.

Contribution to Traditional Security

As the major power in the region, expectations are always high for Brazil's measures to ensure regional security. Brazil's rejection of the use of force in its relations with the neighboring states after the Second World War and its distinctive "diplomatic way" helped shape the character of South America (Kacowicz, 1998:91). With the onset of the debt crisis in 1982 and the gradual liberalization in the region in the early and mid-1980s, Brazil began to demonstrate, in the post-Cold War era, a greater proclivity for collective action (Roett, 2003:198) – on the bilateral, regional, and global fronts.

Bilaterally, the most significant Brazilian initiative concerned relations with Argentina. Historically, the confrontation – which stemmed from the quest by both states for Southern cone primacy –

hindered regional integration, created possibilities for indigenous nuclear weapons development, and jeopardized peaceful settlement of disputes in the region. The dispute started first to diminish in 1979 with the negotiations for the Itaipu-Corpus Treaty and with the outset of multiple nuclear cooperation agreements in the 1980s and 1990s. On the Brazilian side, the Itaipu-Corpus negotiations represented the abandonment of a hegemonic posture regarding the neighboring country that had prevailed off and on for 150 years (Hirst, 1996b: 211). During the Falklands/Malvinas dispute of 1982, Brazil also sided with Argentina, namely by selling Bandeirantes Emb-11 planes at very advantageous conditions, by offering the Brazilian Embassy in London to represent Argentinean interests, and by condemning the boycott of the European Economic Community to Argentina.[22] Even today Brazil defends Argentina's sovereignty claims over the Falkland/Malvinas.

But the rapprochement had economic interests at stake. When Brazilian President José Sarney took power in 1985 he faced growing inflation rates, an increase in unemployment, and ever-higher pressures from the left-of-center political forces and, thereby, had to deal with inflated popular expectations for economic growth and monetary stability (Albuquerque, 2003:280; Oelsner, 2003:194). Moreover, the debt crisis, commercial protectionism of the industrialized world, and the need to isolate the region from the East-West conflict, all encouraged the handshake. In 1986, both countries signed the Program for Economic Integration and Cooperation (PICE), which involved negotiations on sectoral agreements, such as capital goods, technological cooperation, food, and the iron, steel, nuclear and auto industries. In 1988 the integration process was given a boost by the signature of the Treaty on Integration, Cooperation and Development, whose aim was to establish a common market within ten years (see Table 2.3.). The rationale for the rapprochement was, therefore, a need to increase bilateral economic interdependency, which would reinforce their mutual protection against political instability. In addition, economic cooperation was also assisted at this stage by the convergence of unorthodox economic policies domestically (the Cruzado Plan in Brazil and the Austral Plan in Argentina) (Hurrell, 1995:256). The economic growth of Brazil in contrast to the stagnation of Argentina contributed additionally to setting aside the old geopolitical scenarios of bilateral rivalry in favor of concepts that emphasized Brazil's prominence over a weak and indecisive Argentina.

Inspired by the turn of events, the armed forces of Brazil and Argentina have redeployed away from battle-readiness at their border and have frequent exchanges of military information and personnel to reassure each other. The concerns and threats perceptions of the Brazilian military moved progressively away from Argentina towards the Amazon region (Hurrell, 1995:256). Ultimately, cooperation with Argentina provided Brazil with an opportunity to break its traditional geopolitical chains and construct a more flexible foreign policy different from previous stances of caution and balance.

After mitigating the antagonism with Argentina, Brazil arbitrated bilateral disputes where other South American countries were involved. For instance, it has been active in mitigating the territorial dispute between Venezuela and Guyana. Soon after Venezuela refused to renew the Protocol of Port of Spain (1970), where parties agreed to "freeze" the conflict for twelve years, Brazil reached an agreement with Guyana committing itself to construct a road through the area and promote industrial development there. This worked as a check on the possibility of Venezuelan expansion to the east (Oelsner, 2005:96).

In another case, when the border conflict between Ecuador and Peru erupted again in 1995, Brazil was one of the four "guarantors" of a 1940s cease-fire agreement. Along with Argentina, Chile, and the United States, Brazil actively sought to reinstate the cease-fire agreement and to urge the two protagonists to seek a treaty settlement, which eventually occurred. The administration of President Cardoso was indeed a strong supporter of intraregional dialogue. And for the Ministry of External Relations, the intervention in the conflict served to strengthen the image of South America as a beacon of political stability and military détente and underscore the capacity of the countries in the region to act in a cooperative and constructive form in the face of future threats to stability in the region (Oliveira, 1999:148). In retrospect, Luiz Felipe Lampreia, Brazil's then-Minister of External Affairs, classified Itamaraty's role in brokering an end to the forty-four-year-old conflict as one of the most important moments in Cardoso's foreign policy agenda (Burges, 2009:140). On the military front, Brazil also coordinated the Military Observer Mission to Ecuador and Peru's (MOMEP) forces, which succeeded in separating 5,000 intertwined combatant forces without fresh casualties in extraordinarily difficult terrain. MOMEP then added Ecuadorian and Peruvian forces into its peacekeeping operations to enable guarantor diplomats to help the two governments negotiate a lasting peace in the interests of both countries. The 1998 peace between Ecuador and Peru, signed in Brasilia, definitively tilted the strategic balance in South America away from interstate conflict.

President Lula has also been active in mediating in the bitter disputes between Venezuela's President Chávez and Colombia's Uribe. The first time Lula attempted to come in between the two leaders was in

January 2005 when he travelled to the Colombian border to meet Álvaro Uribe in an effort to broker a resolution to a tense diplomatic stand-off between Colombia and Venezuela over the capure of FARC's leader Rodrigo Granda in December 2004. During his second mandate, President Lula has repeatedly tried to let off steam between both leaders, and in 2010 he joined a "group of friend countries" that formed following another verbal clash between Uribe and Chávez at a Summit in Mexico (held in February that year). The group, headed by Dominican President Leonel Fernandez, faded away as Colombia elected President Santos four months later.

Brazil has also participated in minor conflict resolution initiatives. In 2003 it coordinated the OAS Group of Friends (included also Chile, Spain, Portugal, Mexico, and the United States) that was established to facilitate a peaceful resolution to the political crisis in Venezuela after the attempted coup. And in Paraguay, Brazil's Federal Police has been active aiding local police in tracking down EPP guerrilla members.[23] In his inauguration speech, President Lula noted the difficulties in some South American countries and made himself available to find pacific solutions to regional crises. In several occasions the president has actually tried to keep a foot on both sides of the ideological divide in Latin America in order to provide a more balanced and consensual position. For instance, in 2006 during the election for a Latin American rotating place in the UN Security Council, Brazil (and other Mercosur states) supported Venezuela, whereas the United States backed Guatemala. But when it became obvious that neither could get the required two-thirds majority to win, Brazil advocated that both competitors should withdraw. Panama ended up being elected without difficulty (Bourne, 2008:223). Retrospectively, however, Brazil was far from playing the role of a successful mediator, and important crises – such as between Chile and Peru or between Argentina and Uruguay – have been arbitrated by the International Criminal Court in The Hague instead.[24] This has inspired former Uruguayan President Julio María Sanguinetti (1985-1990 and 1995-2000) to exhort Brazil to express its leading role in a "clearer way."[25]

Brazil has also turned its attention to multilateral regional security affairs. In 1986, it hosted the inaugural meeting of what became the Rio Group, originally composed of the Contadora and its Support Group. The Contadora Group was an initiative launched in the early 1980s by the foreign ministers of Colombia, Mexico, Panama, and Venezuela to deal with the military conflicts in Central America. The meeting in Rio had higher goals in mind however. And it eventually led to the creation of a permanent forum for the discussion of the entire agenda of multilateral concerns of the countries involved. Brazil assumed the role of secretary of the Rio Group and undertook a series of initiatives to resolve issues of common concern, namely the debt crisis (see Chapter 15).

Brazil's focus on regional stability was reinforced with President Fernando Henrique. In 2000 he convened in Brasilia a Summit of Presidents of Mercosur and the Andean Community (Chile, an associated member of Mercosur; Guyana and Suriname, members of the Treaty of Amazonic Cooperation, were also invited to this summit). Cardoso's idea was to relaunch the Brazilian strategy of South American integration; but, instead of concentrating exclusively on trade issues, as in the South American Free Trade Area (SAFTA) strategy, the Brazilian president proposed a development and security agenda. The summit served as substratum for the Community of South American Nations, which was formed four years later (Peña, 2008:28). The final declaration of the Summit in Brasília stated that "[T]he consolidation of democracy and peace throughout the region is the foundation for both the historical close ties uniting the South American countries and the resolution of disputes between sister nations through negotiated settlements" (article 20).

The country has also emerged as a leader in the efforts to slow down the arms race and to consolidate the region as a nuclear-free zone. In 1990, Brazil (and Argentina) formally renounced the manufacture of nuclear weapons, and similar measures aiming at cutting down arsenals followed. The 1988 Brazilian constitution even included an article stating that, "all nuclear activity within the national territory shall only be admitted for peaceful purposes and subject to approval by the National Congress" (art. 21-XXIII-a). President Fernando Collor de Mello also took bold steps to control and restrict Brazil's nuclear programs. In September 1990, he symbolically closed a test site at Cachimbo, in Pará State, and one month later he formally exposed the military's secret plan to develop an atom bomb. In November 1990, Presidents Collor de Mello and Carlos Saúl Menem of Argentina signed the second Foz do Iguazu Declaration (Argentine-Brazilian Declaration on Common Nuclear Policy of Foz do Iguazu), in which both governments pledged their commitment to an exclusively peaceful use of nuclear energy and established a Common System for Accounting and Control of Nuclear Materials (Sistema Comum de Contabilidade e Contrôle de Materiais Nucleares – SCCCMN). In July 1991, Presidents Collor de Mello and Menem signed the Agreement for the Exclusively Peaceful Use of Nuclear Energy, which created the Brazilian-Argentine Agency for Accounting and Control of Nuclear Materials (*Agência*

Brasileiro-Argentina de Contabilidade e Controle de Materiais Nucleares – ABACC) (see Table 2.3.). That agreement entered into force in December 1991, after ratification by the legislatures in both countries. With headquarters in Rio de Janeiro, the ABACC provides on-site inspections of nuclear facilities in Argentina and Brazil and maintains an inventory of nuclear material in each country. The most important nuclear accord between Brazil and Argentina was signed in December 1991, however, in a meeting attended by Presidents Collor de Mello and Menem at the headquarters of the IAEA in Vienna. The accord is referred to as the quadripartite agreement, because it was signed by Brazil, Argentina, the IAEA, and the ABACC. The agreement allows for full-scope IAEA safeguards of Argentine and Brazilian nuclear installations. It also allows the two countries to retain full rights over any "technological secrets" and to develop nuclear energy for the propulsion of submarines. Brazil's Senate ratified the agreement in February 1994, but only after considerable pressure by Brazil's Ministry of Foreign Affairs.

The Amazon region has also become a focus of concern for the Brazilian government. Taking advantage of Brazil's extensive and uninhabited border, drug traffickers have found new paths to push their products out of Bolivia, Peru, and Colombia toward large consumer markets in the United States and Europe. Regional threats to Brazil's national interests include the potential for violence to spill over from internal conflicts in neighboring countries, particularly Colombia; people prospecting mineral resources in the middle of the jungle; the smuggling of drugs or people across borders; and the localized depletion of biodiversity that results from the extensive illegal exploitation of regional resources (da Costa, 2001:99). In 1991, approximately forty members of the FARC conducted a raid into Brazilian territory. They attacked a Brazilian Army detachment that was stationed in a semipermanent camp on the bank of the Traíra River at the border between Brazil and Colombia. The Brazilian Army counterattacked by eliminating some of the members, imprisoning others, and recapturing a good part of the stolen military material and equipment. Over the years the belief grew that the FARC could have active cells in Brazil for drug trafficking. The claim was confirmed in May 2010, when José Samuel Sánchez was apreehended in the Brazilian state of Amazonas. Sánchez, who goes by the aliases "Martín Ávila" or "Tatareto," was a suspected drug trafficker who also assisted in the group's logistics and financial planning. In the same period, a leading Brazilian newspaper interviewed a former FARC militant who claimed that the guerrilla operated in the country since the 1990s and had been expanding its drug trafficking operations and increasing its links with Brazilian narcotraffickers.[26] The armed forces of Brazil claim that FARC agents operating in Brazil are not guerilla members but mere drug dealers,[27] but the country's National Defense Strategy, adopted in 2008, stressed the need to protect the Amazon region, stating that "who takes care of the Brazilian Amazon, on behalf of the humanity and of itself, is Brazil" (Art.10).

In conjunction with these regional efforts, the Lula government has also attempted to mediate international conflicts as a part of a proactive global foreign policy. On several occasions the country has voiced its will to mediate peace negotiations in the Middle East, since its participation in the 2008 Annapolis conference in the United States, which brought together a group of countries and representatives of the parties in conflict. In November 2009, over a span of just two weeks, Brazilian President Lula da Silva received his Israeli counterpart Shimon Peres, Palestinian President Mahmoud Abbas, and Iranian leader Mahmoud Ahmadinejad. But Brazil's participation in peace negotiations copycatted the failure of other countries. Lula and his Foreign Minister Celso Amorim constantly argued that "the conflict transcends regional dimensions" and solving it "is a responsibility of all of us."[28] Yet, Brazil's mediation attained no results. The president even visited Israel, the Palestinian territories, and Jordan in March 2010 – the first time a Brazilian head of state had been to this region since a journey by the last Emperor of Brazil, Dom Pedro II, in 1876 – but Brazil's "fresh perspective" was regarded as too farfetched for a middle power with no experience in the conflict.

Even in a more controversial way, Brazil attempted to broker in Iran's nuclear crisis. The country defended Iran's right to develop nuclear technology for peaceful purposes and along with Turkey was able to broker a nuclear fuel-swap deal with Iran in May 2010. However, the agreement was neutralized later by the U.S., European powers, and Iran's opposition and more hard-line forces.[29] The adventurous nature of Brazil's president was severely criticized at home,[30] including former President Henrique Cardoso who called the government "naïve" and accused it of "talking too much."[31] The deal was a high-profile diplomatic coup that catapulted Brazil into the global scene while avoiding the political risk that would accompany establishing a tighter relationship with Iran in defiance of the United States. Beneath the diplomatic fanfare of the nuclear proposal, Lula and his delegation carefully maintained their distance from Tehran and have continued the Brazilian relationship with Washington. But the practical results were indeed poor. According to a Pew Research Center survey released in June 2010, whereas Brazil's government opposed sanctions against Iran, 65 percent of Brazilians were in favor.[32]

Brazil has also long been an enthusiastic peacekeeper, sending troops to about thirty UN operations since 1948. Troops were dispatched, for instance, to Angola (MONUA-UNAVEM, 1988-1997), Mozambique (ONUMOZ, 1993-1994), Ecuador-Peru (MOMEP 1 and 2, 1995-1999), and East Timor (UNMISET, 1999-2001). From 1988 to 2007, Brazil committed more than 10,500 soldiers to UN peace missions. Yet, Brazil has not sent as many troops to UN peace missions as its two neighbors, Argentina and Uruguay. In percentage terms, only 2 percent of Brazil's commissioned officers have peacekeeping experience, and less than 10 percent of the country's military force has been involved in UN peace missions (Velázquez, 2010: 184). Even so, Lula's administration has treated international peacekeeping as a vehicle to project the name of the country internationally and consolidate its national defense strategic objectives. As mentioned by Diniz, "Brazil believes that active participation in the UN is central to its quest for greater political autonomy and recognition in the international scene, primarily because it advocates UN's reform and its acceptance as a permanent member of the Security Council (de Lima, 2005:17; Diniz, 2006:332; Guimarães, 2010:20). This is the context that led President Lula in 2004 to decide to take charge of the United Nations Stabilization Mission in Haiti (MINUSTAH), one of UN's largest missions. In 2005 Brazil boosted its credentials further by opening a peacekeeping school, the *Centro de Instrução de Operações de Paz Sérgio Vieira de Mello* (CIOpPaz) near Rio de Janeiro. CIOpPaz has since trained 15,000 troops. As of October 2013, Brazil had 1,706 troops and police engaged in UN peacekeeping operations. But despite this level of engagement, Brazilian military commanders have resisted committing too many troops for peacekeeping endeavors since such deployments can jeopardize their ability to perform internal security missions. As Velázquez noted, "they commit a limited force, consisting of small units or one battalion, participating only in a couple of PKO [peacekeeping operations], but resisting major or dual deployments" (Velázquez, 2010: 190).

Contribution to Human Security

Over the last decade, Brazil's interest in environmental issues has increased, and more-focused governmental policies have recently born fruits. In 2012, deforestation in the Brazilian Amazon fell to the lowest rate on record, putting Brazil well on track to meet its targets for reducing rainforest destruction. Analysis of satellite imagery by Brazil's National Institute for Space Research (INPE) showed that 4.571 square kilometers of rainforest (three times the size of the city of São Paulo) were cleared in the Amazon in the twelve months ending in July 2012, a 29-percent drop from the year earlier period. Although in the following year (until July 2013) there was an increase in deforestation reaching 5.843 square kilometers, the numbers are much lower than in recent times. In 1995 deforestation reached an historical high of 29,059 square kilometers cleared, and in 2004 it hit 27,772. Between 2000 and 2007, 154,312 km² of forest, an area larger than Greece, was destroyed (Greenpeace, 2009:3). But since 2004 there has been a notable steady decrease.[33] The downtrend is imputed first of all to governmental policies. In 2008, the country unveiled its plan to encourage farmers in the Amazon region to develop sustainable sources of income and turn their backs on the illegal logging that is ravaging the rainforest. The Sustainable Amazon Plan, as it is called, established a R$ 1 billion (U.S.$ 600 million) fund for farmers who adopt environmentally friendly farming methods and includes low-interest loans available to farmers. In the same year Brazilian President Lula da Silva officially unveiled plans for an Amazon Fund, which aimed to raise U.S.$ 21 billion in foreign donations by 2021. Contributors will not be eligible for carbon credits that may be generated by reductions in deforestation, but the money will go towards sustainable development and conservation initiatives in the region.

The other main drivers of deforestation are the beef and soy industries. In 2003, Brazil overtook Australia and the United States to become the world's largest exporter of beef , which stimulated cattle grazing in the Amazon. In 2011 and 2012 Brazil exported 1.1 and 1.2 million metric tons of beef, respectively.[34] According to a 2009 Greenpeace study, 90 percent of the land deforested between 1996 and 2006 is now being used for cattle-ranching (Greenpeace, 2009). On this front, the Brazilian government has done little, it often rejects the association between cattle-ranching and deforestation, and therefore the impact of pastures on the tropical forest is only dependent on market trends. Soya cultivation has been regarded differently. Soy's small and diminishing contribution to Amazonian deforestation is the result of a 2006 moratorium, which was made between soy producers and NGOs, and it prohibited the purchase of soy from newly cleared areas. The Amazon region concentrates 36 percent of Brazil's bovine cattle (over 75 million animals) and 5 percent of soya fields.[35] Brazil's official goal is to reduce the Amazon's deforestation by 80 percent by 2020. A study has shown that the end of deforestation in the Brazilian Amazon would cost between U.S.$ 7 to U.S.$ 18 billion, and it could result in a 2 to 5 percent reduction in global carbon emissions (Nepstad et. al., 2009).

Contrary to recent achievements on the environmental front, Brazil is still lagging behind in urban crime and drug trafficking. The skewed distribution of income in the country (one of the most unequal in the world) may be partially responsible for an endemic and increasing problem of nonpolitical crime. Since returning to civilian government, Brazil has experienced a dramatic increase in the level of crime. The national homicide rate is 27.1 per 100,000 residents (2011) with some states reaching dramatic levels: 72.2 (Alagoas), 47.4 (Espírito Santo) and 40 (Pará) (Waiselfisz, 2013:25). To elucidate, the WHO considers rates above ten homicides per 100,000 residents as epidemic violence. The country (federal government, states, and municipalities) has more than duplicated investments in security from 2003 (R$ 22.5 billion) to 2011 (R$ 51.55 billion), but crime rates remain very high nonetheless (Fórum Brasileiro de Segurança Pública, 2012). As a result, Brazil has one of the largest jail populations in the world. From 1990 to 2010 it increased 450 percent from 90,000 to 498,500 (in the U.S. it escalated only 17 percent).[36]

Drug trafficking can be held responsible for rising criminality and violence in Brazil. In such cities as Rio de Janeiro, Sao Paulo or Vitória, it is linked to other criminal activities such as kidnappings and bank heists. They are organized as a parallel power that challenges the authorities, corrupts the police force, and controls the population of many communities. According to a nationwide study, 98 percent of Brazil's municipalities are affected by the use of crack (a freebase form of cocaine that can be smoked).[37] Although the country has a lower prevalence rate of 0.7 percent of the population aged fifteen to sixty-four, because of its large population, the country has the highest number of cocaine users (900,000) in South America. According to a national survey conducted in 2009 among university students in Brazil, the annual prevalence of cocaine use was 3 percent of students aged eighteen to thirty-five (UNODC, 2011:91). As the country is not a producer of coca, the cocaine trafficked from, and consumed in, Brazil most likely originates in Peru or Bolivia. In 2009, Brazil was the most prominent transit country in the Americas – in terms of number of seizures – for cocaine consignments seized in Europe. The number of seizure cases that involved Brazil as a transit country rose from twenty-five in 2005 (amounting to 339 kg of cocaine) to 260 in 2009 (amounting to 1.5 mt) (UNODC, 2011:109). Narcotics traffickers exploit Brazil's heavily transited and porous border crossings where Brazilian law enforcement agencies only have a minimal presence. Not surprisingly, a poll conducted to two-hundred Brazilian political and social leaders indicated that drug trafficking and organized crime are considered the most serious international threats to the country (82,5 percent of answers) (IRI-USP, 2013).

To combat transborder trafficking organizations, Brazil cooperates with neighboring countries through joint intelligence centers (JIC) in strategic border towns. Brazil is a party to the 1988 UN Drug Trafficking Convention, the 1971 Convention on Psychotropic Substances, the UN Convention against Transnational Organized Crime and its three protocols, and the UN Convention against Corruption. Based on this scenario it is not surprising that according to the policy study cited above, which included the views of approximately 200 Brazilian foreign policy-makers, the most critical threats to the vital interests of Brazil are global warming (66 percent of answers) and the international drug trade (64 percent) (de Souza, 2009:42).

Conclusions

Brazil's traditional foreign affairs strategy has been one of secreting the country's integrated and sustained ambitions for hemispheric and global leadership behind a cloak of indirect and ostensibly technocratic apolitical programs, well wrapped in an added mantle of multilateralism (Burges, 2009:1). In several regional crises, such as in Paraguay (2000 and 2012), Ecuador (2000), Peru (2000), or Venezuela (2002), among others, Brazil employed a combination of collective response with the eschewal of forceful external interventions. The country has been able to resist temptation to impose specific measures and formulas or to intervene militarily to curb crises and conflicts. As often conveyed by Itamaraty, democratic forms and practices must be the result of internal negotiations and agreement, not external imposition. The strong legacy of U.S. intervention in the region, particularly in the creation and manipulation of democratic regimes militated against Brazil's activism. Thereby, the central instrument used by Brazil to advance its leadership project in a consensually hegemonic vein is the creation of regional arrangements. More than anyone, Brazil is aware that the decision to create a region or advance a regional project has the potential to impose costs on other countries in the area. When requested to engage directly to mediate bilateral disputes, Brazil has not shied away (e.g., Venezuela/Guyana, Ecuador/Peru, Venezuela/Colombia), but its preferred path towards regional leadership has been through international organizations, even if, as we shall see in Part IV, they lack organizational capacity and operational expertise in security issues.

Conveniently, Brazil tends to pick the weakest regional organizations to convey its individual messages on a collective stage (e.g., Mercosur, CELAC, UNASUL). Only very seldom has Brazil relied on the OAS, which has the strongest organizational capacity and a mind of its own. Tellingly, according to the poll cited above Brazilians believe that if a violent conflict erupts in the region, it is up to UNASUR (30,5 percent of answers), the UN (29 percent) or the OAS (28,5 percent) to resolve it. Only 5 percent expect Brazil to step in (IRI-USP, 2013).

But although Brazil has achieved regional stardom, its global leadership is still hampered by some obstacles, which are partially related to the relatively domestic credentials of the country. Public security is still a daunting issue in Brazil, with the national homicide rate reaching 26.2 per 100,000 people. Drug consumption is also high in all major cities, and environmental protection has not been fully incorporated in national policies and in people's minds and hearts. Thus, Brazil still needs to do some homework before passing the test of global recognition.

Notes

[1] "UK Backs Brazil as Permanent Security Council Member" (Number10.gov.uk, 27 March 2009), and "UK Backs Brazil Bid for UN Security Council Seat" (*Financial Times*, 9 November 2010).

[2] "France Backs Brazil UN Ambition" (*BBC News*, 23 December 2008).

[3] World Economic Outlook Database. Visited 14 September 2013.

[4] "El Mundo a Nosotros, sin Brasil, No Se Nos Abre, Se Nos Cierra" interview with Luis Almagro (*La República*, 8 February 2010).

[5] "Gigante ou Anão Diplomático" by Jorge Castañeda (*O Estado de São Paulo*, 27 September 2009).

[6] "Perdemos Nossa Relevância Política no Continente" (*Valor*, 30 November 2012).

[7] "Evaluating Brazil's Rise" (*Stratfor*, 22 June 2010).

[8] "O Brasil aos Olhos do Mundo" (*Veja*, 2 January 2012). 7,200 people were interviewed to the poll in eighteen countries.

[9] The estimated cost of the summit, at U.S.$ 2.4 million, accounted for 45 percent of the Brazilian Foreign Ministry's 2005 budget for international meetings.

[10] Despite Brazil's support, the country has not been able to convince African states to vote on Brazil's side in UN resolutions, namely on Iran. See "Planalto Lamenta Apoio de Africanos às Sanções" (*O Estado de São Paulo*, 11 June 2010).

[11] Discurso do Presidente da República, Luiz Inácio Lula da Silva, na sessão de abertura da Cúpula América do Sul – Países Árabes (10/05/2005) (author's translation from Portuguese).

[12] Attendance fell short of Brazil's initial expectations. While the majority of South America's twelve presidents participated, only seven of the twenty-two Arab nations that were invited were represented by heads of state or government.

[13] "WikiLeaks: Lula's Dislike of Pesky Leftist Diplomats" (*The Huffington Post*, 2 March 2011).

[14] Thirty-five Senators voted for the approval, whereas twenty-seven voted against the aprticipation of Venezuela in Mercosur. The voting was held on 15 December 2009.

[15] "Em Defesa da Argentina, Lula Faz Ataque à ONU em Cúpula Regional" (*O Estado de São Paulo*, 24 February 2010).

[16] "Brazil Pushes for Bigger G20 Role" (*BBC News*, 26 March 2009).

[17] See "Protagonismo Inconsequente" by J.A. Guilhon Albuquerque (*O Estado de São Paulo*, 12 December 2009).

[18] "Os Corações Partidos Por Lula no Mundo" by Moisés Naím (*Veja*, 19 May 2010).

[19] This criticism has also been made by former Foreign Ministers Luis Felipe Lampreia and Celso Lafer. See "Brasil Só Blinda Amigos, Diz Ex-Chanceler" (*O Estado de São Paulo*, 25 de Fevereiro 2010) and "Partidarização da Política Externa" by Celso Lafer (O Estado de São Paulo, 20 December 2009). See also "Hubris is Behind Brazil's Ties with Iran" by Andrés Oppenheimer (*Miami Herald*, 21 February 2010); "A Política Externa do Governo Lula" by Rubens Barbosa (*O Estado de São Paulo*, 23 February 2010).

[20] "Brazil president-elect speaks against Iran stoning" (*The Washington Post*, 3 November 2010).

[21] "Falando Francamente" (*O Estado de São Paulo*, 1 September 2013).

[22] During the 2010 crisis over the Falkland/Malvinas, President Lula followed a similar conduct and openly criticized the UN Security Council and Britain for maintaining the status quo in the archipelago.

[23] "PF Ajudou a Investigar Guerrilha Paraguaia" (*Folha de São Paulo*, 29 April 2010).

[24] Colombia's civil war could also prove to be a good case study for Brazil's diplomatic credentials, but in that case it was President Uribe and later President Santos who have not allowed any external meddling (Hofmeister, 2007:81). See "Homem da Guerra e da Paz," interview with Juan Manuel Santos (*Veja*, 1 September 2010).

[25] "Brasil y el Triunfalismo" by Julio María Sanguinetti (*La Nacion*, 2 October 2009).

[26] "Ex-Guerrilheiro Confirma Ligação das FARC com Traficantes Brasileiros" (*O Estado de São Paulo*, 6 June 2010."

[27] "As FARC Aproveitam as Fragilidades da Nossa Fronteira," interview with Luis Mattos (Amazon Military Commander) (*O Estado de São Paulo*, 17 May 2010).

[28] Argentina, Brazil, Spain leaders offer to mediate in Middle East conflict (*MercoPress*, 7 July 2010).

[29] In June 2010 Brazil's foreign minister told the *Financial Times* that his country would step back from its role as a mediator on the Iranian nuclear dispute due to the unfavorable response Brasilia believes its efforts received from the United States. In his words, "We got our fingers burned by doing things that everybody said were helpful and in the end we found that some

people could not take 'yes' for an answer." ("Brazil Ends Role as Iran Broker," *Financial Times*, 20 June 2010)

[30] See "Política Externa Responsável" by Fernando Henrique Cardoso (*O Estado de São Paulo*, 6 June 2010); "'Itamaraty No Improvisa'" by Sérgio Amaral (*O Estado de São Paulo*, 12 June 2010); "O Brasil, o Irã e as Armas Nucleares" by José Goldemberg (*Estado de São Paulo*, 15 March, 2010); "Diplomacia de Palanque" interview with Ambassador Roberto Abdenur (*Veja*, 8 September 2010); "Os Erros da Política Externa", editorial (*O Estado de São Paulo*, 12 June 2010); "Nosso Homem em Teerã" by Demétrio Magnoli (*O Estado de São Paulo*, 27 May 2010).

[31] "País Retrocedeu na Agenda dos Direitos Humanos" interview with Fernando Henriqque Cardoso (*O Estado de São Paulo*, 24 January 2011).

[32] "Brasileiros Apoiam Washington e Castigo a Teerã" (*O Estado de São Paulo*, 18 June 2010).

[33] "Desmatamento na Amazônia Cai e Atinge a Menor Taxa da História" (*O Estado de São Paulo*, 1 December 2010).

[34] Data from the Brazilian Beef Exporters Association. Online at http://www.abiec.com.br/41_exportacao_ano.asp. Visited September 16th, 2013.

[35] "Brasileiros Apoiam Washington e Castigo a Teerã" (*O Estado de São Paulo*, 18 June 2010).

[35] "Desmatamento na Amazônia Cai e Atinge a Menor Taxa da História" (*O Estado de São Paulo*, 1 December 2010).

[35] "O Peso do Homem na Amazônia" (*Veja Especial Amazônia*, September 2009).

[36] "O Brasil Atrás das Grades" (*Veja*, 24 November 2010).

[37] "Epidemia Nacional, Crack Já Está em Pelo Menos 3.871 Cidades Brasileiras" (*O Estado de São Paulo*, 14 December 2010).

7

Chile

"Chile is not free of threats; we know that aggregating the security of each separate country will enhance the security of the international community as a whole. For this reason, Chile is taking enormous strides to adapt to the new security scenarios." —Chile's report on implementation of the Declaration on Security in the Americas/OAS (2010)

Chile was the last South American country to initiate a process of redemocratization. In 1990, a long authoritarian period came to an end, together with an even longer period of search for political projects among polarizing alternatives. The international isolation of the Chilean military junta – in power from 1973 to 1990 – made matters worse. During this period, Chilean foreign policy was marked by the international community's rejection of the Pinochet regime, which resulted in its political isolation and its exclusion from many international arenas. This segregation was also evident in the recurrent condemnation by the United Nations (namely the UN Human Rights Commission in Geneva) and other international organizations. Even so, within the Cold War rationale the United States saw fit to back a regime that had a fierce anti-Communist posture, despite its suppression of democratic institutions and its brutal internal repression. During the period 1974-1976, Chile received U.S.$ 183.6 million in economic aid, as compared to U.S.$ 19.8 million in U.S. assistance given to Chile during the Salvador Allende administration (1970-1973), the first democratically elected Marxist to become president of a country in South America (Morandé, 2003:250).

This was, moreover, a period of mismatch between political reclusion and trade openness. Indeed, between 1984 and 1989, Chile was able to enjoy a constant growth of 6.2 percent, whereas the average for the rest of Latin America was -4.8 percent (Duran, 1996:187).

Moreover, at the end of 1979, Chile's fiscal deficit had been reduced considerably, which again contrasted markedly with the situation in the rest of the region. The strong economic profile of Chile during the military regime gave it some alternatives internationally, but only the reinstatement of the democratic system made it possible to reverse the isolation (Aravena, 1998b:88). In fact, the very notion of multilateralism did not conform to the style of a military regime's foreign policy. Since the central assumptions of the regime's foreign policy rested on its convergence "with a strict conception of realism, any form or instance of negotiation that did not involve a redistribution of international power was considered irrelevant" (Duran, 1996:196).

With redemocratization, a period of consistent search for consensual and national accords on central issues of national development was born (Aravena, 1998b:84). Despite this, the political system inaugurated by the Patricio Aylwin's government (1990-1994) was one of the less successful in the region in subordinating military power to civilian authority. The armed forces' full control of defense policy was part of a formal negotiation with the civil society as one among many preconditions to initiate democratic transition (Hirst, 1998: 105). The military were also unenthusiastic about regional integration and its spillover effects on security affairs. The perception was that closer security relations with other neighbors had to be subordinated to national defense policies.

If this is the political context that has permeated modern Chilean foreign policy, geography has also played an instrumental role. The country is located in the Southern Cone of South America and occupies a long (4,300 kilometers, 2,700 mi) and narrow (on average 175 kilometers, 109 mi) strip of land. The size of the national surface area increases considerably when the Antarctic territory and marine areas are included. These geographic features provide three identities for Chile: it is a South American country, an Antarctic country, and a Pacific Basin country. Because of both its topography and physical shape, Chile confronts a complex situation of security vis-à-vis its neighbors. For that reason, Chile has developed a significant tradition of strategic policies. It was one of the first South American countries to create a well-defined state apparatus, which included armed forces at the national level. And it traditionally overcomes situations of significant tension and crisis by resorting to self-defense and deterrence (Aravena, 1998b:88). Chile has also traditionally resorted to multilateralism to counterbalance politically the pressures from more powerful countries in South America, whether these were bordering nations or not. The basic assumption was that multilateral activity would help partially to overcome the shortage of political resources, opening up a new course of action for Chilean foreign policy and the defense of national interests (Duran, 1996:184-185).

Geography may also explain why legal principles have guided Chilean foreign policy over the last two centuries. Legalism originated with Andres Bello, author of the "Bello Clause," which provided for special tariff concessions for other Hispanic American republics as well as the first Chilean book in international law. He is regarded in Chile as the originator of juridical principles designed to safeguard equality among nations and of the nonintervention principle. The focus on international law has primarily served to defend Chilean conquests, territorial accessions, and modern claims to offshore areas. Once a particular goal, especially a territorial one, has been achieved, it has then been defended patiently and persistently, namely through legal disputes, whether through negotiations, arbitration, or participation in international organizations to protect its position. Chile was the first South American country to make an Antarctic claim (1940), and the first to declare a 200-km economic exclusive zone (1947).

Given this political and geographical context, the principal foreign policy goal of Patricio Aylwin's government was to reinsert Chile into the international system. The drive for acceptance around the world was fuelled in part by the desire to prevent a return to autocratic rule at home through institutionalizing democratic linkages with other states (Mullins, 2006:103). In a short period of time, the country began to occupy a significant space in international forums (namely the Rio Group) and was able to regain its status in the international community. The aim was to resurrect Chile's international image anchored on its democratic institutions and accompanied by the predominance of a domestic political culture that has valued participation in international forums. In fact, before the instauration of the military regime, Chile reached out to the global community. As an example, the Third Assembly of the United Nations Conference on Trade and Development (UNCTAD), held in Santiago in 1971, ratified the policy of creating a wider forum in which developing nations would be able to formulate alternatives to the hegemonic vision of the United States. Also in the 1920, the settlement of the Tacna dispute made then-President Alessandri realize that given Chile's relative power position, the country could no longer afford to be diplomatically isolated (Mullins, 2006:123).

With the transition to democracy in 1990, Chile was able to restore the political legitimacy of its international image, further deepening Chile's economic and commercial ties with the globalized international community. The administrations of Patricio Aylwin, Eduardo Frei

(1994-2000), Ricardo Lagos (2000-2006), Michelle Bachelet (2006-2010), and Sebastián Piñera (2010-2014) have restored the principles of Chilean foreign policy with a strong respect for democratic development and human rights. Over the last decade, Chile often pointed at the connection between regionalism and democracy, maintaining that the former would encourage and perfect the latter. Indeed, though small in population, with just over seventeen million people, Chile stands out on the regional stage by its democratic credentials – low in corruption and high in economic development. But despite Chile's track record in democracy promotion, the military still maintain a high level of influence over the political spectrum. This may be explained by the institutional legacies that constrain the actions of the new democratic authorities; the enduring military hierarchy under the leadership of General Augusto Pinochet; and a strong alliance between the military and right-wing parties (Linz and Stepan 1996; Garreton 1995). The armed forces receive 10 percent of the annual earnings from copper exports by the National Copper Corporation (Codelco). This special budget can be used only for military acquisitions. Chile still is the best example of a South American nation with a high level of military autonomy (Fuentes, 2000: 112).

Beyond its focus on democracy promotion, Chile's foreign policy has also been recognized by its independence and sense of nationalism: the idea of the strong, self-reliant national state, the balancer of power in the Pacific. Diego Portela is considered the founder of Chilean nationalism. He counseled against falling under the influence of any foreign power and opposed the Monroe Doctrine, for example, as leading to United States hegemony (Pittman, 1984:128). He has also originated the ideas that Chile must always predominate in the Pacific and never allow a union of Bolivia and Peru (Pittman, 1988b:175). During the Pinochet era, the government also published guides to "make of Chile a great nation" such as the National Objectives of Chile (1974), the National Objective and General Policies of the Government of Chile (1981), and the Socio-Economic Program (1981). For the Chilean scholar Joaquín Fermandois Chile's culture is still permeated by "an extraordinary self-conscience and self-security as a national State" (Fermandois, 2005:36).

Contribution to Traditional Security

One of the main activities of Chile's democratic governments has been the search for a definitive solution to the pending issue of border demarcation. Economic opening and development, as well as the country's external image, could eventually be put at risk if border tensions resurface. Relations with Argentina made a qualitative jump. Historically, their disputes were primarily a consequence of geographical factors. Faced by the third longest border in the world (5,150 km or 3,200 mi) the two countries first attempt to establish general criteria to determine their borders and resolve disputes was in 1831, when the Borders Treaty was signed. But it was unsuccessful in putting an end to the dispute. The second major cause in delaying the resolution of the bilateral problems was the prevalence of nationalist doctrines in both countries that viewed concessions on territorial issues "purely in terms of a zero-sum game, and felt them as 'losses' and 'dismemberment'" (Oelsner, 2005:106).

The two countries were on the verge of war on several occasions (November 1878, September 1898, December 1901, and especially in December 1978 over the Beagle Islands). In January 1979, under the Agreement of Montevideo, the two nations agreed to withdraw their military forces from the disputed zone, and Argentina revoked its declaration of war. In 1982, at an extraordinary session of the OAS, during the middle of the Falklands/Malvinas war, both countries took their dispute to an intense diplomatic level. Convoked by Argentina in accordance with the Inter-American Treaty of Reciprocal Assistance, the OAS session saw the majority of countries supporting Argentina, whereas Chile preferred to abstain. In the 1980s, however, Chile and Argentina attempted to resolve their issues, and eventually a historic peace and friendship treaty was signed in 1984 (ratified in 1985). The treaty resolved the long-standing conflict over possession of three islands south of Tierra del Fuego and navigational routes in the Straits of Magellan and Beagle Channel. Two commissions were established as a result of the treaty. The first was the 1985 Binational Commission on Economic Cooperation and Physical Integration, intended to encourage economic growth; and the second was the Argentina-Chile Permanent Conciliation Commission, which was set up to arbitrate disputes. The latter called for cooperative development and binational use of free ports and navigational zones, land transportation systems, air navigational routes, electrical interconnections, telecommunications systems, and the like.

Although the Peace and Friendship treaty established the foundation for cooperation and integration, several border disputes remained an issue, and mistrust between the two nations in the political, economic, and military realms persisted for several years. Hence, when Patricio Aylwin came to power in 1990 one of his most important goals was the definite resolution of the border dispute with Argentina and the initiation of close economic and political ties. In August 1991, both presidents signed the Presidential Declaration on the Border between the Republic of Chile and the Republic of Argentina, definitively settling twenty-two border disputes between the two countries. Shortly thereafter, disputes over the Laguna del Desierto and the Southern Patagonia Ice Field (called "Campos de Hielo Sur" in Chile and "Hielo continental patagónico" in Argentina) were also resolved some years later. In the case of Chile there was an anxiety to improve its relations with the outside world after the isolation of the Pinochet years, and the settlement of outstanding issues with Argentina was part of this process. Strategic issues began to drop off the agenda, and trade issues became more important (Mullins, 2006:119). This special relationship reached a peak in 1996 with the agreement of Argentina to supply gas to Chile, leading to a significant increase in Chilean investment in the Argentinean economy (Fermandois, 2011:40). In the same vein, Chile supported the candidacy of former Argentina Presidente Néstor Kirchner, as Secretary General of UNASUR, in spite of muted criticism of some politicians in the center-right coalition of President Piñera (Fermandois, 2011:48).

But despite the positive interactions between Chile and Argentina in the political and economic arenas in the 1990s, both countries continued to base their national security policies on a so-called "hypotheses of conflict" and on a balance of power, rather than on a cooperative regional security program (Arancibia-Clavel, 2007). As Chile's then-Minister of Defense Patricio Rojas (1990-1994) stated: "given the uncertainty of the international system and the transition process following the end of the Cold war, defense policy focused on optimizing deterrent and defensive capabilities in the area of risk and contingency assessment drives the climate in the country" (cited in Arancibia-Clavel, 2007). Although this dynamic has, to a large extent, been replaced by a more cooperative tone, tension still surfaces. In 2010, for instance, old wounds were reopened when Argentine President Cristina Fernández de Kirchner announced that the maps of the Southern Patagonia Ice Field needed to be reassessed.

Relations with Peru have also been rocky even if the termperature has cooled down after the 2014 International Court of Justice (ICJ) ruling over their bilateral maritime dispute. In 2005, the Peruvian Congress unilaterally approved a law, which increased the stated sea limit with Chile. This law superseded the Peruvian supreme decree 781 for the same purpose from 1947, which had autolimited its maritime border to geographical parallels only. Peru claimed that the maritime border was based on two agreements limited to fishery, and that there was no true international border governing sovereignty. Thus, in January 2008 Peru formally presented the case to the ICJ in The Hague, Netherlands. In a formal announcement to the nation, President García declared its expectation that "the Peruvian position will be juridically and irrefutably confirmed by the highest court on the planet" (cited in Elizondo, 2009:226). Chile rejected the Peruvian claim, appealing to international recognition of the existing line. It argued that treaties in 1952 and 1954 between the countries defined the seaborder. The dispute dated back to the 1879-1883 War of the Pacific, in which Chile defeated Peru and Bolivia and gained one-third of its modern territory, in the process acquiring two southern Peruvian coastal regions, Tacna (returned to Peru in 1929) and Arica. Central to the row were 14,633 square miles of fishing-rich sea that Chile currently controlled (see Fig. 7.1). Fueling the inherent geopolitical rivalry were arms purchases, particularly by Chile, before the 2014 ICJ ruling. Chile claimed that its weapons acquisitions were purely for purposes of defense and deterrence, but this offered Peru little consolation given the inherent divergence of security interests and perceptions. In 2009, a new diplomatic row erupted after a Peruvian court ordered the arrest of two Chilean military officers over alleged spying. The court accused the officers of paying a Peruvian air force officer to reveal national secrets. The claims were dismissed by Chile's government, but the issue was put on the table at an UNASUR meeting of Foreign Affairs and Defense Ministers held in Quito in November 2009, which led Peru to storm out of an APEC summit held in Singapore in the same month. The relations between both remained precarious in the following years, leading up to Peruvian President Ollanta Humala's agreement to cede territory claimed by Bolivia against Chile so as to facilitate resolution of the maritime claim. The 1929 Peace and Friendship treaty, which formalized relations between the three states following the War of the Pacific, requires Peru's "prior agreement" to pursue further negotiations for Chile to cede former Peruvian territory to a third party and settle the conflict. Chilean President Sebastian Piñera reacted to the 2014 ruling saying that its implementation would be a gradual process. A few days later, he met with Peruvian President Humala on the sides of the Second CELAC Summit in Havana and reaffirmed the Chilean commitment with the compliance of the ICJ ruling.

With Bolivia Chile does not have pending demarcation issues. What exists is a Bolivian claim for passage to the ocean, a conflict dating back to 1879 when Bolivia lost its coastal territory to Chile in the War of the Pacific. From a Chilean perspective, this is a bilateral issue and not a multilateral one, and therefore no international organization has been able to play a valuable role. In July 2010, the foreign ministers of Chile and Bolivia met in La Paz to begin negotiations on a thirteen-point agenda that includes Bolivia's request for Pacific Ocean access. Chile has, however, shown very strong reservations to ceding territory, and President Piñera has explicitly said this to Bolivian Vice-President García when he visited Santiago in July 2010. In any case, Piñera's government has publicly stated that Bolivia's Evo Morales government is the most stable over the last decades and that Chile should seize the opportunity to resolve the bilateral issue in order to increase its access to Bolivia's markets and natural resources and to use the country as a bridge to reach out to Brazil.[1] When President Morales announced his intent to bring the dispute before the International Court of Justice (ICJ) in The Hague in 2011, the Chilean president showed that he was unwilling to engage in meaningful negotiations. Responding to Morales, Piñera simply said: "there are not unresolved territorial issues between Chile and Bolivia. . . . All issues were definitely settled by the treaty of peace and friendship of 1904. The treaty was duly negotiated more than twenty years after the end of the conflict between our two countries. The Treaty is based on International Law which both Chile and Bolivia must respect and comply."[2] Bolivia's president claimed he opted for an international resolution "because developments were so slow" in bilateral discussions between Chile and Bolivia. And in 2013 when Bolivia did file a lawsuit against Chile at the ICJ, the Chilean government maintained its posture and ruled out any dialogue.

Figure 7.1: Chilean-Peruvian Dispute

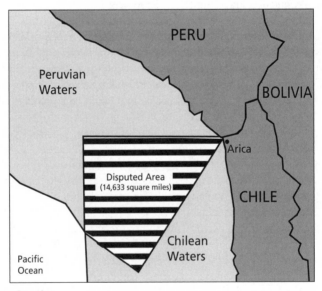

Source: Stratfor

In the regional arena, Chile has lent its strongest collaboration to the deactivation of the conflict between Ecuador and Peru. The last eruption of this enduring conflict broke out in 1995 in the Rio Cenepa area of the Marañon river basin, as result of a territorial dispute in the northern part of the Condor mountain range (see Chapter 3). A previous border dispute between the two countries in 1941 was settled in 1942 when both parties signed the Rio Protocol, guaranteed by Argentina, Brazil, Chile, and the United States. As a "guarantor," Chile played again an important role in 1995 in bringing the two rival countries together. In October 1996, the Foreign Ministers of Peru and Ecuador met in Chile and signed the Santiago Agreement, which provided a framework for the settlement of the border issue.

Moreover, Chile seeks to fortify hemispheric institutionality and redefine hemispheric security. Toward this end, the Fifth Meeting of the Ministers of Defense of the Americas, held in Santiago in 2002, declared that "existing subregional agreements on security and defense contribute to hemispheric security, and should be respected and taken into account in the development of a cooperative security system that emphasizes the prevention of conflicts and recognizes the particular strategic contexts of each subregion in the Hemisphere" (Art.18). Chile was instrumental in designing the text of the declaration. In 1991, Chile had also been one of the main promoters of the Commitment to Democracy and the Renewal of the Inter-American System, approved at the twenty-first regular session of the General Assembly of the OAS, which was also held in Santiago. The Commitment created a mechanism intended to isolate any authoritarian regime that comes to power in the region. Taking its cue from these criteria, the Chilean government determinately supported the auspices of the new Program for the Consolidation of Democracy, which falls under the purview of the Secretariat of the OAS. In 2010, in a meeting with UNASUR's secretary general, the late Nestor Kirchner, Chilean legislators also called for the continental body to add a "democracy clause" in its founding treaty. No doubt, they felt this would demonstrate UNASUR's determination to place its full weight in ostracising any South American regime if ever it seizes power by nonconstitutional means.

In terms of international security, Chile has supported the main initiatives in the area of arms control and limitation. It promoted the Mendoza Declaration, which bans chemical weapons, and it was a participant in the Tlatelolco Agreement, which transformed the region into a nuclear-free zone. In several international forums Chile has reiterated its commitment to nonproliferation and arms control. In 2011, the country (along with Australia, Canada, Germany, Japan, Mexico, the

Netherlands, Poland, Turkey, and the United Arab Emirates) adopted a declaration where they shared a common purpose: to take forward the consensus outcomes of the 2010 Treaty on the Non-Proliferation of Nuclear Weapons (NPT) Review Conference and jointly to advance the nuclear disarmament and nonproliferation agendas as mutually reinforcing processes. The NPT was regarded as "the essential foundation for the achievement of nuclear disarmament, the cornerstone of the global nuclear nonproliferation regime and the basis for the development of the peaceful uses of nuclear energy."[3]

The strong defense of its nonproliferation has not been matched by an equal commitment with peacekeeping, where Chile is a relative novice compared to Brazil and Argentina. While it has experience in conflict resolution that dates back to the 1930s, it has only become a significant contributor to UN operations within the last decade. Its most significant UN operation so far was in East Timor, where Chile provided an aviation brigade, along with some ground forces. But the interest in peacekeeping has grown. As of October 2013, Chile has a total of 498 military and police deployed on UN peacekeeping operations, mainly in Haiti (MINUSTAH). Chile's commitment on peacekeeping is to some extent dependent on the easing of government armed-forces relations. This conflict – about the functional autonomy of the armed forces – manifests itself as bureaucratic infighting within the state apparatus. Chile still faces constant debates and even conflicts about the powers of civilian authorities in the area of defense. Over two decades after the end of the military governments the issues of roles or attributions of the armed forces and human rights remain the main elements of distrust and tension in the political system.

Contribution to Human Security

With fairly low crime, homicide, and drug-trafficking rates, Chile's most lethal nontraditional threats have been nature-made rather than man-made. Extreme weather events and other natural hazards can have far-reaching consequences for the safety and wellbeing of individuals and communities. Such catastrophes tend to exacerbate preexisting problems and inequalities, with vulnerable parts of the population often disproportionately impacted.

Tectonic activity in Chile is related to the eastern subduction of the Nazca Plate (an oceanic tectonic plate in the eastern Pacific Ocean basin off the west coast of South America). In February 2010, an 8.8-magnitude earthquake in Chile was ranked as the fifth-strongest earthquake recorded since 1900, when records were first kept. The most powerful earthquake ever recorded – with a magnitude of 9.5 – was also occurred in Chile, in 1960, and several others ones (in March 1985 and July 1995, for instance) had a magnitude of about 8. The economic and social effects of natural disasters are long lasting and wide reaching in scope. The 2010 quake damaged 1.5 million homes, killed 525 people, and caused U.S.$ 30 billion in damage. Although Chile, a model of economic stability in South America, could raise money relatively cheaply on international markets because it has an investment-grade rating and is considered low risk, the economic impact of the quake was immense. U.S.$ 30 billion represented nearly 20 percent of Chilean GDP. Speaking on his first full day in office, President Piñera acknowledged that he would have to reallocate funds from other projects to pay for the reconstruction, and that the process would take years, not months.

Despite extensive damage and casualties, Chile's good governance played a significant role in limiting the death toll resulting from the 2010 earthquake. Over the years, Chile's effective institutions succeeded in designing and adopting better building codes, which have been periodically upgraded, to take into account previous earthquake experience, innovations in preventative technologies, and the country's growing wealth. Advance planning for earthquakes, including training drills, is an integral part of adult and child education in Chile.

Chile's effective contribution to human security is also detectable in the fight against urban criminality. The country is considered the safest country in South America and the one with the lowest homicide rate (3.7 per 100,000 people) (UNODC, 2013). Reasons for Chile's positive ranking include its good performance on social inequality, employment opportunities, urban segregation, and drug and firearm availability. Law is also fairly well enforced. The role of the Chilean national police forces changed with government and constitutional reforms in the 1990s. The country has two main national law enforcement forces, both of which also have roles in the intelligence community. The *Carabineros*, the national uniformed police, are charged with public safety and border patrols. They also have a paramilitary unit and a counterintelligence arm that combat drug trafficking and enforce border security. The second Chilean police force is the Investigations Police, which employs, among other law enforcement strategies, civilian plain-clothes forces that oversee surveillance and apprehension of suspected criminals and terrorists. A study carried out by a renowned consultancy firm demonstrated that one of the reasons why crime rates were low in Chile was the respect for the country's *Carabineros*.[4]

This does not mean, naturally, that insecurity spots are not detectable. For about one decade now the United States has been monitoring potential terrorist activities in Iquique, a touristic resort town and free-trade zone on Chile's northern Pacific coast. In 2001, the Chilean government confirmed that it was investigating an alleged Arab financial network with terrorist links that could be engaging in money laundering in the region (Hudson, 2003). And it opened an investigation into the activities in Iquique of Brazil-based Lebanese businessman Assad Ahmad Barakat who was suspected of opening two businesses as cover to move money clandestinely to Hezbollah. The investigation did not lead to new information, however. Barakat was arrested in Brazil in June 2002, and the Brazilian Supreme Court ordered his extradition to Paraguay. But suspicion remains. According to a cable from then-U.S. Ambassador to Chile Craig Kelly that was released by Wikileaks, "there is intelligence information indicating that Iquique groups contribute to fundraising for Islamic charitable organizations and possibly others."[5]

The Chilean Government is a consistent and active supporter of U.S. counterterrorism efforts and works with the Embassy in Santiago in the monitoring of Chile's Muslim organizations. But Chilean authorities have not been particularly proactive given the small size of Chile's Muslim community (3,000-5,000 people) and a likely lack of conviction that there is a serious threat.

In recent years Chile has increased its military visibility in the Northern part of the country. In 2009, some 1,800 troops, pilots and air force personnel from Argentina, Brazil, Chile, the United States, and France carried out the Salitre II military exercises, based in the desert regions surrounding the cities of Iquique and Antofagasta in northern Chile. In 2011, the Chilean Armed Forces also conducted the Hurricane Iquique Exercise, involving 10,000 troops. Yet, despite the geographical location of the exercises, it is highly unlikely that they were associated to a growing concern over Arabic militant presence in the region.

The antiterrorism law is one of Chile's harshest laws. It includes harsher penalties for some offenses, makes pretrial release more difficult, enables the prosecution to withhold evidence from the defense for up to six months, and allows convictions on testimony by anonymous witnesses. The application of this law has often run into controversy. Human Rights Watch, for instance, has recommended that the antiterrorism law be modified to ensure that only the gravest crimes of violence involving attacks on life, liberty, or physical integrity are considered terrorist crimes, and then only when the other conditions specified in the law are met.[6] Chilean authorities have often used the antiterrorism law to prosecute the indigenous Mapuche population in

Southern Chile for common crimes, such as arson and destruction of machinery and equipment. Indeed, the current version of the law lists arson as a "terrorist" offence. The Mapuche (which means "people of the land" in their language, Mapuzungun) are Chile's largest indigenous group, numbering nearly one million among Chile's population of more than sixteen million. In the late nineteenth century, the state wrested the Mapuche lands from the people in southern Chile by force. A century later, in the early 1990s, Mapuche communities and organizations began to lay claim to their ancestral territories through a strategy of occupying private lands, which are often in the hands of lumber companies, and protesting logging and mining initiatives and garbage dumps that have serious environmental impacts near their communities. The Mapuche consider insufficient the 667,457 hectares of land restored to them by government since 1994. In 2011, four Mapuche involved in land conflicts were sentenced to twenty and twenty-five years in prison. The following year, Chilean President Sebastian Piñera invoked again the antiterror law to pursue those responsible for setting a number of wildfires that killed seven firefighters, burned dozens of homes, and destroyed around 123,000 acres of woodland and brush. The violence of the punishments has caused more distress and distrust. According to data from Chile's Attorney General Office the number of reported crimes in La Araucania linked to the Mapuche conflict increased 77 percent in twelve months: from 169 in 2011 to 300 in 2012.

Conclusions

Chile's democratization process had to convince a successful military government to turn over political power peacefully and constitutionally. The route was not necessarily perfect, but had the capacity to nullify the isolation that the country had experienced during the military regime. Indeed, one of the first steps of democratic Chile was to reject the polarized politics of the Cold War (even before the collapse of the Soviet Union) and to make a significant contribution to Southern Cone security, namely by solving intricate border conflicts with Argentina. The foreign policy program of the first democratic government showed a clear language of "democratic internationalism" and highlighted the need to reduce "foreign dependence". The reestablishment of ties with its neighbors and trading partners would serve to facilitate the penetration of overseas export markets and to attract much-needed foreign investment. Although the internationalization of the country was successfully achieved (mainly through economic diplomacy) and Chilean leaders are respected abroad (President Michelle Bachelet was the Executive Director of UN Women between 2010 and 2013 and President Ricardo Lagos was UN special envoy for climate change from 2007 to 2010), the pacification process is still far from over. Chile's relations with Peru, Bolivia, and even Argentina are marked by cyclical episodes of tension and animosity. It is the issue of Bolivian access to the Pacific Ocean that has been the most intricate problem. The failure to resolve this matter has seen bilateral relations frozen in a way that resembles the nineteenth century.

The mixed results are also seen internally. While Chile is the country that enjoys the highest human development indexes in South America, it nonetheless faces domestic conflicts, namely with indigenous groups. The official line of argument followed by the democratic governments that have ruled Chile since 1990 is that violent indigenous groups represent a small minority within the one-million strong Mapuche community, and that the main problem involving the country's largest indigenous group is reducing the high poverty levels that they face. The subordination of the military to civilian rule has lifted the impediments to a more cooperative attitude, but the application of antiterrorist laws has left little space for cooperation, and ignited the problem rather than solved it.

Notes

[1] "Este Es un Gran Momento Para Resolver el Tema Marítimo con Bolívia" interview with Jaime Ravinet (*La Tercera*, 1 August, 2010).

[2] "Chile and Bolivia Have Heated Argument over Ocean Access in UN" (*Digital Journal*, 22 September 2011).

[3] Berlin Statement by Foreign Ministers on nuclear disarmament and nonproliferation, 30 April 2011, Art. 2.

[4] "Uruguay, Chile and Costa Rica Rated as Safest Countries in Latinamerica" (*Mercopress*, 30 April 2010).

[5] Online at: http://ciperchile.cl/2011/02/28/cable-38339-comunidad-musulmana-en-chile/. Visited January 22nd, 2012.

[6] Human Rights Watch (2010), "Chile: Amend Anti-Terrorism Law and Military Jurisdiction." Online at: http://www.hrw.org/news/2010/09/27/chile-amend-anti-terrorism-law-and-military-jurisdiction. Visited January 22nd, 2012.

8

Colombia

"Don't forget that we still have a conflict. . . . " —Juan Manuel Santos, president of Colombia, 2012

One of the most permanent characteristics of Colombia's international relations has been the impact of the United States on the country's foreign policy. Although relations between both countries were tense in the early twentieth century as the U.S. supported the independence of Panama in 1903 (until then a part of Colombia), they soon normalized. The close relationship between Colombian and U.S. political elites, which started with President Marco Fidel Suárez's (1918-1921) "Polar Star Doctrine," was an important source of stability for the Colombian political system throughout the twentieth century (Ebel, Taras and Cochrane, 1991: 141). The onset of the Cold War brought about no changes in this dynamic as the main political forces in the country – the Liberals and Conservatives – were ideologically committed to fighting communism both at home and abroad. Colombia was the only South American country to send troops to Korea in 1951, and it also participated in a UN emergency force deployed to the Suez Canal in 1956. In exchange for its loyalty, the country received substantial military and economic assistance from the U.S. Colombia was one of the three largest recipients of U.S. military assistance in Latin America and the second largest recipient, after Brazil, of U.S. economic aid between 1949 and 1974 (Tickner, 2003:170). Colombia also played host to the founding conference of the OAS in 1948 and, as a result of its close ties with the United States, it was able to provide the first secretary general, Carlos Llheras Camargo. And it strongly supported the creation in 1960 of the Latin American Free Trade Association (LAFTA), which was intended to establish a free trade among member states through annual tariff reduction.

The ascendance of Ronald Reagan to the presidency in 1981 provided a prime opportunity for Colombia to align its foreign policy even further with that of the United States, given the ideological affinities between both executives. As a result, the country adopted a high anticommunist profile on an international level, in consonance with U.S. foreign policy imperatives, which reached its maximum expression in Central America and the Caribbean (Pardo and Tokatlian 1989: 140). While gaining the favor of the United States, this posture tended to isolate the country diplomatically from its South American neighbors. Colombia's decision to abstain from voting on the application of the Inter-American Treaty of Reciprocal Assistance in the Falklands/Malvinas war (1982) provided a poignant statement of the distance created by the Turbay administration (1978-1982) between Bogotá and other countries of the region. President Turbay recognized in 1978 that there were critical situations in which the military were called to govern in order to assure the survival of a given society (Buitrago 1989). Turbay's statements, which allowed the military to exercise an open repression against communism, coincided with U.S. Ambassador to Colombia Diego Asencio's acquiescent approach to extreme anticommunist tactics.

The honeymoon with the United States came to an end when President Belisario Betancurt (1982-1986) expressed his determination to develop an "independent" foreign policy. During President Reagan's visit to Colombia in late 1982, Betancur urged him to abandon U.S. interventionism in Central America and proposed the renegotiation of Latin American debt (Bagley and Tokatlian 1987: 178). The Colombian president was also critical of United States' drug policy, and consequently refused to eradicate illicit crops, as well as to enforce the extradition treaty that the two countries had signed in 1979 (Tickner, 2001). In his attempt to adopt an independent foreign policy, he called Colombia to join the Non-Aligned Movement and joining with Mexico, Venezuela, and Panama created the Contadora Group as a counterbalance to "the Reagan administration's hardline policies in Central America" (Bagley and Tokatlián 1985: 41). Betancur's alternative approach to Regan's tough anticommunist strategies made it possible for the FARC to regard the creation of the Unión Patriótica (UP)[1] as a means to access the political system and bring about the changes they were fighting for. Betancur's shift in foreign policy reflected the changes he was to implement in domestic politics in order to "confront the regime's deepening legitimacy crisis and the problem of continuing political violence" (Bagley and Tokatlián 1985: 35).

The end of the Cold War did not produce any major transformation in Colombia's foreign policy. The external relations of the administration of Virgilio Barco (1986-1990) exhibited a relative degree of continuity with that of Betancur's government. Barco continued to emphasize the nonideological nature of the country's international relations, intensified efforts to diversify them, and asserted Colombia's independence in relation to the United States. His administration opposed the U.S. bombing of Libya, opposed U.S. intervention in Panama in 1989 to overthrow Manuel Noriega, and criticized Israel's occupation of Arab territory (Randall, 2011:143). The external relations were pursued primarily through explicit emphasis upon foreign economic diplomacy, and the expansion of commercial and diplomatic relations with other regions of the world, rather than those political measures characteristic of the Betancur period. The diversification of the country's external relations was viewed essentially as a means of increasing its international negotiating capacity (Tickner, 2001).

The administration of César Gaviria (1990-1994) maintained emphasis on certain objectives introduced by the previous administration, such as the preservation of a relative degree of autonomy, the search for an active economic diplomacy, the modernization of the country's foreign policy apparatus, the improvement of national negotiating power and the diversification of Colombia's political ties on an international level (Tokatlian and Tickner, 1996:108). In consequence, the Colombian government participated actively in regional integration schemes such as the ALADI, G-3 and the Andean Group, while signing a number of new bilateral trade agreements with neighboring countries.

Notwithstanding efforts undertaken during both the Barco and Gaviria administrations to diversify Colombia's international economic relations, these remained concentrated in the United States and, to a lesser degree, Europe. For example, by the end of the Gaviria period Colombia continued to export 35 percent of its products to the United States, while 40 percent of its imports originated in that country as well. The approval of the Andean Trade Preference Act (1991) in the United States, and the Special Cooperation Program in Europe (1990), designed to assist drug-producing nations in the Andean region to diversify their commercial relations, reinforced this tendency (Tokatlian and Tickner 1996: 109; Tickner, 2001). The salience of the drug issue in Colombian-U.S. relations beginning in the 1980s reinforced the dependent relations between these two countries. In November 1993, the Gaviria Administration released a new national strategy against violence under the name Security for the People, where the government argued that the borders between drug trafficking, guerrillas, and common crime had blurred. Gaviria thus unified a punitive-police approach against all forms of violence. It was the first time that a Colombian president acknowledged these connections.

With the inauguration of President Samper (1994-1998), the bilateral relationship with the United States experienced a severe breakdown following revelations that his presidential campaign had received financial contributions from the Cali cartel. During the 1980s and halfway through the 1990s, the so-called Medellín and Cali cartels came to control more than 70 percent of the Colombian drug exports (Guizado and Restrepo, 2007:74). Increasingly, the U.S. began to refer to Colombia as a "narcodemocracy" or as a "narcostate," rather than an ally (Tickner, 2003:178). This was what Joe Toft, the U.S. DEA officer in charge of the Bogotá office, called the country on Colombian national television in September 1994. In fact Cali cartel bosses adopted a survival strategy that opted for penetrating the state by financing politicians' campaigns and buying their loyalty rather than violent confrontation. This strategy was so successful that with their contribution they were able to influence the presidential race in 1994, when Ernest Samper was elected. During the subsequent debate in Congress, "nearly one third of its members, as well as some kind of high-ranking state officials, were denounced for having had some kind of relationship with the Cali drug lords" (Guizado and Restrepo, 2007:78). Several congressmen, as well as high officials, lost their seats and went to prison.

As speculations in Colombia grew regarding Samper's level of awareness and involvement in the campaign scandal, U.S. policy toward the country became markedly aggressive and intransigent, reducing the country's margins for international action even further. Although, arguably, the U.S. government may not have identified Samper's removal from power as an explicit policy objective, the weakening of the Colombian president clearly became the policy of some, if not many, State Department officials (Franco 1998: 53; Tickner, 2001). Not only was Colombia ostracized by the U.S. but it became increasingly identified as a pariah state within the global community. The Clinton administration went as far as denying Samper a visa in 1996. During his entire period, Samper received only two official state visits by the neighboring heads of state of Venezuela and Ecuador (Tickner, 2003:180). Colombia went from being an ally of the U.S. to become a victim of "coercive diplomacy" (Buitrago, 1989: 101).

The election of Andrés Pastrana (1998-2002) was considered a key opportunity for reestablishing a cooperative tone to the bilateral relationship. Pastrana established a clear distinction between Colombia's domestic priority, which revolved primarily around seeking a peaceful solution to the armed conflict and U.S. interests in the country, based essentially on the drug problem (Tickner, 2003:180). As we saw in Chapter 4, Pastrana proposed a "Plan Colombia" when he came into office in 1998, asking foreign governments to collaborate on a plan of economic aid to Colombia's neglected countryside in order to promote peace. This plan received practically no response internationally. In 2000, however, due to increased concerns about drug production, the stability of the Colombian government, and the potential failure of the peace process, the Clinton administration decided to support Plan Colombia, but it demanded major amendments to the original text (Randall, 2011:147). Thus, following initial attempts to gear Colombia's foreign policy toward domestic priorities (peace), rather than U.S. concerns (drugs), President Andrés Pastrana was forced to resort to a "drug war logic" in order to secure sorely needed U.S. support. In practice, this shift signaled the return to a strong alignment with the United States, which had characterized Colombia's foreign policy in the 1950s-1970s. Plan Colombia did not exclusively aim at the U.S. carrying out a subtler intervening role in the hemisphere; instead it was also designed to solve the "external threat" that drugs posed to U.S. society. It not only benefited the United States but also Colombia. The Pastrana administration's acquiescence in the "drug war" was also conceived as a way to increase the country's military strength.

When President Álvaro Uribe (2002-2010) took office internal security became his highest policy priority. While the Uribe administration had a mixed record on the other pillars of its stated policy agenda – modernizing the state apparatus, battling corruption, balancing the budget while reviving economic growth and reducing unemployment – it made clear that security must come first. To achieve its objectives, the government devised what it called its Democratic Defense and Security Policy (DSP), which sought to regain control of the country by increasing the numbers and capacity of troops and police units and by deploying them across the country to challenge the guerrillas. This has been accompanied by a major increase in the eradication of illicit crops, aimed as much at denying revenues to the guerrillas and paramilitary groups as at reducing coca and opium poppy production. According to DSP, Colombia's democratic institutions and Colombian citizens are threatened by six factors: terrorism; drug trafficking; illegal financing; trafficking of arms, ammunitions and explosives; extortion and kidnapping; and homicide. In 2004, as part of the DSP, Uribe adopted the Patriot Plan, intended to get military presence to the most remote areas of Colombia, where the guerrillas had enclaves, and enable the introduction of social programs. The U.S. government supported the democratic security policy of Álvaro Uribe, who proved to be one of the United States' only remaining allies in a region where critics of U.S. foreign policy did well at the polls. Uribe endorsed the Bush administration's war on terror in the aftermath of 9/11 and supported the U.S.-led invasion of Iraq. He went as far as to support several policies favored by Washington but controversial at home: the antidrug application of herbicides over nearly a million rural hectares, and a free-trade agreement that preserved many U.S. agricultural subsidies and quotas. As a show of support for the often-beleaguered Colombian president, President Bush twice visited Colombia during his presidency – Cartagena in 2004 and Bogotá in 2007, the first to the Colombian capital by a serving U.S. president since 1982.

The close bilateral relationship was predicated on Plan Colombia – an aid package that established Colombia as the largest U.S. aid recipient outside the Middle East. The statistics of the bilateral cooperation are noteworthy. Between 2000 and 2010, Washington gave Columbia U.S.$ 8 billion worth of aid. And between 2000 and 2008 Colombia sent 68,452 men to the U.S. for professional training. Colombia became the primary country in which U.S. counterdrug, counterinsurgency, and counterterrorism agendas converged.

In October 2009 the Uribe administration also announced that it had reached an agreement on the terms of a decade-long lease to allow U.S. military personnel to use seven Colombian military bases to conduct antidrug trafficking and antiterrorism operations. The increased access would serve to replace the U.S. lease at Manta, Ecuador, the only U.S. base of operations in South America until the lease was allowed by the Correa administration to expire. The agreement stoked the flames of regional conflict as it was severely criticized by virtually all South American leaders (except Peru). Reacting to the deal, President Chávez called Uribe a "mafia leader" and said that the region was on the "brink of war." In August 2010 the Colombian Constitutional Court suspended the proposed deal on the grounds that the joint agreement was "an arrangement which requires the State to take on new obligations as well as an extension of previous ones" and that it should be an "international treaty subject to congressional approval." Uribe claimed the deal was merely an extension of the Plan Colombia defense pact with the United States and thus did not require authorization beyond his signature.

In August 2010 President Juan Manuel Santos – Uribe's former defense minister – assumed office after receiving the highest number of votes obtained by any candidate in the history of Colombian democracy. Santos did not stray far from Uribe's hardline security policies against the FARC, but he had an interest in differentiating himself from his predecessor when it came to dealing with the explosive Colombian-Venezuelan relationship. He broadened his country's friendships in the region, first by resuming diplomatic ties with Ecuador and second, by striking a truce with Venezuela.[2] In his own words, "We didn't have a relationship with Venezuela and we insulted each other on and off; some people even talked of war. . . . We've changed that 180 degrees."[3] Uribe's defense relationship with the United States and tumultuous relationship with Venezuela had long alienated Colombia from much of the region. While Uribe centered Colombia's foreign policy on an alliance with the United States, Santos maintained good relations with Washington yet also kept some distance, becoming more of an independent player in South America. He won praise for being a pragmatic bridge builder. While remaining the United States' most solid ally in the region, he also lobbied for Cuba to have a seat at international forums. This historic turn has been openly discussed by Santos. In an interview with the *Washington Post* in August 2011, he declared that,

> "Yes, they [relations with Venezuela] were not almost at an end [as the reporter had suggested]; they were at an end. We had no diplomatic relations, no trade. The only discussions we had were through the media and we were talking about war, which is inconceivable. So I decided to have cordial and cooperative relations not just with Venezuela, but also with Ecuador, a country with which we also had no relations. What we decided is that it is in our interest to have a region that is not on the verge of war."[4]

Contribution to Traditional Security

Colombia's civil conflict is the longest and the most intricate in the continent. President Álvaro Uribe pursued a hardline stance against left-wing guerrillas while making tentative peace overtures. Uribe's father, a wealthy landowner, was killed by the FARC guerrillas during a 1983 kidnapping attempt, and while in power Uribe always priorized a strategy of military confrontation rather than political negotiation. In fact, it may be argued that he won the 2002 elections because he was in tune with the majority's feelings of frustration towards a failed peace experiment during Andrés Pastrana's government. Uribe built a coherent policy that involved all governmental instruments around a same cause: defeating the FARC in all military, political, economic, and diplomatic aspects. The guerilla faction shrank to less than half its 2001 peak of 20,000 fighters and lost several of its leaders: FARC's founder, Manuel Marulanda succumbed to a heart attack in 2008, and Alfonso Cano, who replaced him as the group's leader, was shot dead in 2011. President

Juan Manuel Santos called Cano's elimination, "the most resounding blow against the organization in its entire history."[5] The government's security build-up drove the FARC from heavily populated central Colombia to remoter areas and caused disarray in the ranks. Moreover, several media-prone cases such as the bombings at Raúl Reyes' Ecuadorian guerrilla camp, or the operation that freed former senator Ingrid Betancourt, were hard setbacks to the FARC. These events led FARC to be open to discuss a truce, and therefore in September 2012, President Santos announced publicly the beginning of peace talks to be conducted in Norway and Cuba. The agreement did not include a ceasefire nor the granting of a safe haven, as occurred in the last peace talks, which ended in failure in 2002. While the Cuban and Norwegian governments are the "guarantors" of the discussions, Venezuela and Chile are "participants." The agenda for discussion includes six central points: agrarian reform, political participation, drug trafficking, victims and reparations, ending the conflict, and implementation of the peace deal. It took as long as nine months of negotiations for a draft agreement to be reached on the first point and an additional three on the second, indicating that the process could be lengthy.

If tackling leftist guerrillas meant facing them militarily or verbally, tackling the right-wing paramilitaries presupposed demobilizing them. Colombia's Justice and Peace Law came into effect in 2005 with the purpose of negotiating the transit to peace of the right-wing paramilitary groups by offering them incentives to give up fighting, and at the same time redressing the victims, ensuring justice and finding the truth. The law "enabled criminal acts to be known and tackled that would have been impossible to reveal under other circumstances." In other words, it is an additional mechanism to reduce impunity rates and it "is a window of opportunity, which, despite its weaknesses, had never been opened in Colombia's history" (Ideas Para la Paz). During Uribe's administration, about 30,000 right-wing paramilitaries were demobilized and integrated into civilian life through education and training.[6] A report published in 2010 by the Office of Justice and Peace Promotion revealed that 4,112 excombatants of the paramilitary United Self Defense Forces of Colombia (AUC) confessed to having committed 30,470 murders in a twenty-year period – from mid-1980s to 2003, when it would have begun the process of demobilization. The death toll puts the paramilitary groups in Colombia at the same level of dictatorships in the region.

Colombia's relations with its neighbors – namely Venezuela – have also been strained. One of the dents in the relationship is the territorial dispute centered on control over the entrance to the Golfo de Venezuela. The key to establishing this control was ownership of the Islas Los

Monjes, a chain of three tiny islands lying at the gulf's northern mouth. The roots of the conflict stretch back to colonial times as the borders of the nations that emerged from the wars for independence were not clearly defined. In 1881, Venezuela and Colombia appealed to King Alfonso XII of Spain to arbitrate their conflicting claims but Venezuela rejected the eventual arbitration decision because of a disagreement over the location of the source of the Río Oro. Negotiations have had ups and downs ever since. After an abortive effort in the early 1970s and an adamant refusal by Venezuela to submit the dispute to international arbitration, the two governments announced in 1981 a draft treaty popularly known as the Hypothesis of Caraballeda. When Venezuela's foreign minister presented the draft to representatives of the officer corps, however, he received an extremely negative reaction. Opposition to the treaty quickly spread, forcing the government to withdraw from further negotiations with the Colombians. There have been no formal talks dedicated to the maritime boundary since that time.

Over the last decade, moreover, relations with Venezuela have been troubled by a myriad of personal and ideological rivalries. Ties between the two neighbors, always tense, took a turn for the worse after a March 2008 attack by Colombian forces on Ecuadorian soil that resulted in the death of Raúl Reyes, a high ranking official of the FARC. The attack set off one of the worst diplomatic disputes in recent years in South America, complete with bitter recriminations over sovereignty and foreign influence in the region. Shortly before leaving office in August 2010 Uribe went to the OAS to once again accuse Venezuela of harboring FARC rebels; Venezuelan President Hugo Chávez responded by breaking all ties with the neighboring country. The contribution of President Uribe to mend the problems with Venezuela was weak. Despite the relevance of the Venezuelan market to Colombian exports, sharp divergences in personal style and ideology marked the relations between both presidents. It can actually be argued that the bilateral crisis was partially inflamed by the domestic agenda of Colombia (and of Venezuela) since the dispute was a clear opportunity to instigate nationalist feelings and increase the popularity of the president.[7] The value of bilateral trade topped U.S.$ 7 billion in 2008 before falling to U.S.$ 4.6 billion the following year, and nearly collapsing entirely in 2010 amid the diplomatic spat between Uribe and Chávez. Despite this truculent heritage, Santos and Chávez reestablished diplomatic links between their countries in August 2010, when the former took power. Since then, both presidents have had a friendly relationship focused on boosting trade, development in the border area, and the fight against drug trafficking. At the end of 2011 the two leaders signed a bilateral agreement to extend a Venezuelan pipeline to Panama and Ecuador and announced the bilateral lifting of tariffs on 3,500 products. Santos also traveled to Caracas to sign a number of symbolic bilateral initiatives on agriculture, trade and security.

In 2013, however, Santos became involved in a tense dispute with Venezuelan new president, Nicolas Maduro, after the Colombian leader decided to meet with Venezuela's main opposition leader, Henrique Capriles. There were fears of a come back to those years when relations and commercial ties were frayed by ideological differences and volleys of insults between heads of state. But soon both leaders met personally to turn the page on the diplomatic spat and to announce the opening of a "new chapter of neighbourly relations."

Although Colombia's contribution to regional security has naturally been focused on the resolution of its own domestic and bilateral problems, the country has periodically contributed to foreign security efforts. For instance, it became a central figure in the Contadora Group, created in January 1983 with the goal of counteracting U.S. interventionism in the Central American crisis by creating an alternative conflict resolution mechanism. Moreover, at the beginning of the Gaviria administration, the Rio Group was accorded a high degree of importance in Colombia's Latin American policy agenda, reflecting the country's desire to establish itself as a protagonist in regional affairs and to strengthen South America's negotiating power on a global level. For Colombia, the major worth of this group resided in its political significance and its potential for cohesive dialogue with the United States and Europe in particular. The centrality of issues such as human rights, narcotics, multilateral organizations, and commercial cooperation in the Rio Group's agenda coincided with the priority that these topics received in Colombia's foreign policy (Tokatlian and Tickner, 1996:113-114).

Contribution to Human Security

No other country in the world is so immediately connoted with drug trafficking as Colombia. National legislation against consuming, trading, and producing certain drugs originated with Law 11 of September 1920. Since then there has been clandestine traficking in drugs, aimed at establishing a connection between drug consumers and producers. According to official U.S. documents, Colombia during the 1930s was already integrated into the secret drug network that linked Europe – where the main producers of manufactured drugs were to be found – with consumers from the Caribbean countries (Guizado and Restrepo,

2007:63). Colombia's role in this industry has evolved over the past decades. In the 1970s, a boom in marijuana cultivation along Colombia's Atlantic Coast created a class of newly rich traffickers supplying the U.S. market. In the late 1970s, Colombia's new cartels, first in Medellin and then in Cali, expanded from marijuana to the processing and export of cocaine. Led by a small number of powerful drug kingpins, these family-based empires came to control a billion-dollar cocaine industry that processed coca grown primarily in Bolivia and Peru.

It was first during the administration of Liberal leader Julio César Turbay Ayala (1978-1982) that the Colombian government raised the stakes in its war against drug traffickers. Turbay was the first Colombian president to declare war on the traffickers, prompted by the reality that by the late 1970s Colombia had become the primary producer and exporter of marijuana to the U.S. market (Crandall, 2008b:23). Beginning in 1989 with the Andean Strategy, U.S. funds, equipment, logistical support, and personnel from the DEA, the CIA, and other agencies have played a leading role in counternarcotics operations in Colombia. U.S.-assisted operations resulted in the killing of Pablo Escobar in 1993 and the jailing of the heads of the Cali Cartel in 1994. However, the breakup of the two largest cartels did not lead to a long-term decline in Colombian drug trafficking. These drug syndicates have since been replaced by smaller, more vertically integrated trafficking organizations whose nimble, independent traffickers are much more difficult to detect and infiltrate. These traffickers employ new and constantly changing shipping routes through Central America, Mexico, and the Caribbean for moving cocaine and, increasingly, heroin.

Both the extent and pattern of global cocaine production have changed significantly over the last four decades. From the end of the Second World War until the late 1990s, almost all the world's coca bush (the raw material for the manufacture of cocaine) was grown in Peru and Bolivia, and since the 1970s, most of this output was refined into cocaine in Colombia. This increased over time, and in 1997 coca cultivation in Colombia exceeded that of the traditional growers for the first time. In the twenty-first century, the pendulum has swung back again. Coca cultivation in Colombia decreased dramatically from 2001 (145,000 hectares) to 2011 (64,000), mainly due to large-scale eradication. At the same time, it increased in Peru (from 46,000 to 64,400) and in Bolivia from (20,000 to 27,200), and both of these countries have acquired the ability to produce their own refined cocaine (UNODC, 2013a:xiii). The success in confronting the trafficking has also impacted the national homicide rate. Although the country still has one of the world's highest, it has seen a massive drop in its homicide rate from 70 per 100,000 at the beginning of the decade to 33 in 2011 (UNODC, 2013). Hence, Colombia provides "an example of a country that has succeeded in reversing escalating levels of lethal violence through strict law enforcement measures, reducing both drug trafficking and the homicide rate" (UNODC, 2011:53).

In 2011, Colombia adopted the country's new Comprehensive Security Policy for Prosperity (PISDP), a road map against guerrilla groups, narco-traffickers and gangs. The policy is also aimed at reducing homicides, kidnappings, extortions, pirating of land, and other crimes by 50 percent by 2025. The PISDP also has five other central goals to strengthen the Andean nation's fight against terrorism: (i) a substantial improvement in intelligence; (ii) strengthening of the leadership and control; (iii) strategic protection of the population; (iv) strategic application of force; and (v) respect for human rights and international humanitarian rights. PISDP represents an appropriate combination of continuity and change. Continuity with the Policies of Democratic Security (2002-2006) and the Consolidation of Democratic Security (2006-2010) have been embraced by Uribe's administration, but it adopts a more comprehensive approach and recognizes that Colombia is mired in an internal conflict.

Despite these recent accomplishments, it has been argued that to successfully confront Colombia's drug problem one has to look at the problem not in a criminal or military way, but as a health problem. Promoting this view, the American Commission on Drugs and Democracy (led by Fernando Henrique Cardoso, former president of Brazil; César Gaviria, former president of Colombia; and Ernesto Zedillo, former president of Mexico) concluded that Colombia's antinarcotic policies have failed. "Over the last 30 years, Colombia implemented all conceivable measures to fight the drug trade in a massive effort where the benefits were not proportional to the resources invested. Despite the country's achievements in lowering levels of violence and crime, the areas of illegal cultivation are again expanding."[8]

Conclusions

Colombia's foreign policy and contribution to security are centered on the dynamics of its civil war, which has caused at least 50,000 deaths since its inception in 1964. Since the end of the Cold War, the country's relations with neighbors Ecuador and Venezuela and with the United States, the level of support it gives to regional arrangements, and its international voting profile, are all molded by the need to halt the conflict and to blockade the trafficking of drugs that provides most of the income to the FARC. The importance of military issues in the Colombian context has then eroded the influence of the Foreign Ministry and increased the relative importance of other ministries, including Defense. To a significant degree, practical domestic political considerations have driven foreign policy, in particular, because the two dominant domestic issues, drug trafficking and the guerilla insurgency, have had international implications. Relations with neighboring countries, marked by a mix of pragmatism and ideology, have hence been tense over the last decades (more acute during Uribe's administration) due to accusations that these countries support Colombia's insurgent groups ideologically, logistically, and financially. The claims have been proved a few times, but have not stopped the current President Juan Manuel Santos from engaging in an unprecedented, albeit discreet, movement to pacify relations with its neighbors. Cooperation with Andean and Amazon countries is, indeed, crucial for antidrug trafficking initiatives to bear any concrete result. Colombia seems to be on the right track with coca cultivation decreasing significantly and with homicide rates dropping steadily. But the protracted conflict, even it has lost vigor and lethality, is still active.

Notes

[1] The UP was a leftist political party founded by the FARC and the Colombian Communist Party in 1985, as part of the peace negotiations that the guerrillas held with the Conservative Belisario Betancur administration.

[2] "Homem da Guerra e da Paz," interview with Juan Manuel Santos (*Veja*, 1 September 2010).

[3] "Santos Highlights Foreign Policy Victories" (*The Miami Herald*, 8 August 2012).

[4] "An interview with Colombian President Juan Manuel Santos" (*The Washington Post*, 26 August, 2011).

[5] "Top Dog Down" (*The Economist*, 12 November 2011).

[6] See "Not yet the promised land" (*The Economist*, 30 December 2009).

[7] "Po70 per 100,000 at the beginning of the decade to 33 in 2010lítica Interna Move Crise Entre Bogotá e Caracas" (*O Estado de São Paulo*, 28 August 2010).

[8] "The War on Drugs is a Failure" by Fernando Henrique Cardoso, Ernesto Zedillo and César Gaviria (*The Wall Street Journal*, 23 February 2009).

9

Venezuela

"Who is not *chavista*, is not Venezuelan." —Hugo Chávez, president of Venezuela, in a rally in 2012

Venezuela's recent political history has comprehended a short-lived democratic experience (1945-1948), a dictatorship (1948-1958), a democratic period established by the Pacto de Punto Fijo (1958-1998), and a military-populist regime (1998-). Thus, strongly impacted by regime change, foreign policy moved between adaptation and resistance to the challenges presented by the initiation, intensification, transformation, and termination of the Cold War (da Silva and Hillman, 2003:146-147).

For a long time Venezuela's international reputation and institutional stability was due both to its consolidated democracy and to its oil wealth, which are the key components of a foreign policy whose goals extend beyond those of countries of a similar size (Sanjuán, 2008:146). The first two presidents of the democratic era, Rómulo Betancourt (1945-1948 and 1959-1964) and Raúl Leoni (1964-1969), took courageous stands against tyrannies of the right and the left. Betancourt shared with other political leaders a vision of civilian control based on a depoliticized and professional military confined to a narrow sphere of activities. (Trinkunas, 2000: 89). The Betancourt Doctrine, whereby Venezuela refused to maintain diplomatic relations with governments formed as a result of military coups, was followed by both administrations and eventually led to some isolationism as most other South American nations were dominated by nonelected regimes. This period was described iconically by Naím as:

> "While wars raged in Central America, Venezuela was completely at peace. While military dictators throughout the region stifled freedoms and 'disappeared' their opponents, Venezuela held peaceful,

competitive, and fair elections every five years, with the opposition often actually replacing the party in power. While hyperinflation, high unemployment, and irresponsible economic management were the norm in most of Latin America, the oil-fueled Venezuelan economy seemed immune to the economic catastrophes that beset its neighbors. Whereas the unimaginable poverty and hopelessness elsewhere in the region inspired countless novels, doctoral dissertations, and journalistic dispatches, even the Venezuelan poor seemed to be better off than their neighbors in the region" (Naím, 2001:18).

During the 1980s, however, Venezuela's relative stable position suffered several significant transformations. The combined effects of the decline in oil prices on the international market and the impact of the external debt provoked an unprecedented economic crisis that called into question the very stability of Venezuela's democracy (Serbin, 1996:90). In the late 1980s, deficits in the external account, fiscal and monetary problems, and the unwillingness of the international banks to grant loans worsened economic conditions.

It was in this context that late Carlos Andrés Pérez was reelected to president (1989-1993). Soon after his inauguration, he began a major policy orientation in Venezuela (*gran virage* or turnabout) grounded in the need both to reorient the country's economic policy to counteract the effects of the economic crisis and to reorganize the political system to adjust to this economic imperative. But these changes, and its social and economic costs, generated a strong reaction from various sectors of the populations and led in February 1989 to the *caracazo* massive riots and looting in important cities. It left hundreds of victims and great material losses. In a society that many considered a model of democratic stability and prosperity, the revolt revealed exhaustion of the political and economic model that governed the country. The successful repression of the rebellion strengthened the resolve of some military leaders, namely the Bolivarian Revolutionary Movement (MBR-200) that the political regime had to change and that neoliberal economic policies had to be rejected. The movement supported a populist strategy and called for the development of a constituent assembly to reconstruct Venezuela's democracy. The MBR-200 attempted to overthrow Andrés Pérez's government in February 1992, and sympathizers of their cause attempted again to remove the government in November 1992. Both coups failed as neither was able to obtain support across the armed forces in a substantial and effective manner (Avilés, 2009:1557). The U.S. condemned the 1992 coup attempts against the neoliberal regime, issuing a declaration that "the basis of U.S. policy in the region is the support of democracy, and even if we understand that Venezuela, among other nations, is going through a difficult period, authoritarianism is not the solution" (cited in Romero, 2002).

Venezuela was hence constrained once again by troubles common to the region. In this context, the country's foreign policy rapidly lost its image of democratic exceptionality and oil affluence, and it had, thereby, to undergo a radical shift beginning in the 1990s (da Silva and Hillman, 2003:154). In May 1993, President Péres became the first Venezuelan president to be forced out of the office by the Supreme Court for the misappropriation of 250 million bolívars belonging to a presidential discretionary fund, furthering the idea that the democratic credentials of Venezuela was a thing of the past. The commitment to economic integration and liberalization, promotion of democracy, and cooperative approaches to border issues was compromised by this episode. But despite growing domestic streess, President Pérez attempted, and to a large extent succeeded, to improve credibility in foreign policy occasioned by improvements in international relations. He proposed a series of steps that would liberalize trade and would promote integration and the expansion of economic activity so that the country's nontraditional exports might be diversified and increased. Within this context, regionalization – namely in Central America and in the Andean region – became an essential component of Venezuela's new foreign policy, and it sought to maximize the country's previous successes in economic cooperation, political consensus, and geoestrategic alliances (Serbin, 1996:93-94). During the Péres administration, the United States played the role of an ally. It was Venezuela's principal market for its oil exports and chief source of its imports. In 1991, more than half of Venezuela's exports and nearly 70 percent of direct exports of petroleum and its derivates went to the United States (Serbin, 1996:96). Since the beginning of the *gran viraje*, the importance of this traditional alliance was reaffirmed by Venezuela, especially during the political turmoil of 1992, when many feared that a military government could take over in Caracas (Serbin, 1996:96).

After the transition government of acting President Octavio Lepage (May-June 1993) and of President Ramón J. Velázquez (June 1993-February 1994), the second Rafael Caldera administration (1994-1998) took office with a new party and an *ad hoc* coalition. Foreign policy, which during the inconclusive Pérez administration had been a high priority in public policy, was reduced in importance and modified in direction as well as in its thematic and geographical focus (da Silva and Hillman, 2003:156). Soon after his inauguration he pardoned Hugo Chávez, who was serving time in jail for a coup attempt in 1992. During his second term he also revoked some constitutional guarantees, including protection against arbitrary searches and arrests by the police.

Venezuela excluded the armed forces from politics for more than forty years until the 1998 elections that brought to power retired lieutenant colonel Hugo Chávez, one of the leaders of the failed military uprising of February 1992. His administration adopted a program that gave participatory democracy a prominent role, resulting in a strongly presidential and centralized regime with a weak system of checks and balances. The new international agenda of Venezuela is also closely knit with the president himself whose polices reflect his charismatic, personal, military, Christian, and antihegemonic attitudes. The country started to practice a foreign policy that, according to Chávez's interpretation, "promotes a socialism of the twenty century" (Urrutia, 2006:159). This attempt to shift the international image of the country was allegedly inspired by a new sense of independence, sovereignty, nationalism, Latin American unity, and antihegemonic orientation. It was also predicated on the notion that the main actors of the Bolivarian revolution were the armed forces and the people, a permanent dichotomy that would be responsible for the leveraging of social development. These ideas were revealed both in the principles written in the new constitution and executed in the foreign policy of President Chávez (da Silva and Hillman, 2003:157). In fact, the guidelines of Venezuelan foreign policy were set out by the 2001/2007 National Development Plan, which aimed to promote the democratization of international society, Latin American and Caribbean integration, the strengthening of South-South relations and Venezuela's position in the world economy. In order to implement these policies, oil would be used as the basis for a "socialist" regional integration project (Lima and Kfuri, 2007).

In addition, Chávez repeatedly criticized the U.S. government for its unilateralism and regularly pointed out how the world's financial and trade institutions, such as the World Bank, IMF, and WTO, were generally operating in the interests of the developed North. Indeed, Venezuela and the United States could hardly be further apart in terms of their foreign policy agendas. Venezuela and Cuba are two of the few countries in the world that are fundamentally opposed to U.S. hegemony.[1] But the relationship is full of contradictions as Venezuela needs the U.S. as a market for its oil and the U.S. needs Venezuelan oil. The oil sector accounts for roughly 30 percent of GDP, 90 percent of export earnings, and more than half of the central government's ordinary revenues. In July 2010, in the wake of another diplomatic flare-up with Colombia and after breaking off relations with Colombia and recalling its ambassador, Venezuela threatened to cut off oil exports to the United States in the event of a U.S.-Colombian invasion. But it was a largely empty threat, as sixty-seven percent of Venezuela's crude exports go to the United States and such a move would harm Venezuela. As noted by Santoro and Valente, "we know, for example, that the ease with which Chávez verbally attacks the United States is inversely proportional to the difficulty he would have in ceasing to supply oil to that country" (Santoro and Valente, 2006). Hence, often the U.S. is guided by the "Maisto thesis," which reflects the U.S. Ambassador John Maisto assumption that Chávez should be judged by his actions and not by his declarations, implying that nothing would come of his radical rhetoric. Communication media is Chávez's worldwide political promotion instrument. It makes his acts resonate both positively and negatively, consolidating him as a political character of the international system (Vigevani and Cepaluni, 2009: 125).

Chávez's foreign policy also stressed multipolarity through the promotion of Latin American integration, which he did first by having Venezuela join Mercosur in July 2006 (ratified in 2012). The move was a major diplomatic triumph for Chávez and provided a stronger institutional framework for the already existing bilateral agreements Venezuela has with Brazil and Argentina. Chávez also pushed for closer ties between the CAN and Mercosur. In December 2003, with the Chávez government pushing particularly hard, an agreement was struck between the two regional organizations to form a CAN-Mercosur trade agreement, whose goal was to establish a free trade zone in South American by 2015. Venezuela has also been instrumental in the creation of UNASUR (along with Brazil), the Bolivarian Alliance for the Peoples of Our America (ALBA) (along with Cuba) and supported the establishment of the Community of Latin American and Caribbean States (CELAC) (spearheaded by Mexico and Brazil).

ALBA – a top priority of the Chávez government – is an international cooperation organization based on the idea of social, political, and economic integration between the countries of Latin America and the Caribbean. It is associated with socialist and social democratic governments and is an attempt at regional economic integration based on a vision of social welfare, bartering, and mutual economic aid, rather than trade liberalization as with free-trade agreements. It was proposed in December 2001 by Chávez at the Third Summit of the Heads of State and the Government of the Association of Caribbean States, held in Isla de Margarita. Calling for a revival of the Bolivarian dream of unity, he sketched the lines of a project resting on the principles of solidarity, cooperation, similarities, and reciprocity.

The idea was to herald a new dawn for the historical endeavor of such nineteenth-century leaders as Francisco de Miranda, Miguel Hildalgo, Marina Moreno, Simon Bolivar, José Artigas, Bernardo Monteagudo, Cecilio del Valle, or José Marti (Dabène, 2009:210).

The union, originally called the Bolivarian Alternative for the Americas, was meant to serve as the antidote for the U.S.-backed Free Trade Area of the Americas (FTAA). The proposed FTAA, which is abbreviated with the acronym ALCA in Spanish, served as both the visual and ideological antithesis of President Chavez's ALBA. The FTAA intended to reduce trade barriers among all American countries with the exception of Cuba. ALBA, meanwhile, sought to promote trade with the goal of economic development.

Three years after it was proposed, ALBA became a reality with an initial bilateral agreement between Venezuela and Cuba. Although since its inception in 2004, the alliance has grown to include eight countries,[2] and a Strategic Plan was agreed upon in April 2005, the project is still more a declaration of intention than a thorough program, and includes a strong emphasis on poverty reduction. The whole idea was to invent a form of regionalism not centered on trade but rather on social issues (Dabène, 2009:210). Although Venezuela-led regional integration is frequently demonized by being too politically centered, it has at least been able to recoup the integration tradition of Latin American history inaugurated by Bolívar and followed by Martí, Sandino, and Mariátegui (Fernandes, 2008:236). In fact, it is important to note that more than a political priority, regional integration in Venezuela is a juridical obligation. The 1999 constitution states that, "The Republic shall promote, and encourage Latin American and Caribbean integration, in the interest of advancing toward the creation of a community of nations, defending the region's economic, social, cultural, political and environmental interests . . . the Republic may transfer to supranational organizations, through treaties, the exercise of the necessary authorities to carry out these integration processes" (article 153).

Chávez also pursued a policy of diversifying foreign relations namely by promoting South-South relations. In this context, the Venezuelan government has particularly pushed for closer relations with Organization of the Petroleum Exporting Countries (OPEC) countries, India, Iran, and China. Within hours of his election in 1998, Chávez announced he would leave on a nine-day tour to the ten other OPEC member-nations. As the leader of OPEC this year, by virtue of a regular rotation, he also called for the first meeting of OPEC heads of State since 1975, and invited all the other heads of OPEC states to come to Venezuela for a summit meeting in September 2000. The purpose of the summit, he made clear, was to forge a strong bond between OPEC leaders. Within the context of South-South relations, the Chávez administration also promoted links with China, with whom it struck a U.S.$ 20 billion loans-for-oil deal in 2010. "The relations between China and Venezuela extend from below the surface of the Earth to outer space," Chávez said, in reference to the oil deal and Venezuela's first satellite, which China built and launched into orbit in 2008. This rapprochement with nontraditional allies was reinforced at the Fifty-Sixth Meeting of the UN Commission on Human Rights in 2000, where Venezuela backed China and Afghanistan over their handing of human rights. Despite their geographical distance, Venezuela and Iran have also forged increasingly close ties, a lot of which correlates with their shared anti-Americanism. They have signed a series of deals to promote industrial and security cooperation, and since September 2006 the Iranian state oil company Petropar has been participating in exploration of the Orinoco oil belt along with state companies from China and India.

Chávez foreign policy moved into a more radical phase in 2002. The administration adopted a confrontational and insolent attitude towards the United States – and specifically towards President George Bush – and began supporting social movements abroad that could bring about Bolivarian socialist revolutions, namely in countries such as Bolivia, Peru, Ecuador, and Brazil. The support was not only political but presupposed also the transfer of large sums in the form of donations, loans, oil selling at favorable prices, infrastructure, buying of external debt (e.g. Argentina and Ecuador), arms purchases or building of refineries. The Agreement for the Application of the Bolivarian Alternative for the Peoples of Our America and the Peoples' Trade Agreements signed in April 2006 by the presidents of Bolivia, Cuba, and Venezuela further consolidated President Hugo Chávez's continental Bolivarian project. The treaty was designed to counter U.S. efforts to forge a free-trade area of the Americas. In more recent times, the growing visibility of Venezuela in the region coupled with the stridency, radicalization, and the simplistic administration of complex issues have all contributed to the polarization of Chávez's image. To stay in power, in 2007 Chávez also decided to create a militia. Venezuela's National Bolivarian Militia (NBM), not a particularly skilled or well-trained force, included as many as 300,000 members recruited primarily from poorer, rural parts of the country selected for their loyalty to Chávez and his ideology more than anything else. Though the NBM might not be a formidable fighting force currently, simply keeping a loyal and sizable militia force in reserve allows the president to significantly reduce the risk of a coup by potential dissenters.

In March 2013, Chávez died and was replaced by Nicolas Maduro, who had played a leading role in crafting some of his country's best known foreign policy and regional integration initiatives. Serving as Hugo Chavez's foreign minister from 2006 to 2012, Maduro made a name for himself in the foreign policy world through his more radical policy (toward states such as Syria, Iran, and Libya) and at times, more pragmatic approach (especially toward Colombia). But in his role as president, Maduro's foreign policy agenda has diminished. Stabilizing his grasp on power and Venezuela's economy has dominated his agenda. Venezuela's noisy withdrawal from the OAS Inter-American Court of Human Rights in September 2013, after opposition leader Henrique Capriles sent documents to the OAS accusing Maduro of election fraud, had more to due with domestic than with international politics.

Contribution to Traditional Security

Venezuela has pending territorial issues with Guyana and Colombia. Although Chávez spearheaded a turnaround in Venezuela's foreign policy, its policies regarding territorial disputes mantained, to a large extent, the same line of conduct as his predecessors (Sánchez et.al., 2005:213). This is clearly the case with Guyana. Relations with the eastern neighbor have been strained for decades by Venezuela's claim to all territory west of the Essequibo River, more than half the present size of Guyana. A 1966 tripartite agreement in Geneva established a Guyana-Venezuela commission to discuss the dispute. In 1970, President Caldera agreed to a twelve-year moratorium on the issue. In fact, until the 1980s, Venezuela applied diplomatic pressure to get Guyana to enter into bilateral negotiations and strongly opposed what it saw as Guyana's attempt to "internationalize" the conflict by seeking the Non-Aligned Movement's censure of Venezuela for alleged aggression. But when the nonaligned states merely reaffirmed the necessity of reaching a peaceful solution in accordance with the 1966 Geneva Agreement, Venezuela reversed its position on direct talks, and along with Guyana, agreed to accept UN mediation (Hazleton, 1984:167). The UN appointed Alister McIntyre as the first UN Good Officer to the region in 1990. McIntyre began to make progress in 1993 when President Jagan of Guyana visited Venezuela. Further progress was made in 1996 when Venezuela's foreign minister visited Guyana, where they discussed possible cooperation in the disputed region. However, the two could not come to a final solution on resource development cooperation within the disputed territory. Venezuela proposed such a solution in 1998 whereby the two nations would work together on considering mining and logging projects in the region, but Guyana found it unacceptable, largely because of internal opposition to the ruling party giving up any sovereignty in the Essequibo. It was in this context that in 1998 both countries agreed to create a High Level Bilateral Commission (*Comisión Bilateral de Alto Nivel – COBAN*). This Commission has allowed the parties to systematically explore opportunities for cooperation in different areas, even as the border dispute goes through the channels provided by the Geneva agreement. The pace, however, has alternated between slow and intermittent and, therefore, in 2011 the OAS decided to appoint a new mediator in the territorial dispute between both countries (Jamaican Professor Norman Girvan). That year, Guyana made an application to the UN to extend its continental shelf towards a region where Venezuela had granted natural gas concessions to foreign companies, putting an additional dent into the resolution of the bilateral dispute.

In Venezuela, one of the arguments about the "need to recover" Essequibo is geo-strategic: the territorial waters of that region would be Venezuela's Atlantic façade, her one guaranteed direct outlet to the ocean beyond the patchwork of territorial waters in the Caribbean Sea. Even though the treaty signed with Trinidad in the early 1990s helped take some of the pressure off this issue of access, it is one that is taken seriously even in the army. Another related concern is the impact that certain activities have on the environment on the Venezuelan side of the border. For instance, there have been repeated complaints about the levels of mining-related pollution that come with the river waters that flow out from the Essequibo region.

With Colombia the relationship is even more complex. Colombia is the country that most resembles Venezuela in terms of history, culture, and interconnections between the two peoples (Wilpert, 2007:164). However, at the same time, there are many tensions between both countries, ranging from border disputes and access to natural resources along the border, to tension generated by border crossings of various Colombian regular and irregular armed forces, such as the FARC, the ELN, Colombia's military forces, and the AUC. In some ways, tensions between the two countries can be traced back to material differences between the liberator Símon Bolívar and the more conservative Francisco de Paula Santander, seen by the establishment as the real founding figure of independent Colombia (Raby, 2011:166).

As we saw earlier, the border disputes between both countries date back to the very founding of each, when what used to be one country, *La Gran Colombia*, was divided in 1833. The border issue has always been very sensitive for the two countries because much oil and mineral wealth is located in this border region (Wilpert, 2007:165). In August 1987 the border dispute heated up when a Colombian Navy corvette, the *Caldas*, entered an area of the gulf that has traditionally been patrolled by Venezuela. On and off for almost a week, the *Caldas* apparently sought to assert Colombia's claims to sovereignty in the area. Venezuela responded with a diplomatic protest note and sent naval, army, and air force reinforcements, including a squadron of United States-made F-16 fighters, to its western frontier as tensions rose. The situation cooled down only after the mediation of OAS Secretary-General João Baena Soares and Argentinean President Raúl Alfonsín, who asked Colombia to withdrawl the corvette from the disputed area.

The other bone of contention between Venezuela and Colombia is the alleged Chávez and Maduro's support and harbor of one or both of Colombia's guerrilla groups.[3] The Venezuelan government shares a leftist ideology with the FARC that is often cited as the main factor linking the two. But in reality, just as Pakistan has backed Kashmiri militants against India and Iran backs Hezbollah against Israel, Venezuela's support for the FARC is primarily designed to constrain its main regional adversary — and thus distract Bogotá from entertaining any military endeavors that could threaten Venezuela's territorial integrity, particularly the resource-rich Lake Maracaibo region. Venezuela's fears of Colombia are also amplified to a large degree by the close defense relationship Bogotá shares with Caracas's other key adversary, the United States.[4]

The claim that Venezuela is supporting Colombia's guerrilla groups was initially triggered by the covert capture in December 2004 of Rodrigo Granda – a top Colombian FARC insurgent – in the Venezuelan capital Caracas. Colombia insisted that Venezuela was harbouring "terrorists" wanted by the Colombian authorities, while Venezuela withdrew its ambassador to Bogotá in protest and unilaterally suspended trade links. The suspicions evolved into facts when the computer disks belonging to Raúl Reyes, head of FARC's International Committee (COMINTER) were seized by Colombian armed forces in a raid in March 2008 on Devía's camp inside Ecuador. The analysis of the data conducted by the International Institute for Strategic Studies (IISS), which was given the disks by the Colombian government, demonstrated that FARC's relationship with Venezuela ultimately acquired a strategic dimension characterized by various forms of state support (IISS, 2011). Although the accusations were systematically denied by Chávez, Venezuela's attitude toward the guerrilla movements damaged relations between the two neighbors and undermined the legitimacy of the country's traditional mediating role. These tensions were exacerbated by increased agreement between the United States and Colombia regarding terrorism, trade, and Plan Colombia. Plan Colombia was severely criticized by the Venezuelan government because of the military component of the U.S. aid and the risks of regional conflict escalation (da Silva and Hillman, 2003:159). The bilateral row was also fueled by the personal animosity between Chávez and former President Uribe who showed no inhibitions in insulting each other in public in numerous multilateral summits,[5] and, as we saw, by the demands of Venezuela's (and Colombia's) domestic agenda. With popularity rates and oil revenues dropping in inverse proportion to criminality, Chávez used the specter of a foreign threat to create a sense of embattlement and to spark national cohesion.[6] Even if the relationship with Colombia improved after Santos took office, Chávez used populist tactics until his death.

Venezuela's regional track record also demands some analysis. During the Carlos Pérez and Ramón Velásquez administrations, the country promoted a regeneration of the OAS and supported the idea that it should play a more active role and enlarge its scope to include themes such as narco-trafficking, Cuba-U.S. relations, or guerilla groups (Sanjuán, 2008:156). Venezuela was also a prominent promoter of Resolution 1080 and supported the creation of a Unit for the Promotion of Democracy in the OAS (1990) aimed to respond immediately and collectively "to the sudden or irregular interruption of the democratic political institutional process or of the legitimate exercise of power by the democratically elected governments." It was in this context that it condemned the extraconstitutional powers assumed by President Alberto Fujimori of Peru in 1992.

However, with Chávez, Venezuela's backing of OAS's role in democracy promotion faded. As an example, the Chávez government considered the ostensible threats to democratic institutions in Paraguay and Ecuador in 1999 and 2000, respectively, as questions of a strictly domestic nature. And it openly condemned a report on Venezuela by the Inter-American Commission on Human Rights, published in December 2009, that warned the "absence of due separation and independence between the branches of government," found that "not all persons are ensured full enjoyment of their rights irrespective of the positions they hold vis-à-vis the government's policies," and concluded that "the State's punitive power is being used to intimidate or punish people on account of their political opinions" (Inter-American Commission on Human Rights, 2009). The report followed the same track of other Amnesty International and Human Rights Watch reports.

Contribution to Human Security

Drug trafficking and crime are major threats to Venezuelans. In the 1980s and 1990s the orientation of Venezuela's antidrug policies followed the proposed guidelines of the U.S. to the Hemisphere. Drug trafficking was associated with national security in 1981, and Venezuela was the first country in the region to do so (Sanjuán, 2004:354). In the same period, Venezuela created the National Commission against Illegal Use of Drugs (Conacuid) and signed the Quito Declaration against Traffic in Narcotic Drugs (August 1984). With the emergence of Hugo Chávez in Venezuela's political scenario, the situation changed significantly. Drug smuggling through Venezuela has exploded since Chávez ordered police and the military to sever most ties with the U.S. law enforcement agencies. In the summer of 2005, Venezuelan officials suspended collaboration with the U.S. DEA over Caracas' allegations that the U.S. agency had engaged in spying. In response, Washington decertified Venezuela as a cooperative antinarcotics partner, and labeled it as one of two countries worldwide that "failed demonstrably to make substantial efforts"[7] in the antidrug campaign. The amount of cocaine flowing into Venezuela from Colombia has skyrocketed, going from an estimated 60 metric tons in 2004 to 260 metric tons in 2007. That amounted to 17 percent of all the cocaine produced in the Andes in 2007. As the Colombian Government has taken greater control of its territory, traffickers are making more use of transit countries such as Venezuela. The White House Office of National Drug Control Policy estimates that as much as 24 percent of the cocaine shipped out of South America in 2010 passed through Venezuela, accounting for more than 200 tons,[8] and according to the UN, between 2006 and 2008, over half the maritime shipments of cocaine to Europe detected came from Venezuela (UNODOC, 2010:26). The information was denied by Venezuela's Interior Minister.[9] Corruption at high levels of President Hugo Chávez's government and state aid to Colombia's drug-trafficking guerrillas have made Venezuela a major launching pad for cocaine bound for the United States and Europe. In fact, Maj. Gen. Henry Rangel Silva, Venezuela's chief of strategic operations for the armed forces and a Chavéz loyalist, was thought to be one of the chief drug traffickers in the Venezuelan armed forces. In 2008, the U.S. Treasury Department listed Rangel Silva and Director of Military Intelligence Hugo Carvajal as drug kingpins involved in financing the FARC.

Drug trafficking goes hand-in-hand with high urban violence, as forewarned by the UNODC:

"[Venezuela has experienced] significant declines in cocaine seizures while the homicide rate increased steadily to 49 per 100,000 population [in 2010]. Whilst the activities of drug trafficking organizations certainly play a significant role in Venezuela, the increase in homicide in this case may also be linked to other factors including general conventional crimes" (UNODC, 2011:54).

Crime, according to the 2011 Latinobarómetro report, is the biggest problem in Venezuela, say 61 percent of respondents (Corporacion Latinobarómetro, 2011:66), reflecting an homicide rate of 45.1 in 2010 (UNODC, 2013). According to official figures reported by a survey on victimization carried out by the National Statistics Institute (INE), the Venezuelan capital was, in 2009, the deadliest city in the world: 233 homicides per 100,000 inhabitants. An August 2010 a *The New York Times* headline highlighted that Venezuela was "More Deadly than Iraq."[10]

Conclusions

Venezuela, under Chávez and Maduro, has become a strident actor in international relations. Chávez, in particular, was often rebutted by the international community for his demagogic, improvisational and nationalistic style, advocating populist economic policies that failed in the past. Despite this clout, some have been quick to identify the social achievements of the "Bolivarian Revolution," but Chávez's contribution to regional and domestic security was weak. None of the pending territorial conflicts with Guyana and Colombia were fully resolved. Claims over Essequibo and the Islas Los Monjes are still on the agenda and still taint relations with Venezuela's neighbors. Over the last decade, the country has also intervened directly or indirectly in the internal affairs of several Latin American states leaving a populist trail that achieved only mixed results. It is fairly well documented that Hugo Chávez, in clear violation to UN resolutions, sided with the FARC, providing them logistical and financial support, in order to gain leverage vis-à-vis Colombia, a country that balances out Venezuela in terms of military capacity.

Chávez took a successful step in diversifying its portfolio of partners as part of a quest for multipolarity. But this amplification of Venezuela's options did not result in an increase in the country's pragmatic contribution to conflict resolution in the region (or elsewhere). At home, Venezuela's track record is not better. The country has the highest homicide rate in South America and one of the worst crime rates on the continent. Venezuela was once regarded as a natural leader in the region and a beacon of democracy. These credentials no longer apply. Venezuela's great asset on the international stage is, of course, oil. Its position as a leading petroleum exporter gives it the means to play a role out of proportion to its size. But nothing will really transform the region except good leaders with broad popular support implementing sound, pragmatic political, economic and educational programs over the long term. There is indeed a discrepancy between Venezuela's economic assets and its contribution to internal and external peace.

Notes

[1] Under Chávez, Venezuela's relations with Cuba have become very close. Beyond fluid cooperation in political, economical, and social issues, Cuba has dispatched approximately 500 military consultants to Caracas that have ensured protection to Venezuela's President and his interests. See "Venezuela's Military Ties with Cuba Stir Concerns" (*The New York Times*, 14 June 2010).

[2] Founding members Cuba and Venezuela, Bolivia (2006), Nicaragua (2007), Dominica (2008), Honduras (entered in 2008 and withdrew in 2010), Ecuador (2009), Saint Vincent and the Grenadines (2009), and Antigua and Barbuda (2009).

3 General Jim Jones, President Obama's former national security advisor, has stated this frequently. See "FARC Atuam Também na Venezuela," interview with Jim Jones (*O Estado de Sao Paulo*, 6 August 2009).

[4] See "Colombia-Venezuela Cooperation against the FARC" (*Stratfor*, 8 October 2010).

[5] Such as in the second Latin American and Caribbean Summit on Integration and Development (Mexico, February 2010).

[6] "Política Interna Move Crise Entre Bogotá e Caracas" (*O Estado de São Paulo*, 28 August 2010).

[7] "US Anti-Drug Report Faults Venezuela, Burma" (*Voice of America*, 17 September 2007).

[8] "Cocaine's Flow Is Unchecked in Venezuela" (*The New York Times*, 26 July 2012)

[9] "Caracas Rejeita Relatório de Drogas da ONU" (*O Estado de São Paulo*, 25 June 2010).

[10] "Venezuela, More Deadly than Iraq, Wonder Why" (*The New York Times*, 22 August 2010).

PART 3

REGIONAL ACTORS

10

Regionalism

"Existing subregional agreements on security and defense contribute to hemispheric security, and should be respected and taken into account in the development of a cooperative security system that emphasizes the prevention of conflicts and recognizes the particular strategic contexts of each subregion in the Hemisphere." —Declaration of Santiago, Fifth Conference of Ministers of Defense of the Americas, 2002, Art. 18

Regionalism in South America or in the Americas in general is not a new phenomenon. Understood both as an expression of regional identity, and as an attempt to give that identity institutional form, it dates back to the 1826 Congress of Panama (also called Amphictyonic Congress in homage to the Amphictyonic League of Ancient Greece) convoked by Simón Bolivar, and to a series of Pan-Hispanic American conferences in the middle and late nineteenth century (Lombaerde, Kochi and Ruiz, 2008: vii; Fawcett, 2005). The Congress proposed creating a league of American republics with a common military, a mutual defense pact, and a supranational parliamentary assembly. But it was under the auspices of the International Conferences of American States (1889-1954) (Peck, 1998:140) that the first permanent inter-American organization was created: the Commercial Bureau of the American Republics (at the first conference in 1889-90), which became the Pan American Union at the fourth conference in 1910 (Scott, 1931; Connell-Smith, 1966). Created to promote international cooperation, it offered technical and informational services to all the American republics, served as the repository for international documents, and was responsible through subsidiary councils for the furtherance of economic, social, juridical, and cultural relations.

Regionalism derives thus from the early idea of the Americas, postulated by independence fighters and thinkers like Simon Bolívar and Andrés Bello, incorporating a distinctly Hispanic interpretation of

American identity. Regional cooperation was believed to confront the perception of a potentially aggressive recolonization ambition by Spain and other Western European powers (Thomas and Magloire, 2000:3). In the end, it did not prevail. Former Spanish colonies were seldom connected to one another, and territorial as well as regulative disputes were conducive to rivalry and competition (Malamud, 2010:638).

The failure led to U.S.-driven pan-Americanism. The first statement about the Americas as a whole came in 1823 from U.S. president James Monroe, who declared unilaterally that the Americas were not to be considered as subjects for future colonization by any European powers. Later, when the United States emerged as the principal industrial power of the world, economic engagement with Latin America became an even stronger source of interest (Fishlow, 1999:16). In the twentieth century, Pan-Americanism reached its peak with the formation of the postwar inter-American system, after the signining of the Inter-American Reciprocal Assistance Treaty in 1947 and the creation of the OAS in 1948.

Debates about new forms of regional cooperation continue, and the literature is already vast. In fact, since the early 1990s there has been a revitalization of subregional integration projects throughout Latin America (Lombaerde and Garay, 2008:8; Banega, Hettne and Söderbaum, 2001:236; Grugel, 1996:132; Hurrell, 1995:250). Regional and subregional integration arrangements are being revised and new groupings formed – often they take the shape of a complex picture of overlapping initiatives and memberships. Regionalism is viewed as a precondition for securing effective competitiveness, improved positions in global markets, and increased negotiation capacity in the field of international economic and political relations (van Klaveren, 2000:135).

Latin America's two great powers, Mexico and Brazil, have chosen contrasting routes to regionalism, promoting two visions of American order: one putting an emphasis on the relations with the United States, and the other focusing on subregional affairs. Lesser powers join them in an increasingly complex web of hemispheric, regional, and subregional networks (Fawcett, 2005:43-44). But one of the most visible contradictions of South American experiences with integration is the very modest level of integration achieved through the years, "as compared to the inflated agenda of topics discussed by the presidents during their summits, or the great variety of norms adopted by the numerous organs" (Dabène, 2009:107). In fact, regionalism in South America could be regarded as symbolic, ceremonial, or summit-based (Dabène, 2009:203). The integration process lacks a supranational administrative structure with sufficient political and financial power to influence the formulation of national policies of each member country (Junquera, 2008:63). And therefore it is driven mostly by the summits of regional leaders. They embody the unification of the South American family and the spirit of brotherhood but do not necessarily pave the way for deeper and sustainable integration processes. Photo opportunities do not necessarily mean integration opportunities. For instance, although in the Santo Domingo Summit of the Rio Group (March 2008) and in the inaugural summit of UNASUR (in May 2008) Colombian President Uribe, Ecuador President Correa, and Venezuelan President Chávez displayed fraternal gestures in public, in private they were involved in a serious conflict over Colombia's military incursion into Ecuadorian territory to eliminate a FARC guerilla camp. At the second Latin American and Caribbean Summit on Integration and Development, held in Mexico in 2010, the presidents of Venezuela and Colombia became involved in a violent verbal clash, and Honduras was not even invited due to the outcome of its presidential elections. But that did not inhibited Mexican President Calderón to claim that Bolivar's ideal "of a united America is more alive than ever."[1]

Whether these organizations are moved by symbols or by content, it is unquestionable that security issues are increasingly gaining space in the agenda. In fact, the adoption of common rules and norms by a small group of states at the regional level is more palatable than the consensual acceptance of security policies at the world level. As the Fifth Conference of Defense Ministers of the Americas agreed in Santiago, in November 2002, "existing subregional agreements on security and defense contribute to hemispheric security, and should be respected and taken into account in the development of a cooperative security system that emphasizes the prevention of conflicts and recognizes the particular strategic contexts of each subregion in the Hemisphere" (art. 18).

Currently, South American states belong to the amazing number of eighteen international agencies and arrangements. The region has the highest concentration of international organizations in the world. Out of these eighteen, eight have legal capacity to undertake security-related activities: Andean Community of Nations (CAN), Caribbean Community (CARICOM), Community of Latin American and Caribbean States (CELAC), Organization of American States (OAS), Union of South American Nations (UNASUR), Africa-South American Summit (ASA), Ibero-American Summit, and the Summit of South American-Arab Countries (ASPA). Out of these eight, all but ASA and ASPA have undertaken security-related activities. The following chapters will assess their role as agents of peace and security, with the exception of CARICOM, given that its operational focus is dominated by Caribbean affairs (and not South American).

In the following chapters the book will examine the capacity of these organizations. Capacity includes *legal capacity, organizational capacity,* and *operational experience.* The first relates to the legal capacity (mandate) of an organization in security matters, whereas organizational capacity indicates its institutional capacity to make decisions, as well as the existence of organs, rules, and procedures necessary for their implementation. Operational experience encapsulates the procedural ability of an organization to undertake action in the field to maintain peace and security. This depends on the mechanisms that it has developed to put into action the decisions it may have taken in conflict prevention,[2] peacemaking,[3] peacekeeping,[4] peace enforcement[5] or peacebuilding.[6]

Notes

[1] "Calderón Quer Região 'À Imagem de Bolívar'" (*O Estado de São Paulo*, 23 February 2010).

[2] "Actions, policies, procedures or institutions undertaken in particularly vulnerable places and times in order to avoid the threat or use of armed force and related forms of coercion by states or groups, as the way to settle the political disputes that can arise from destabilizing effects of economic, social, political and international change" (Michael Lund, *Preventing and Mitigating Violent Conflicts: A Revised Guide for Practitioners* (Washington, DC: Creative Associates International, 1997), 3. It includes: (a) preventive diplomacy: mediation, conciliation, negotiation; (b) preventive deployment: the fielding of peacekeepers to forestall probable conflict; (c) preventive disarmament: destroying old weapons and reducing small arms in conflict areas; and (d) structural prevention: political, institutional and developmental efforts at root causes.

[3] Peacemaking refers to the use of diplomatic means to persuade parties in conflict to cease hostilities and negotiate a pacific settlement of their dispute. It involves negotiation, enquiry, mediation, conciliation, arbitration, judicial settlement, good offices – applied after a dispute has crossed the threshold into armed conflict.

[4] Peacekeeping is distinguished from peace enforcement in two fundamental ways: first, the mission is dependent on the consent of the host member state; and second the mission has a mandate to use force only in self-defense. Peacekeeping may be seen as of two types: *traditional* includes the stabilization of conflict situations after a ceasefire, and the creation of an environment for the parties to reach a lasting peace agreement; whereas *modern* is broader and comprises assistance in democratization, good governance and economic development

⁵ Peace Enforcement signifies the use of force by a UN or UN partner against one of the parties to enforce an end to hostilities or maintain stability once hostilities have ended. On several occasions the Security Council has authorized member states to use "all necessary means," including force, to achieve a stated objective (within the mission's mandate contained in the Security Council resolution under Chapter VII) in situations where consent of the parties is not required. Peace enforcement is often referred to as "robust peacekeeping," but it is suggested here that, for the sake of clarity, the term "peacekeeping" should be confined to missions with a Chapter VI (or "six-and-a-half") mandate as described in the preceding footnote.

⁶ Peacebuilding refers to "posthostility actions, military and civilian, taken to forestall future eruptions by strengthening structures capable of consolidating a political settlement" (Alex P. Schmid, *Thesaurus and Glossary of Early Warning and Conflict Prevention Terms* (London: FEWER, 1998).). This term pertains to assistance to countries and regions in the transition from war to peace.

11

The Andean Community of Nations

"There are very serious conflicts and tensions within the CAN, which must be taken into account." —Rafael Correa, president of Ecuador, 2009

With transnational security threats, a political-ideological rift, and opposed geopolitical projects and international alliances, the Andean states have a long way to go toward the establishment of a functional regional security architecture. Thus far, the most important attempt towards Andean integration is the Andean Community of Nations (CAN),[1] which was founded in 1969 by the Cartagena Agreement to encourage industrial, agricultural, social, and trade cooperation. The advent of the Andean Pact (as it used to be called) was a direct consequence of the failure of the Latin American Free Trade Association (LAFTA) which had been established in 1960 with the aim of improving the conditions for participation of the less-developed countries encompassed by the LAFTA agreements, and developing a common market in Latin America. But it made little progress due to regional heterogeneity and divergent national interests (Malamud, 2010:640). There was an absense of a supranational authority that would propose and coordinate common policies (Farías, 2008:28). Moreover, demands for exceptions in combination with continued protecticionism against Third-World countries led only to economic stagnation.

When it was created, the Andean Pact was one of the most ambitious integration schemes in all of the Third World (Malamud, 2008:145; Malamud, 2010:641). But the ambitious plan soon proved short-lived. The external debt crisis that Latin America experienced during the 1980s led to the application of adjustment policies by the Andean countries reducing the trade preferences exercised among them and leading to trade reduction during the mid-1980s. Moreover, the inward-looking and protectionist conception of integration implicit in the original arrangement made little progress in the 1970s and 1980s. The intraregional trade was as low as 1.2 percent in 1970 and in 1985 it had grown to a modest 3.2 percent (World Bank, 2001:191). While between 1970 and 1982, the intraregional exports had been growing at an annual average of 21.8 percent, during the period between 1982 and 1989 they decreased at an annual average of 1.8 percent (Farías, 2008:33). Moreover, a lack of agreement on the economic direction within the grouping led to Chile's withdrawal in 1977 and to the abandonment of the original integration benchmarks. Soon, an internal split into two blocs was formed by: Colombia, Venezuela, and Ecuador, trading 70 percent of their goods within the Pact; and Peru and Bolivia, trading with Argentina, Brazil and Chile. One of the remedies proposed to overcome the crisis was to build up institutions able to settle conflicts between members: the result was the creation of the Court of Justice and the Andean Parliament in 1979. However, they lacked real weight, and the integration process stalled for a decade (Malamud, 2010:642).

It was not until the late 1980s that the inward-looking arrangement was replaced by an open-regionalism approach – which did not discriminate in trade or investment terms against nonmembers of the bloc – and a new institutional structure allowed the integration process to move forward and establish a partial custom union (Prada and Espinoza, 2008:20). The Andean Pact reactivated itself with the Quito Protocol, signed in 1988 and later modified by the Galápagos Declaration (1989), the La Paz Accord (1990), and the Caracas Accord (1991). This last document resulted from a review of the Cartagena Agreement. The emphasis shifted from closed regionalism (inward integration) to open regionalism (outward integration) with the rest of the world. To mark the change, in 1996 the Trujillo Protocol was signed, changing the name of the organization from "Andean Pact" to "Andean Community."

Despite the renovated impetus, progress toward regional integration has been slow and is mostly due to the inadequate commitment of the Andean countries. If in the 1990s (CAN's "golden age") stability and a minimum policy consensus permeated the whole region, "today it is difficult to talk about a shared vision for the economic and political future of the CAN" (Prada and Espinoza, 2008:23). The more divergent the political visions of each member state, the more regional cooperation becomes a lower priority in national projects. CAN members are unequally prepared to pay the price of true integration and are subject to the strong attraction of other regional centers: the United States to the north, and Mercosur to the south and the east (Venezuela defected in 2006 to join it). Bolivia, which is currently an associate member of Mercosur, is showing inclinations to become a full-fledged member. This institutional wrangle is the consequence of an ideological divide in the subregion. President Chávez of Venezuela left the CAN because Peru and Colombia had signed FTAs with the United States (Márquez, Sánchez and Quevedo, 2006:2). The country accounted for a third of the bloc's economic strength, and its departure was a harsh blow to the CAN. In July 2004, at the XV Andean Presidential Summit in Quito, President Chávez warned his Andean neighbors that signing free trade agreements with the United States could put regional integration in jeopardy:

> "We respect the decision of Colombia, Ecuador, Peru, of any fellow country. However, it concerns us because the integration proposed by the United Status is a risk for our citizens. . . . We won't reject integration with the North (the United States), but all the countries that make up the Andean regional organization should reconsider the timeline. . . . The priority of the Andean Community should be to consolidate its integrative process in order to later negotiate with the North on fair conditions, not in conditions of subordination."

During the negotiation process, the United States government demanded that tariff preferences extended to Andean countries through the free trade agreement not be extended to Venezuela. The Cartagena Accord establishes that if one of the member countries concedes benefits or preferential treatment to a country or countries outside the subregional block through a commercial negotiation, those benefits should apply to all other member countries. Bolivia, under President Morales, and Ecuador, under President Correa, share the same disapproval of the traditional free-trade policy, but unlike the Venezuelan government, they remained in the CAN, they argue, in order to change it from within and reestablish Andean integration on new values, with protection of the environment, as well as protection of social and cultural rights, prevailing over commercial considerations. In contrast to this "antiglobalization" view, Alan Garcia's Peru and Alvaro Uribe's Colombia remain determined advocates of "open regionalism" and free trade, concerned first and foremost with economic development and productivity, interested in the Asian markets, and unwilling to get trapped in an overly exclusive regional framework.

Andean integration is also hindered by the multiple political problems of the Andean countries that jeopardize political stability, democracy, and the protection of human rights. For developing countries of medium and small size the margin of autonomy is smaller, and the countries struggle with internal problems such as the lack of state presence, weak political institutions, internal conflict, predicaments of political parties, lack of identity and political will, and contrast in the political projects of the different countries (Ardila, 2005:128). There is, for instance, no real regional consensus over the handling of the Colombian conflict; and the existence of insurgent groups (arms and narco-trafficking) jeopardizes free-trade negotiations (Cárdenas and Höwer, 2004:xiii and xvii). Internal instability is also generalized. Ecuador, for example has had seven presidents from 1996 to 2008, whereas Peru has been under the authoritarian fist of Alberto Fujimori for ten years (1990-2000) (Buitrago, 2008: 466-7). The systematic internal problems of these countries tend to project themselves externally making relations with neighbors more difficult to handle.

In 1999, CAN and Mercosur began negotiating a merger with a view to creating a South American Free Trade Area (SAFTA). In December 2004 the Andean Community signed a cooperation agreement with Mercosur, and it published a joint letter of intention for future negotiations towards integrating all of South America in UNASUR. Similar to other regional good-will initiatives, neither the SAFTA nor the full integration into UNASUR have materialized. Mercosur, UNASUR and CAN are likely to resist any merging attempt and will at best cooperate amongst themselves. Tellingly, when Peru held the rotating presidency of CAN, the country's foreign minister José Antonio Garcia Belaunde noted that CAN and UNASUR's work should complement each other [not merge] so as to create "synergy that will allow us to overcome our difficulties."[2]

Legal Capacity

CAN is a subregional organization endowed with an international legal status (Art. 48 of Cartagena Agreement), and given the territorial contiguity of its members it may be regarded as a regional agency under Chapter VIII of the UN Charter. Its foundation treaty, however, includes no provisions on the issue of security, and therefore CAN would be legally handicapped to operate in this arena. This handicap started to be overcome in 1989 when member states adopted the Andean Commitment to Peace, Security and Cooperation, contained in the Declaration of Galapagos. The Declaration proposed the interchange of information and the meeting of military staff and created conditions for the political coordination of drug trafficking. Most of the proposals, however, stayed on paper. The first step to reverse this came in 1991 when the presidents of the Andean Group adopted the Cartagena Declaration on Renunciation of Weapons of Mass Destruction, reaffirming their committment to renouncing the possession, production, development, use, testing, and transference of all weapons of mass destruction, be they nuclear, biological, toxic, or chemical, as well as the storing of acquisition of such weapons. An additional key step forward arrived in 2002 with the adoption of the Lima Commitment: Andean Charter for Peace and Security and Limitation and Control of the Expenditure on Foreign Defense, agreed at a meeting of the Andean Council of Foreign Ministers with the Ministers of Defense. The Charter is one of the most comprehensive security legal documents adopted by regional organizations worldwide. It defined a Common Andean Policy on External Security; characterized a Peace Zone in the Andean Community; limited military spending in order to use those funds for social investment purposes; pledged the eradication of anti-personnel landmines; and intensified cooperation to fight terrorism and illegal arms trafficking, among other matters. The Lima Commitment set the stage for the adoption, two years later, of the Guidelines of the Andean Policy on External Security which listed as objectives:[3]

- To confront any threats posed to the security of the Andean Community in a cooperative and coordinated manner.
- To develop and consolidate the Andean Peace Zone, as an area free of nuclear, chemical and biological weapons, promoting mechanisms that ensure the pacific settlement of disputes, the building of reciprocal confidence, and that contribute to overcome factors susceptible of generating disputes among the Member Countries.
- To prevent, combat and eradicate the new threats to the security, and their interrelations, when appropriate, through cooperation and coordination efforts to confront the challenges that such threats represent for the Andean Community.
- To contribute to the economic development and social welfare of the Andean Community population by reinforcing the security of the subregion.
- To contribute to the consolidation and the enhancement of the Peace Zone and South American Cooperation within the framework of a South American integration area.
- To promote the participation of the Member Countries in the definitions and procedures of the collective, hemispheric and world security.

The Guidelines also called for the adoption of an Andean Plan Against Terrorism (VI-5), which according to a follow-up presidential meeting[4] should include, among other elements, subregional cooperation, the exchange of information, and legal mutual assistance for preventing the international circulation of terrorists, and ensuring the processing of anyone participating in the planning, financing or perpetration of terrorism acts. Despite the high expectations, the Plan has not yet been implemented.

At the First Meeting of the High-Level Group responsible for the semiannual evaluation of the progress made in implementing the Lima Commitment (held in 2003 in Bogotá), the Andean vision of security was defined as "a situation in which the State and society are protected from threats or risks likely to affect the overall development and welfare of the citizens, as well as the free exercise of their rights and freedoms within a context of full democratic rule" (italics added).[5] From this perspective, security has a "multidimensional and comprehensive nature" and encompasses "political, economic, social and cultural matters, which are reflected in the policies in spheres as diverse as the strengthening of democratic institutions and the rule of law, defense, health, the environment, the economy, economic development, and the prevention of natural disasters, among other areas."

This concept of security was reinforced when in June 2003 member states adopted the Andean Plan to Prevent, Fight and Eradicate Illicit Trafficking in Small Arms and Light Weapons in all its Aspects (Decision 552). This comprehensive vision of security is in tune with OAS's Declaration on Security in the Americas adopted four months later. Both postulate that a meaningful definition of security cannot be limited to traditional military operations, but must adopt an integrated approach that addresses the conditions creating social instability. The inclination of both organizations to adopt such a concept is even more relevant if we consider that the atrocities of 9/11 produced an understandable obsession with preventing future acts of a similar kind and relied mostly on traditional military action to do so.

The CAN security concept encompassed, for instance, the threat of trafficking in small arms. This is generally recognized as being a nuclear problem in Andean security. In the same vein, the above-mentioned Plan states that illicit trade in small arms and light weapons constitutes "a serious threat to the peace, security, governance, stability and democratic and institutional order of Andean Community Member Countries and conspires against the aspiration of our societies to attain higher levels of political, economic, social and cultural development that are sustainable in the long term" (Introduction). Consequently, the Plan provides for specific mechanisms and lines of action at the national, subregional, and international levels. It should be noted that Decision 552 is the first binding instrument at the subregional level to be derived from the United Nations Program of Action to Prevent, Combat and Eradicate Illicit Trafficking in Small Arms and Light Weapons in all its aspects.

The major threat to Andean security is, however, narcotrafficking, from which derive other threats such as urban criminality, funding for illegal armed groups, and terrorism. To address this regional cancer CAN has adopted two declarations. The first and most important is the Andean Cooperation Plan for the Control of Illegal Drugs and Related Offenses (Decision 505) adopted in Valencia, Venezuela, in June 2001. The Plan acknowledges that drug trafficking is one of the "most harmful and dangerous forms of organized transnational crime, that makes use of the globalizing logic of the markets, disrupts the social dynamic, distorts the economy, undermines the state of law, and subverts the public order" (Art.1). It includes a Plan of Action that provides guidelines on the reinforcement of national, binational, and CAN strategies to address the serious problem. The second is the Andean Regulation for the Control of Chemical Substances Used in the Illegal Manufacture of Narcotic Drugs and Psychotropic Substances, adopted in 2004, which reinforced the application of the control and surveillance procedures concerning the traffic of chemical substances that are likely to be used for the production of illicit drugs, cocaine, and heroin in particular.

Finally, CAN adopted in 2004 the Declaration of San Francisco de Quito on the Establishment and Development of an Andean Peace Area, which defines the geographic space, grounds, criteria, and objectives of the Andean Peace Zone. It also lays down guidelines to promote its consolidation and international projection. In July 2001, member states of the Andean Community, Mercosur and the government of Guyana and Suriname had already established a South American Cooperation and Peace Zone. The declarations are, however, confined to the declaratory sphere and have little impact in reality. Tellingly, all the Andean countries have been arms suppliers to the Colombian conflict at one or the other of its stages.

Yet, where legal competence is concerned CAN has become an international lighthouse in the security field. It may even be argued that CAN is the most robust organization in this regard having adopted unmistakable legal documents to address both traditional and nontraditional aspects of security. Even so, CAN members have not been tempted to build on this strong, normative framework to develop common security regional policies. While the broad legal framework provides some regional sense on security matters, it does little to forestall internal conflict. Indeed, the development of Andean integration is being scattered by centrifugal forces, such as the divergent priorities of the member governments and their reluctance to give up certain national powers. As mentioned by Buitrago, "in the Andean countries there is no vision of shared security against threats, not as a result of different perceptions or different national security agendas, but rather due to the political incapacity of governments in the region to reach consensus" (Buitrago, 2008: 469).

Organizational Capacity

CAN has two sets of institutions: intergovernmental bodies in which the members are representing the interests of their country of origin (the Andean Presidential Council, the Andean Council of Ministers of Foreign Affairs, and the Andean Commission) and Community bodies in which the members are independent from their country of origin and defend the Community interest (the Andean Court of Justice, the Andean Parliament, the Secretariat General of the Andean Community (SG CAN), the Andean Development Corporation (CAF), and the Latin America Reserve Fund (FLAR).

The Presidential Council comprises the presidents of the member countries. It has a chairman who represents the Andean Community at the highest political level and holds that position for a period of one calendar year, after which it is rotated successively. The body meets regularly once a year and may meet in special session any time it deems it advisable. The Council orients and promotes actions on matters of interest to the subregion, namely security and foreign policy. It also evaluates the course and results of the integration process; examines all issues and matters connected with the progress of integration and its relations with the world. For example, in the Council meeting held in Valencia, Venezuela, (June 2001), the contours of a common security policy started to be drawn.

The Council of Ministers of Foreign Affairs is the body responsible for the definition and coordination of the Andean Common External Security Policy. It is the political leadership body. It signs conventions and agreements on global foreign policy and cooperation issues with countries or groups of countries, or with international organizations. It also coordinates the joint position of the member countries in international forums and negotiations on matters within its sphere of responsibility. Other responsible organs are the Executive Council of the Andean Common External Security Policy and the Andean Security

Network, constituted by political, business, academic, and other organizations of the civil society together with the governmental and intergovernmental organizations of the subregion.

"[T]he legal principle of direct effect and the preeminence of community law evokes a level of formal institutionalization, only behind the European Union" (Malamud 2005: 11). Still, the CAN has not been uplifted by its network of institutions. Malamud argues that the member countries are "naïve regarding their faith in supranationality" (Malamud, 2005: 16).

Operational Experience in Traditional Security

The Andean Group has progressively made the integration process a much-diversified one. Despite the dominant focus on trade, 34 percent of all decisions (238 in 707) taken by CAN from 1969 to 2008 have been on external relations, human rights, and security (Dabène, 2009:123).[6] But despite the numerous accords and decisions, the Andean Community has never been able to contain or resolve the serious conflicts that emerged in the region in the 1990s: the negative externalities of the Fujimori regime, the war between Ecuador and Peru, the recurrent governance crises in Ecuador, the successive disputes between Colombia and Venezuela, or the issue of guerilla warfare in Colombia (Sanjuánn, 2008:169). A truly regional approach to solving the latter problem has been absent mainly because Colombian heads of state refuse to recognize the internationalization of the conflict for fear that doing so has transterritorial implications and could, consequentially, lead others to challenge their sovereignty. But this and other conflicts are unquestionably regional in nature. As alerted by Andrew Hurrell, "the liberalization of economic exchanges facilitates illicit flows of all kinds, especially when this liberalization forms part of a more general shift in power from the state to the market. Such illicit activities may then spill over into interstate relations" (Hurell, 1998b: 540). Whatever the cause of CAN's passivity, the organization has made limited progress in enhancing security in the region and its contribution has been mostly declaratory and often only in vague terms (Arias, 2011). It has for instance conveyed its support to President Fernando de la Rua of Argentina during the political crisis of 2001. At the time the Andean group observed that:

> "In light of the importance to the Andean Community of its political dialogue with the Mercosur, the Presidents reiterate their full solidarity with the Republic of Argentina in the face of the political situation it

confronts and express their unrestricted backing for the democratic institutions and the Constitutional Government of that country."[7]

But this is far too little. Although the CAN is framed by a thick legal web that would permit a resolute role in conflict resolution and built on a tense and demanding security environment, the Community has remained uninvolved in conflict prevention, peacekeeping, peacemaking, or peacebuilding.

Operational Experience in Human Security

Despite the fact that CAN has attempted to mitigate a wide range of nonsecurity threats – such as small arms proliferation[8] – it is in drug trafficking that its contribution becomes more salient. As we saw, in June 2001 the Andean Council of Foreign Ministers gave its approval to the Andean Cooperation Plan for the Control of Illegal Drugs and Related Offenses, which provides for preventive and interdiction measures, reduction of illicit crops, and alternative development, as well as the control of the diversion of chemical precursor substances, asset laundering, and traffic in arms, ammunition, and explosives. The Plan explains the principles and objectives, establishes the mechanisms for carrying them out, and contains a biennial Program of Action. The Plan was defined as "a key issue of Andean political cooperation" (Art. 6) and the proposal is made to consolidate the CAN as "the moving force for a South American and hemispheric strategy for the control of illegal drugs and related offenses" (Art. 7). The Program of Action is aimed at reinforcing national, binational, and Community strategies. In the area of national strategies, it provides for a series of measures to control the production, smuggling and diversion of chemical precursor substances, the technical eradication of illicit crops, the promotion of alternative development to replace the drug production-based economy, and the dismantling of drug-trafficking production and transportation infrastructure and organizations. The Program establishes a series of measures to cope with asset laundering and proposes a succession of steps to cut down the demand, ranging from prevention campaigns to programs for the rehabilitation and social reinsertion of drug-dependent individuals. Insofar as the reinforcement of binational strategies is concerned, the bilateral agreements on drug control will be evaluated with a view to their updating and perfecting, at the same time as bilateral mechanisms designed specifically for application to border areas will be promoted. In the Community area, the exchange of intelligence among the competent authorities of the Andean countries will be reinforced and the coordination of national authorities responsible for drug control will be strengthened and their training promoted. Criminal legal assistance agreements will be advanced, and the harmonizing of national legislation on criminal and procedural law boosted.

In an effort to amply its fight against illegal drugs, the Andean Community adopted in 2004, as we saw, the Regulation for the Control of Chemical Substances used in the Illegal Manufacture of Narcotic Drugs and Psychotropic Substances. The purpose of this legal instrument was to protect and shield the Andean Community's customs territory from the diversion of imports or exports of certain chemical substances for the illegal production of narcotic drugs and psychotropic substances, particularly cocaine and heroin. Finally, and in order to offer alternatives to the people who have benefited from coca plantations, member states adopted in 2005 the Andean Integral and Sustainable Alternative Development Strategy to contribute, with an integral and sustainable approach, to poverty reduction and social cohesion.

This legal framework indicates that Andean governments have not simply followed the guidelines of multilateral agencies and accepted without question discourses and practices relating to "the fight against drugs." In contrast, members of the Andean Community are frontline actors in the development of standards for global cooperation against the manufacture, trafficking, and consumption of drugs for purposes other than medicine and science. CAN members' diplomacy has influenced the definition of the phenomenon as a threat to the security of society and state, and their foreign policy has included the principle of "shared responsibility" and the goal of "development alternative" in multilateral cooperation against illegal drug trafficking. Although it is not possible to affirm that there is a functional Andean regional security system for the "war on drugs," the Andean Community has mechanisms, procedures, and technical agencies to coordinate actions against production, trafficking, and consumption of narcotic drugs (Cruz, 2010). At multilateral forums such as the UN and OAS, Andean countries have been inclined to adopt common positions and actions, and diplomats meet frequently in Washington, Geneva, Brussels, and Vienna to discuss common approaches.

In 2010, the European Union and the Andean Community agreed to take their partnership to fight drug trafficking and global warming to a higher level of committment. In fact, the fight against drugs has always been high on the agenda of the political meetings between the EU and the CAN. The EU-CAN High Level Specialised Dialogue on Drugs was established in the mid-1990's to bring together high level experts from both sides to exchange views on how best to address the drugs phenomenon and how to coordinate efforts. But in 2010, the sides met after a summit between the EU, Latin America and the Caribbean in Madrid that included officials from sixty countries and more than thirty heads of state or government. European Commission President José Manuel Barroso, who characterized drug trafficking as a threat to security and democracy, pledged that the European Commission will fund the program with EUR€ 257 million.

Conclusions

The Andean Community has evolved from a regional organization based predominantly on economic cooperation to one that encompasses a myriad of shared issues, including security. Despite enlarging its scope and adopting a strong legal framework, its contribution to conflict resolution has remained nugatory. Although it adopted many reforms, and democracy gradually settled down in all Andean Community countries, the political situation in the Andean Community countries has remained very fragile. This is one of the reasons why regional integration has never been the number-one priority, if at all more than a formality or pure rhetoric (Farías, 2008:7). The objective of integration as such often fails to convince, and one can note an enormous distance between the Andean Community's institutions, the respective governments, and with civil society at large. This situation is aggravated by the strong ideological and political differences between its members, who advocate different rhythms for the integration process and seem not to converge on priorities and interests. As argued by Malamud, "no spillover effects have taken place, and only joint national intervention could put back on track the integration process" (Malamud, 2005:11). There is a lack of common belonging and a generalized social ignorance towards the process of integration that is taking place.

CAN's internal crisis became even more evident in 2008, when at a summit leaders failed to come up with a new strategy to suit the different economic and ideological circumstances of its member countries and resolve the identity crisis threatening its survival. At the end, CAN's Secretary General Freddy Ehlers told journalists that it was time to "rethink the Andean development model, because the present one is unsustainable." The president of the Andean Parliament, Ivonne Baki, also told the press that, "the disagreements in the CAN are not just ideological; they are caused by [competition for] political leadership," and added that, "We are going through the most difficult time. What do we do? Do we continue or not? We have to make a decision. We can't carry on playing with people."[9] UNASUR is increasingly being seen as a viable alternative for regional integration. In 2012, Peruvian President Ollanta Humala, as president pro tempore of UNASUR, said that the integration processes of CAN and UNASUR were one of the pritorities of Peru's foreign policy. In 2013, President Correa of Ecuador also advocated that Mercosur and CAN should merge into UNASUR. In the same year, the foreign ministers of Peru, Uruguay and Ecuador, the countries then chairing UNASUR, Mercosur, and CAN, respectively, also agreed on the need to move towards greater integration of these blocks. But the decision has not yet been taken.

Notes

[1] It currently comprises four countries: Bolivia, Colombia, Ecuador, and Peru. Venezuela joined in 1973 but withdrew in 2006, and Chile withdrew in 1977. Chile withdrew due to the incompatibility of the group's protectionist economic policies with the neoliberal economic strategy adopted by the Chilean military government. Peru suspended its membership in 1992 but resumed it in 1997.

[2] Peru Aims for Close Work Between CAN, Unasur (*Andina*, 7 August 2009).

[3] Decision 587, Guidelines for the External Security Policy of the Andean Community (10 July 2004).

[4] Minutes of the Lima Presidential Meeting Democracy, Development and Social Cohesion. Sixteenth Andean Council of Presidents.

[5] http://www.comunidadandina.org/ingles/Exterior/security.htm. Visited 26 February 2012.

[6] In the same period, CAN has taken 311 decisions on trade, the equivalent to 45 percent of all decisions.

[7] Declaration of Santa Cruz de la Sierra (30 January 2002) (Art.24). Online at http://www.comunidadandina.org/INGLES/documentos/documents/santacruz.htm. Visited 23 March 2011.

[8] In 2003, CAN members adopted the Andean Plan to Prevent, Combat and Eradicate Illicit Trade in Small Arms and Light Weapons.

[9] "CAN Fails to Overcome Internal Crisis" (*Infosur Hoy*, 2008)

12

The Organization of American States

"Our new concept of security in the Hemisphere is multidimensional in scope, includes traditional and new threats, concerns, and other challenges to the security of the states of the Hemisphere, incorporates the priorities of each state, contributes to the consolidation of peace, integral development, and social justice, and is based on democratic values, respect for and promotion and defense of human rights, solidarity, cooperation, and respect for national sovereignty." —Final act of the commemoration of the fifth anniversary of the Declaration on Security in the Americas (2009)

In 1947 regional cooperation reached an important landmark. The experience of the Second World War convinced hemispheric governments that unilateral action could not ensure the territorial integrity of the American nations in the event of extracontinental aggression. This inspired twenty Latin American states to sign the Inter-American Treaty of Reciprocal Assistance (Rio Treaty), which provides for collective defense, not only from foreign attacks but also from any action or threat posed by one member against another. In this light, acts of aggression are subject to sanctions that may include the recall of diplomatic missions, the breaking of diplomatic relations, the partial or complete interruption of economic relations, and the use of armed force (Art. 6). The treaty was invoked numerous times. For instance, in the 1950s economic sanctions were levied against the Dominican dictator Rafael Trujillo following an assassination attempt on Venezuelan President Rómulo Betancourt. According to Pastor, despite the Rio Treaty "few would call the region a 'security community,' a region in which there were no expectations of conflict" (Pastor, 2005:210). The emergence of democracy had dampened the likelihood of war but, in part because many of the democracies were fragile, there were still conflicts.

In parallel, the International Conferences of American States produced myriad conventions and treaties. These ranged from the establishment of unions and confederations to promotion of hemispheric solidarity and defense alliances to peaceful settlement procedures (Scott, 1931; Tacsan, 1998:95-97). These meetings culminated in the birth of the Organization of American States (OAS) as it stands today, with the signature by twenty-one American countries of the Charter of the Organization of American States in April 1948 (in effect since December 1951) at the ninth international conference. The meeting also adopted the American Declaration of the Rights and Duties of Man, the world's first regional human rights instrument, and the American Treaty on Pacific Settlement (also known as the Pact of Bogotá), whose purpose was to impose a general obligation on the signatories to settle their disputes through peaceful means. The treaty was adopted in fulfillment of some of the principles of the OAS Charter.

Following the League of Arab States established in 1945, OAS is the oldest regional organization in the world, covering the totality of the American continent's thirty-five member states (and of South America's twelve states).[1] The OAS has a wide mandate (e.g., cooperation in the fields of culture, education, science and technology, human rights, international law, foreign trade, drug trafficking), including an explicit mandate to act in the arena of peace and security. But despite its bold objectives, OAS was paralyzed in the 1970s and 1980s by the deep divisions that existed between the United States and Latin America over the crisis in Central America, the unilateral decisions by the United States to intervene both in Grenada in 1983 and in Panama in 1989, and the marginal role OAS played in the Falklands/Malvinas War (Hurrell, 1995:265; Herz, 2003:215; Tacsan, 1998:92-93). The Cuban Revolution in 1959 and the United States' response to the domestic issues in that country also preempted any effective or institutional response and influence by the Organization. Yet the salience of OAS has increased dramatically in the 1990s, prompted by a wide sense of failure, the admission of Canada in 1990, different interests of regional actors, and the wider debate on the redefinition of the concept of security. Although its role in the traditional field of peace and security remains somewhat limited, it has adopted a much more forceful position with the regard to the support of democracy. The first sign of a significant move toward a prodemocracy doctrine came in 1979 with the passage of a resolution condemning the human rights record of the U.S.-backed Somoza regime in Nicaragua (Cooper and Legler, 2006:24).

Even if the Americas constitute a region in which the bonds connecting the various subregions are more symbolic than substantial (Pastor, 2005:210), many now see the effective collective defense of democracy as forming the heart of a renewed and strengthened inter-American political and military system (Herz, 2003:213). The Summit of the Americas, a sequence of summits led largely by the United States bringing together the countries of the Americas for discussion of a variety of issues (first in 1994), has also provided OAS with a renewed agenda.

Legal Capacity

The OAS's explicit mandate in security matters is enshrined in its founding document, where it coins itself as a regional agency for UN purposes (Chapter VIII of the UN Charter), one of the few regional actors to do it so clearly. Furthermore, member states also proclaim in the charter that the purposes of OAS include "to strengthen the peace and security of the continent" (art. 2-a), "to promote and consolidate representative democracy, with due respect for the principle of nonintervention" (art. 2-b), "to prevent possible causes of difficulties and to ensure the pacific settlement of disputes that may arise among the Member States" (art. 2-c), and "to provide for common action on the part of those States in the event of aggression" (art. 2-d). The mandate for peaceful settlement of disputes is further elaborated in article 3-i where it is stated that "controversies of an international character arising between two or more American States shall be settled by peaceful procedures." This mandate is encapsulated in Chapter V ("Peaceful Settlement of Disputes," arts. 24-27), which enumerates the peaceful procedures for the settlement of disputes available to the organization: "direct negotiation, good offices, mediation, investigation and conciliation, judicial settlement, arbitration, and those which the parties to the dispute may especially agree upon at any time" (art. 25). The dispute settlement capacity of the organization is reiterated in the above-mentioned 1948 American Treaty on Pacific Settlement (Pact of Bogotá).

The OAS Charter also envisages a collective defense mechanism, set out in article 3-h, which states that, "an act of aggression against one American state is an act of aggression against all the American states" and is further elaborated in Chapter VI ("Collective Security," arts. 28-29). The same disposition can be found in article 3 of the Rio Treaty. This regional mechanism established during the Cold War to address Soviet threats is still in place and was in fact invoked, at Brazil's initiative, in the aftermath of the September 11 bombings in the United States. Yet, history demonstrates that collective security, when applied to the Americas is hardly an easy concept. In the imbalances of power, which existed in U.S./South American military relations, definitions of aggression, victory, and rights were all relative to the circumstances, to perceptions of security interests, as well as to the states involved. As pointed out by Thomas and Magloire,

> "The Anglo/Argentinean War in 1982 over the Falklands Islands was perhaps the most serious issue on the interpretation of the application of "the external aggression provision" that Latin American/U.S. relations had to engage and endure. Irrespective of what might have been a propriety regional response, the unambiguous alliance of the United States in that conflict and the position taken by at least two other Latin American states of the Hemisphere, were clear indications that the interpretation of that principle in relation to the Hemisphere was and would be at best conflictive and, at worst, potentially disruptive" (Thomas and Magloire, 2000: 23-24).

Thus, unlike NATO and the Warsaw Pact, the OAS has never been modeled to a collective security organization to the Americas, and member states have been more concerned about nonmilitary threats, such as threats to democracy (Shaw, 2003:128). In fact, this concept of "multidimensional security" gradually established itself over the years in a number of agreements, but especially those arising out of the thirty-second regular session of the OAS General Assembly held in Bridgetown, Barbados, in 2002; the Special Conference on Security held in Mexico City in 2003, which adopted the key Declaration on Security; and the Special Summit of the Americas in Monterrey, Mexico, in 2004.

In the Declaration on Security member states unequivocally contended that their "new concept of security" in the hemisphere includes "traditional and new threats," and is based on "democratic values" (see the following text box). Also significant in the Declaration is the shift from state security – so characteristic of South American states – to human security (Table 7). During the 2003 conference, the differences in perspectives between the countries became clear. The argument of Chile's governments were based on the concept of human security; Colombia's representatives stressed the threat posed by illegal armed groups – drug trafficking, and terrorism; and Argentinean and Brazilian officials focused on poverty as a threat in itself (Herz, 2011:40-41). The landmark declaration ended up therefore identifying a comprehensive program for addressing ever-changing security threats in the Americas through action in a number of areas. These include strengthening democracy, combating terrorism, fostering the peaceful resolution of conflict, furthering confidence and security building measures between states, curbing the proliferation of weapons of mass destruction, combating transnational organized crime and illicit trafficking in firearms, preventing and mitigating the effect of natural disasters, and addressing issues of health and poverty.

In order to keep the Declaration alive in ongoing political discussions, the OAS has organized regular events, including a Special Meeting to review progress in implementing the Declaration (2007), the Commemoration of the Fifth Anniversary of the Declaration (2009), and the Follow-up to the Special Conference on Security (2010 and 2012). Member states and OAS organs are invited to submit progress reports with detailed updates on their contribution to the implementation of the Declaration. While there is a long way yet to go and much work remains, cooperation is increasing and a number of important joint initiatives have begun and are bearing fruit.

Declaration on Security in the Americas (excerpt)

II. Shared values and common approaches

2. Our new concept of security in the Hemisphere is multidimensional in scope, includes traditional and new threats, concerns, and other challenges to the security of the states of the Hemisphere, incorporates the priorities of each state, contributes to the consolidation of peace, integral development, and social justice, and is based on democratic values, respect for and promotion and defense of human rights, solidarity, cooperation, and respect for national sovereignty.

4e. In our Hemisphere, as democratic states committed to the principles of the Charter of the United Nations and the OAS, we reaffirm that the basis and purpose of security is the protection of human beings. Security is strengthened when we deepen its human dimension. Conditions for human security are improved through full respect for people's dignity, human rights, and fundamental freedoms, as well as the promotion of social and economic development, social inclusion, and education and the fight against poverty, disease, and hunger.

Source: OAS website,
http://www.oas.org/documents/eng/DeclaracionSecurity_102803.asp

The OAS also adopted legal instruments to face terrorism. The inaugural agreement was the Convention to Prevent and Punish Acts of Terrorism Taking the Form of Crimes Against Persons and Related Extortion That Are of International Significance, signed in 1971. It included the pledge by member states to take all measures "to prevent and punish acts of terrorism, especially kidnapping, murder, and other assaults against the life or physical integrity of those persons to whom the state has the duty according to international law to give special protection" (Art.1). Back then the United States was more preoccupied with native groups such as the Black Liberation Army, an underground, black nationalist-Marxist militant organization that operated in the United States from 1970 to 1981, than with Islamic terrorism. It was only in the 1980s and 1990s that the page was turned. The Declaration of Lima to Prevent, Combat, and Eliminate Terrorism and its plan of action – adopted at an OAS Specialized Conference on Terrorism held in 1996 – urged cooperation between and among states on issues of exchange of information, border security, transportation and travel documents, and other steps to eliminate terrorism. The declaration clearly extended security concerns to other government agencies and opened the door for security cooperation across the range of government portfolios (Hayes, 2007:84). A second Inter-American Conference on Terrorism was held in 1998 in Mar del Plata, with ministers of interior in attendance. They adopted the Commitment of Mar del Plata condemning terrorist acts as serious threats to the stability of elected governments. They also recommended creation of an Inter-American Committee Against Terrorism (CICTE), which would coordinate cooperation among states. Created in 1999 and reinvigorated after September 11, it promotes cooperation on border-security mechanisms, controls to prevent terrorist funding, law enforcement, and the exchange of counterterrorism intelligence and information.

In 2002, OAS members took an important step forward by adopting the Inter-American Convention Against Terrorism at the OAS General Assembly meeting in Bridgetown, Barbados (entered into force in July 2003). The Convention commits state parties to endeavor to become party to ten international conventions and protocols relating to terrorism (listed in the Convention), consistent with UN Security Council Resolution 1373. The Convention also commits state parties to take certain measures to prevent, combat, and eradicate the financing of terrorism and to deny safe haven to suspected terrorists. The Treaty further requires that the terrorist acts covered under the specified international conventions and protocols be criminalized as predicate crimes to money laundering. The Convention provides for enhanced cooperation in a number of areas, including exchanges of information, border control measures, and law enforcement actions.

Moreover, the OAS has also built a legal basis to disarmament. In 1997 it approved the Inter-American Convention against the Illicit Manufacture of and Trafficking in Firearms, Ammunition, Explosives, and Other Related Materials. This was the first multilateral treaty designed to prevent, combat, and eradicate illegal transnational trafficking in firearms, ammunition, and explosives. Two years later, member states signed the Inter-American Convention on Transparency in Conventional Weapons Acquisitions, whose objective was to contribute more fully to regional openness and transparency in the acquisition of conventional weapons by exchanging information regarding such acquisitions. In addition, in June 2010 the foreign ministers of the OAS issued a call to promote arms control in the region by limiting conventional weapons and preventing the proliferation of weapons of mass destruction in the region known as the Lima Declaration. The Declaration was spearheaded by Peru, which criticized its neighbor Chile for the high military expenditures.

The OAS has also adopted legal instruments to confront drug trafficking. The Hemispheric Drug Strategy was adopted by the OAS General Assembly in Lima in June 2010, opening a new phase in regional cooperation in dealing with the world drug problem. The preparation of the Strategy, chaired by Brazil, involved a year-long dialogue including four face-to-face meetings. The Hemispheric Drug Strategy replaced the Anti-Drug Strategy in the Hemisphere of 1996 as member states agreed that the previous strategy lagged behind on some key issues, such as the need to integrate human rights and scientific evidences in the implementation of drug policies. The new strategy also regards drug dependence as a chronic, relapsing disease that should be treated as a public health issue. As noted by James F. Mack, the Executive Secretary of the Inter-American Drug Abuse Control Commission (CICAD), "the new Strategy regards drug-dependent persons as men and women suffering from an illness that requires medical attention, just as those suffering from diseases such as diabetes, hypertension or asthma require medical management of their chronic, relapsing illnesses."

Finally, the organization has also adopted legal tools to prevent the emergence of domestic political crises. In 1991 OAS foreign ministers approved the Declaration on the Collective Defense of Democracy (Santiago Commitment), which promised firm support for democracy and resolved that any "sudden or irregular interruption of the democratic political institutional process" of any of them would result in the calling of an emergency meeting of foreign ministers (Hurrell, 1995:265). Resolution 1080,[2] which accompanied the declaration, creates automatic procedures for convening the OAS Permanent Council in the event of a coup or other disruption of constitutional order. It states that, "representative democracy is an indispensable condition for the stability, peace, and development of the region" (Preamble) and includes an automatic procedure to respond to democratic breakdown – allowing the OAS to undertake a wide range of collective activity so long as these actions are approved by the foreign ministers of its member states and/or the General Assembly. Once this door was open, the OAS made sure there was no way back. The Protocol of Washington of 1992, which amended the Charter, made the OAS the first regional political organization to permit suspension of a member whose democratically constituted government is overthrown by force. In 1993, the Organization adopted the Declaration of Managua for the Promotion of Democracy and Development, where member states expressed their conviction that the Organization's mission is not limited to the defense of democracy wherever its fundamental values and principles have collapsed, but also called for ongoing and creative work to consolidate democracy as well as a continuing effort to prevent and anticipate the very causes of the problems that affect the democratic system of government. In 2001, the OAS also adopted the Inter-American Democratic Charter whose main purpose was the strengthening and upholding of democratic institutions throughout the continent. The Charter defines democracy and its relationship to integral development and the war on poverty, and it specifies how it should be defended when under threat. Democracy promotion became one of the most important attributes of the Organization.

Organizational Capacity

The principal decision-making body, convening annually to establish the work plan and the political agenda of the OAS is the General Assembly, composed of heads of state and government. It replaces what used to be known as the Inter-American Conference in the organization's original charter of 1948. This change came in 1967 at a special conference in Buenos Aires. The exact role of the Assembly in relation to the peaceful settlement of conflicts by the OAS is not specified in the charter. However, among the duties of the Assembly, as outlined in the charter, are "to decide the general action and policy of the Organization, determine the structure and functions of its organs, and consider any matter relating to friendly relations among the American States" (art.53).

The implementation of the General Assembly decisions is carried out by the Permanent Council consisting of the permanent ambassadors to the OAS. The Council keeps vigilance over the maintenance of friendly relations among the member states and, for that purpose, effectively assists them in the peaceful settlement of their disputes. It includes a committee on hemispheric security with a mandate that includes handling of actions against antipersonnel mines, arms trafficking, cooperation for hemispheric security, or natural disaster reduction.

The main coordination and implementation body of the OAS is, however, the General Secretariat, managed by the Secretary-General, who might bring to the attention of the General Assembly or the Permanent Council matters that might threaten the peace, security, or development of member states (Herz, 2003:216). In the 1990s the Secretary-General has been involved in facilitating negotiations between Belize and Guatemala, Costa Rica and Nicaragua, and Ecuador and Peru (Peck, 1998:143; Shaw, 2003:126). Within the secretariat, the major departments handling security issues are the Secretariat for Multidimensional Security, which coordinates OAS actions against organized crime, illegal drugs, border control, and other threats to public security, and the Secretariat for Political Affairs, responsible for political dialogue, international security and democracy.[3] Within the latter, the Department of Sustainable Democracy and Special Missions provides technical expertise in matters pertaining to conflict resolution, threats to democracy, good governance, and democratic dialogue. The Department also manages the Fund for Peace (established in 2000) and the Inter-American Peace Forum (created in 2008). The first supports negotiations concentrating on peaceful settlement of territorial disputes. It is more than a mere material fund. It offers the disputing parties a series of negotiation and mediation mechanisms and affords them access to OAS technical expertise in conflict resolution, including its experience with diplomacy and international and inter-American law. Complementarily, the Inter-American Peace Forum operates within the framework of the Fund for Peace and it seeks to create an opportunity for the development of programs aimed at creating a culture of regional peace. It also maintains an exhaustive database of institutions and NGOs involved in promoting peace and peace research, in order to facilitate the exchange of information, experiences, and best practices.

Finally, the OAS has established several specialized organizations such as the Inter-American Human Rights system (commission and court) and the Inter-American Defense Board, all of these bodies being accountable to the General Assembly. The Inter-American Commission was established in 1959 and began its work in 1960, long before it had the legal foundation of the American Convention on Human Rights, which entered into force in 1978. The commission represents all member states of the OAS, and its principal function is to promote the observance and protection of human rights and to serve as a consultative organ for the organization (Shaw, 2003:144).

The OAS security structure was originally designed for collective security operations and diplomatic consultations. Regarding conflict between states in the hemisphere, the emphasis lay on peaceful means for the settlement of disputes. Nevertheless, in recent years the range of activities in which the organization is involved has grown considerably, and new capabilities have been generated (Herz, 2003:214). We will turn our attention to OAS organizational capacity in conflict prevention and early warning.

Conflict Prevention and Early Warning

One of the principal contributions that the OAS makes toward structural conflict prevention is through democratic institution-building in member states. In 1991, the Unit for the Promotion of Democracy (UPD) was created within the General Secretariat to support the consolidation of democracy in the region (in the meantime it was dismantled in 2006 and its functions were distributed between the Department of Sustainable Democracy and the Department of State Modernization and Governance). In 2001, the UPD established the Special Program for the Promotion of Dialogue and Conflict Resolution to assist member states in developing national and subregional capacities in dialogue, consensus building, and conflict resolution. The mission of the Special Program was to contribute to the development of responses to deep-rooted, sociopolitical conflicts and critical challenges facing member states and their societies.

The adoption of Resolution 1080, the Protocol of Washington, and the Inter-American Democratic Charter were also major breakthroughs allowing the OAS to engage in conflict prevention. Peck has pointed out that "these developments mark a real turning point in the organization's history, in which domestic political circumstances (the interruption of a democratic government) can become the grounds for collective action" (Peck, 1998: 142). In South America, Resolution 1080 was applied in Peru (1992) and in Paraguay (1996). One may argue that, next to the Council of Europe, the OAS has the most well-developed and active human-rights machinery of any regional organization.

Also associated with conflict prevention is early warning. The General Secretariat of OAS does not have an indicator-based, conflict early warning center at the time of writing. However, the Department of Sustainable Democracy and Special Missions through its Political Analysis and Multiple Scenarios System (SAPEM) works to enhance OAS's capacity for early warning and response.[4] The system aims at designing and implementing a comprehensive early-warning mechanism, including the use of political analyses, to monitor, assess, and address nascent threats to democratic stability.

Operational Experience in Traditional Security

Even if the OAS Charter envisaged a collective defense mandate for the organization, in reality OAS experience is largely focused on peacekeeping, conflict prevention, peacebuilding, and to a smaller extent also on peacemaking. The OAS is one of the world's organizations with the largest experience in conflict management. Zacher compared the efficiency of the OAS, the Organization of African Unity (OAU), and the Arab League to conclude that in "wars, the frequencies of intervention and success by the OAS are considerably greater than those of the other bodies" (Zacher, 1979:213).

Concerning peacekeeping, the only intervention in South America was the OAS Special Mission to Suriname (1992-2000). Its mandate was to assist the government in formalizing and safeguarding a durable peace, and in strengthening national institutions and democratic order. It was directly involved in the negotiations between the government and illegally armed groups that brought peace, and it served as a deterrent to those who might attempt again to disrupt democracy. The mission also helped collect and destroy weapons from armed groups that had operated throughout Suriname's rural areas. In 1993 and 1994, the OAS monitored compliance with the peace accord and assisted in the removal of land mines (Herz, 2011:52). Although the OAS has deployed peacekeeping missions in other Latin American states (Costa Rica/Nicarágua, Dominican Republic, Honduras/El Salvador), the OAS is still more a political than military institution. And since it operates best when guided by the consensus of its member states – and it is constituted by countries equal in juridical terms but unequal in size and power – it is unrealistic that the OAS frequently uses force to solve a given problem (Muñoz, 1994:200). The focus is hence on conflict prevention, peacemaking, and peacebuilding.

Conflict Prevention and Peacemaking

The OAS has systematically intervened to prevent conflicts from emerging in the first place (or to prevent a conflict from reescalating in a postconflict phase). On the evening of December 24th, 1990 the Army of Suriname overthrew the elected Government of President Ramsewak Shankar and Vice-President Henck Arron in a bloodless coup d'etat. Promptly, the OAS called (at Venezuela'a request) a special session to condemn the seizure of power. Some months later, it sent a forty-person delegation to observe the National Assembly elections. In accordance with Suriname's constitution, Jules Ajodhia and Ronald Venetiaan, both of the New Freedom Coalition Party, were elected vice-president and president of Suriname, respectively. An independent audit conducted by the OAS mission concluded there was no fraud in the tabulation of official results.

Two years later, it acted more vigorously in Peru. In April that year, after Alberto Fujimori pulled off an *autogolpe* and suspended various civil rights, Resolution 1080 was invoked. Within days, the Foreign ministers met and stated that they "deeply deplored" President's Fujimori's actions; they urged the restoration of democratic rule in Peru and called on the Peruvian authorities to fully respect human rights. At the same time the ministers appointed a special diplomatic mission to travel to Peru to promote negotiations between the government and opposition forces for reestablishing full democracy. The OAS exerted pressure, which added to positions of many other actors, and elections were held for a constitutional congress seven months after the coup. An *ad hoc* committee of foreign ministers resolved that the November constituent assembly elections had "represented an important phase in the process of reestablishing democratic institutional order" and that consequently the OAS investigation could come to an end (Arceneaux and Pion-Berlin, 2007:16).

Eight years later the OAS became involved again in the country. Concerns over electoral fraud[5] led to the adoption of Resolution 1753, which sent a High Level Mission led by OAS secretary general César Gaviria and Canadian foreign minister Lloyd Axworthy to the country. Their visit resulted in the establishment of an OAS-facilitated *mesa de diálogo* (roundtable), where Peruvian government, opposition, and civil society representatives discussed a concrete reform agenda and negotiated a consensual and peaceful solution to the political crisis. Despite widespread initial skepticism both in Peru and internationally, this OAS initiative filled the institutional vacuum caused by the polarization of political forces in Peru following the elections. It provided a mechanism for important democratic reforms, eased the transition from Fujimori to an interim government in November 2000, helped prevent a slide toward further state repression, and laid the foundations for a new and successful round of elections in April 2001 (Cooper and Legler, 2005; 2001: 124). Letting the Fujimori government completely off the hook would have seriously damaged the OAS's reputation in the run-up to the Windsor OAS General Assembly and the 2001 Summit of the Americas, at which democracy was to be a major theme. McClintock, on the other hand, downplays the contribution of the OAS arguing that the negotiations at the *mesa de diálogo* became fruitful "only after the September 14 release of the video that showed security chief Vladimiro Montesinos bribing an opposition congressman-elect. Two days after the release of the video, Fujimori promised new elections for 2001" (McClintock, 2001:139).

The OAS has also intervened in Paraguay. In April 1996, Paraguayan Army Commander General Oviedo attempted to force President Wasmosy to resign. In the face of this threat to democracy, the OAS Permanent Council met and called for a meeting under Resolution 1080. But by the time it convened the critical moments of the Paraguayan standoff had passed. Secretary General Gaviria ended up traveling to Paraguay to express support for President Wasmosy, but the successful resolution of the Paraguayan crisis was heavily dependent on the strong leadership of key members of the diplomatic community in Asunción and the willingness of officials in several countries to improvise a plan of direct contacts and visits aimed at supporting the defenders of the constitutional order (Valenzuela, 1997:54). The OAS has often issued declarations on the country. In 1999, the Permanent Council strongly condemned the assassination of Paraguay's Vice-President Luis María Argaña in Asunción. And in 2000 it strongly rejected the coup attempt against President Macchi and expressed "full support . . . for the constitutional government of Paraguay."[6] In 2012, however, the impeachment of President Fernando Lugo demanded a more determined intervention by the organization. Although the OAS acknowledged that Article 225 of the Constitution of Paraguay empowers the Chamber of Deputies to initiate impeachment proceedings, and the Senate to act as a court, there were concerns about the lack of respect for due process and the right of legitimate defense (the trial lasted less than six hours). Within one week, the Secretary General led a fact-finding mission to assess the situation and developments surrounding the impeachment, and then reported to the Permanent Council. His report about the postremoval situation in the country plus human- and civil-rights conditions was positive, which led to the decision not to sanction Paraguay for the removal of Fernando Lugo from the presidency.

In 1992, in Venezuela, the OAS condemned the abortive coup d'état led by Hugo Chávez directed against the Carlos Andrés Pérez government. Ironically, in April 2002 business leader Pedro Carmona and some military units led a coup attempt against Hugo Chávez, which was also repudiated by the OAS. The Permanent Council convened to "condemn the alteration of constitutional order," called for normalization of democratic institutionality, and sent a fact-finding mission headed by Secretary General César Gaviria (who would also offer his good offices. Initially, President Chávez was reluctant to offer the international community a role in a national process but, as confrontations with the opposition intensified, he invited the OAS, the Carter Center (TCC), and the United Nations Development Program (UNDP) to contribute to a resolution. The OAS acted swiftly, but the coup fell apart from internal pressures, as Carmona quickly alienated his early supporters (Arceneaux and Pion-Berlin, 2007:14). In February 2003, the Venezuelan government and the opposition jointly signed the Declaration of Principles and the Declaration Against Violence and for Peace and Democracy. These agreements set a common understanding for moving forward with the negotiations. Implementation of the accord was difficult at times and hampered by political polarization between supporters and opponents of President Chávez. Nevertheless, Venezuela's National Electoral Council announced in June 2004, that a presidential recall referendum would be held in August 2004. Chávez won the referendum convincingly by a margin of 59.3 percent to 40.7 percent, according to the CNE's final official results.

In October 2003 in Bolivia, a proposal to export natural gas through Chilean territory instigated massive demonstrations. They left more than one hundred people dead, forcing President Guillermo Sánchez de Lozada to resign, and his vice president, Carlos Mesa Gisbert, to replace him. As the crisis unfolded, the Permanent Council met to "reiterate its full and decisive support" for the Sánchez de Lozada government and to identify the protests as "acts of violence" that "endanger [Bolivia's] constitutional order" Just seven days later, the council met again "to express its full support for the constitutional and democratic succession" to the government of Mesa (Arceneaux and Pion-Berlin, 2007:19). President Mesa met the same fate as his predecessor in June 2005. Protesters had first called for higher taxes on foreign oil and gas companies, then for the companies' nationalization and constitutional changes to increase indigenous representation in Congress, and finally for Mesa's resignation. The OAS General Assembly issued a declaration expressing "the need for the resignation of the president of Bolivia to be considered in terms of the statutory channels established in the country's Constitution" and noting its "regret" over the "political crisis." Ambassador Horacio Serpa of Colombia, designated special representative of the Secretary General, also facilitated political dialogue. In December 2005, President Evo Morales was elected, through a process considered free and fair.

But the OAS had to intervene again. In 2008 Eastern Bolivia erupted in violent anti-Morales protests and the president declared martial law in the remote region of Pando and arrested its governor, Leopoldo Fernandez. During the protests anti-Morales groups ransacked and occupied dozens of government buildings, blocked highways and sabotaged natural gas pipelines, temporarily cutting off exports to neighboring Argentina and Brazil. The OAS played an active role in fomenting institutional strengthening and governability in the country. In October, in Cochabamba, the OAS participated in the dialogue process between the Executive Branch of the government and the regional opposition self-named CONALDE (Governors of the eastern regions of the country). The OAS also participated in November in the Congress dialogue, which facilitated the Constitutional referendum held in January 2009.

In February 1997, after Ecuadorian Presidency Bucaram was dismissed by the congress on grounds of alleged "incapacidad mental" (mental disability), the OAS Secretary General visited him, but the organization took no formal position on those matters (Halperin and Galic, 2005:138; Fox and Roth, 2000:181). In January 2000, the OAS intervened again in the country. The Permanent Council gathered to express its decisive support for the constitutional government of the president of Ecuador, Jamil Mahuad, and the institutions under the rule of law. It also condemned firmly the attempt against the legitimately established democratic order. In April 2005, the Organization stepped in again after the Ecuadorian Congress voted to overthrow President Gutiérrez on grounds of his having abandoned office. The OAS Permanent Council passed a weakly worded resolution that "encouraged all sectors . . . to strengthen governance and ensure full respect for democratic order" and sent in a fact-finding mission. In the face of some ambiguity and domestic resistance to foreign interference, the OAS deferred to principles of sovereignty and nonintervention, refusing to invoke sanctions, as also allowed under the Democratic Charter (Arceneaux and Pion-Berlin, 2007:19). In any case, Secretary General Insulza appointed two jurists as his special representatives to observe the selection process to the Supreme Court of Justice; and new members were sworn in, in November 2005.

Five years later, the OAS intervened again in the country. In September 2010, following a police uprising and a subsequent attempt at a coup d'etat in Ecuador, the OAS Permanent Council convened in an emergency session and adopted a resolution to repudiate the action and express its firm support for the constitutional government of President Rafael Correa. The Secretary General of the OAS, Jose Miguel Insulza, traveled to Ecuador to support President Correa and inform him about the Organization's determination to demand the observation of the principles and norms enshrined in the Democratic Charter.

In 2008, the OAS attempted to broker a deal aimed at ending the acrimony between Colombia and Ecuador that resulted from the former carrying out a raid in Ecuador in a cross-border attack. Soon after the incursion, the OAS adopted several decisions to mediate between the two countries and prevent the escalation of the conflict. It is worth noting the Twenty-Fifth Meeting of Consultation of Ministers of Foreign Affairs of the OAS, where member states declared that the attack violated International law and requested Secretary General Jose Miguel Insulza to lead a delegation (which included representatives from Brazil, Argentina, Peru, and Panamá) to both countries to ease tension and to prepare a report with recommendations to mitigate the conflict. Although tension was high, Venezuela and Colombia resumed diplomatic relations one day after the OAS's delegation visit. Less than two weeks later OAS Foreign Ministers met again to discuss the report and to adopt another resolution rejecting the attack and establishing that "no state or group of states has the right to intervene, directly or indirectly, for any reason whatever, in the internal or external affairs of any other state" (Art. 19).

Peacebuilding

The OAS has been heavily involved in peacebuilding activities in South America, namely in the fields of disarmament, demobilization, and reintegration (DDR); truth, justice, and reconciliation; rule of law, human rights, good governance, and electoral assistance. In 2004, the government of Colombia officially invited the OAS to verify and accompany its efforts to implement a peace agreement with illegal armed actors in the country. The OAS Mission to Support the Peace Process (OAS/MAPP) was created with the objective of providing a broad and flexible accompaniment of these efforts. It has participated in DDR activities aimed at demobilizing armed structures like the paramilitary United Self-Defence Forces of Colombia (AUC) and in reintegrating them into civilian life. From the beginning, the OAS Mission has documented the peace process in Colombia, making it more visible, and highlighting the challenges and achievements of the process through one of its primary tools for disseminating information – the quarterly reports that the Secretary General presents to the OAS Permanent Council. In the first two years alone, the Mission verified the demobilization of 31,651 members of paramilitary groups and the turning in of 18,002 weapons (13,734 rifles).

OAS/MAPP decided to concentrate its verification and monitoring efforts in the regions where communities have been most affected by the violence. The Mission has served as a bridge and supported institutions involved in peacebuilding, giving special attention to the accompaniment of the victims of violence through specific programs and projects in the most remote communities of the country. The OAS Secretary General summed it up with the following: "OAS/MAPP has been able to implement its mandate with creativity and commitment as it takes on the enormous challenges presented by the process, and it has consolidated itself as the continent's primary support mechanism for the peace process in Colombia."[7] But it has not been an easy task. In 2011 it issued a key report expressing alarm over the activities of paramilitary successor groups and noting that, "massacres have continued, wiping out entire families." Beyond Colombia, the OAS has also deployed de-mining programs in Ecuador (completion by 2004) and Peru (completion by 2003).

Operational Experience in Human Security

Although the OAS has a long history of technical cooperation on matters related to natural resources and environmental management, only in 1991 did it bring the environment – viewed as a new security issue – to the political level. The Inter-American Program of Action for Environmental Protection was approved, creating a Permanent Committee on the Environment within the Permanent Council, and various activities were initiated – ranging from publications to seminars and training workshops – to comply with the recommended measures of the Inter-American Program of Action. The Organization carries out several mandates designed to protect biodiversity, strengthen environmental law, manage water resources, raise awareness on climate change, and promote sustainability, among others.

The OAS and its predecessors have also a long history of dealing with the narcotics problem. But beginning in the mid-1980s, as the problem intensified, it introduced new programs and initiatives. An OAS narcotics program was launched at the Inter-American Specialized Conference on Traffic in Narcotic Drugs in April 1986 – the first Western Hemisphere meeting to deal with all aspects of the drug problem. In accordance with the program of action adopted at that meeting, the OAS General Assembly in November 1986 created the Inter-American Drug Abuse Control Commission (CICAD) to develop, coordinate, evaluate, and monitor the Program of Action of Rio de Janeiro Against the Illicit Use, Production and Trafficking of Narcotics Drugs and Psychotropic Substances. CICAD's main objective is the elimination of illicit drug trafficking and drug abuse in the Inter-American region through hemispheric cooperation. In 1996, CICAD served as the forum successfully to negotiate a Hemisphere Anti-Drug Strategy, as called for by the 1994 Summit of the Americas. And, as we saw, in 2010 it was instrumental in designing the Hemispheric Drug Strategy and worked on a Plan of Action to define core policy guidelines and recommendations in key policy areas: institutional strengthening, demand reduction, supply reduction, control measures, and international cooperation.

The OAS track record in combating terrorism is also worth analysis. Under the auspices of the OAS, member states met in Lima, Peru, in 1996 in the largest gathering of countries to discuss counterterrorism. The meeting approved an action plan listing practical steps members should take to combat terrorism. The states also endorsed the characterization of terrorist acts, regardless of motivation, as criminal rather than political crimes. After the September 11 attacks, the OAS role on counterterrorism became more salient. The Inter-American Convention against Terrorism, adopted in 2002, seeks to prevent the financing of terrorist activities, strengthen border controls and increase cooperation among law enforcement authorities in different countries. In addition, the Inter-American Committee against Terrorism plays an important role in carrying out efforts in this field and is considered a model for other regional organizations involved in counterterrorism. The Committee's areas of work include border control, critical infrastructure protection (cyber and tourism security), legislative assistance and terrorism financing. Its activities are in line with the Inter-American Convention against Terrorism and international law. In 2012, the Committee set new ground when adopted a declaration on "Strengthening Cyber Security in the Americas", leading member states to set up their National Computer Security Incident Response Teams (CSIRTs). Terrorists and criminals have shown a keen ability to manipulate the internet to outpace and outwit and governments and law enforcement agencies. The OAS has been showing forward thinking to address this threat.

Conclusions

For an organization founded approximately six decades ago the OAS has shown over the last decade a substantial capacity to adjust to new political situations and to find a new raison d'être. The core of its activities is presently centered on the nexus between democracy and security. The latter is defined by the organization in a modern and comprehensive way: the Declaration on Security states that, "the traditional concept and approach [of security] must be expanded to encompass new and nontraditional threats, which include political, economic, social, health, and environmental aspects" (II-4i). But OAS still has a long path ahead in order to fulfill its potential.

The first shortcoming is related to the adherence to consensus decision-making and the sacredness of sovereignty. "Given the history of state formation among the different nations, the struggle for independence during the first decades of the nineteenth century, and the difficulty in realizing the Westphalian model in the face of great power influence and lack of central government authority over parts of the territory in several cases" (Herz, 2003:215), South American states were compelled to be sensitive about sovereignty and separation. Even if the OAS has extended its mandate to allow it to take bold measures when the democratic credentials of a member states are in jeopardy, the phantom of intervention still prevails. National sovereignty comes hand-in-hand with consensus decision-making, as the search for consensus serves as a mechanism for guaranteeing the protection of state sovereignty. Some authors look at the decision-making capacity of the OAS with more optimistic lenses. In this close examination of how institutional rules have affected the power of the organization, Shaw finds that institutional rules – procedural, structural, and normative – affect state and organizational decisions in the highly germane area of conflict resolution. Consensus decision-making, one of those institutional rules,

". . . is highly valued by member states. They believe that decisions adopted consensually carry more weight than those with only the requisite two-thirds vote. In addition, regional solidarity, which strengthens regional stability, is maintained if compromises can be reached rather than passing disputed proposals by a majority vote. Because members prefer to act consensually, the decision-making process within the organization involves bargaining among members to reach mutually acceptable agreements on issues where members have divergent preferences" (Shaw, 2004:4).

Although consensus decision-making might strengthen behavioral norms, on higher-profile issues where there are profound differences of opinion, it is prone to some considerable stalling if not immobilization (Cooper and Legler, 2006:33). This was most obvious in the case of Haiti in 1994, over the issue of coercive intervention after the overthrow of President Aristide and the invocation of resolution 1080. The OAS was only able to send a small grouping (eighteen members) of a civilian mission known as OAS-DEMOC. In fact, research has shown that the OAS has been selective in its interventions on behalf of democratic promotion. The organization responds more forcefully when the problem presents a clear and present danger both to the offending state and to other members. As threats become weaker or more ambiguous, the OAS tends to act more timidly, unless domestic constituencies cry out for its assistance or the United States puts its full weight behind the effort (Arceneaux and Pion-Berlin, 2007).

Second, there is a lack of a coherent policy regarding the extent and role that the organization should have in intrastate conflict prevention and resolution at various levels. Coupled with this, there is also a need to increase public awareness (among its member states as well as the international community) of the organization's acquired expertize and successes in the peacebuilding and postconflict reconciliation arenas. A striking example of this is the popular idea that the OAS has a camouflaged U.S. agenda (Grugel, 1996:134; Banega, Hettne and Söderbaum, 2001:236). In fact, research has demonstrated, on the basis of a thorough study of thirty cases of conflict resolution in the OAS over a fifty-year period, that relations among member states are more nuanced than many observers might anticipate. Not every case involved tensions between U.S. and Latin American preferences. And if there are cases when the U.S. dominated the organization, there are also cases when Latin American members resisted U.S. pressure and rejected U.S. proposals (Shaw, 2003:88).

Third, particularly when enforcement becomes a requirement for success, the OAS is not prepared for robust operations and does not even present a formal mechanism for compulsory cost-sharing for peace missions. The regional culture does not support this option. In countries where a violent conflict is protracted, such as today's Colombia, the organization does not have the political clout or the necessary resources to make an impact (Herz, 2003:226; Tacsan, 1998:106).

Finally, although the Summit of the Americas held in Miami in 1994 has tagged the OAS as the main organization for the defense and consolidation of democracy within the Americas, other overlapping initiatives have also come about. As noted by Cooper and Legler, there has been a proliferation of agencies sharing this agenda, including the Rio Group, the Andean Community of Nations or CARICOM (Cooper and Legler, 2006:31). The division of labor is far from being clear. Institutional proliferation is not only expensive but leads to political competition, deviation of resources, and unaccountability. It is true, however, that in certain instances, like the 2008 dispute between Colombia and Ecuador, the OAS is the only organization with a specific mandate to contribute to the prevention of potential squabbles in the fragile border area between the two countries. But the OAS suffers from lack of funding for this kind of mediation activity.

Notes

[1] The OAS member states are: Antigua and Barbuda, Argentina, The Bahamas, Barbados, Belize, Bolivia, Brazil, Canada, Chile, Colombia, Costa Rica, Cuba (excluded from participation since 1962), Dominica, Dominican Republic, Ecuador, El Salvador, Grenada, Guatemala, Guyana, Haiti, Honduras, Jamaica, Mexico, Nicaragua, Panama, Paraguay, Peru, Saint Kitts and Nevis, Saint Lucia, Saint Vincent and the Grenadines, Suriname, Trinidad and Tobago, U.S.A., Uruguay, and Venezuela.

[2] AGRES 1080, 5 June 1991. Resolution 1080, on Representative Democracy, stipulates the actions that the organization can take in case of "sudden or irregular interruption of the democratic political institutional process or of the legitimate exercise of power by the democratically elected government in any of the Organization's member states." Available at www.oas.org/juridico/english/agres1080.htm

[3] The Secretariat for Political Affairs was created in 2006; and the former Department of Crisis Prevention and Special Missions, the Unit/Department for the Promotion of Democracy, the Department for Democratic and Political Affairs and its Office for the Prevention and Resolution of Conflicts were dismantled and their functions harmonized and integrated in the new organizational structure.

[4] The other two units of the Department are the Fund for Peace and the Special Missions unit, which includes the work of the Mission to Support the Peace Process in Colombia (MAPP-OAS).

[5] The OAS election observation team that was sent to Peru to follow the Presidential election concluded that "with respect to international standards, the Peruvian electoral process is far from being considered free and fair" (cited in McClintock, 2001:137). For the first time in the history of OAS election observation, a Latin American election had clearly and carefully been judged illegitimate.

[6] Arrests Follow Failed Paraguay Coup (*BBC News*, 20 May 2000)

[7] Online at http://www.oas.org/en/americas/article.asp?df_sCodigo=5860. Visited 10 March, 2012.

13

The Union of South American Nations

"Within the framework of UNASUR we hope to deepen our mutual understanding in order to create a common vision of defense and security for the region, consolidating South America as a zone of peace and democracy." —Lula da Silva, president of Brazil, 2010

The origin of the Union of South American Nations (UNASUR),[1] formally established in 2008, can be traced back to the First South America Summit, which took place in Brasília in 2000 with the objective to revitalize the old aspirations of South American integration. In the Summit, even if South American leaders decided not to step into the mined terrain of security, they agreed to the creation of the Initiative for the Integration of Regional Infrastructure in South America (IIRSA). IIRSA's guiding vision was to facilitate multisectoral integration within the three main coastal zones of South America – Caribbean, Atlantic, and Pacific – and to link these with the continent's internal regions. One year later, in 2001, another step was taken towards the integration of the region when Mercosur, CAN, and Chile agreed to the establishment of a Mechanism of Dialogue and Political Coordination, whose purpose was to make it easier to coordinate joint measures in the areas of political cooperation, economic integration, and physical infrastructure. In 2002, the Second South America Summit, held in Guayaquil, Ecuador, decided to reinforce the instruments for implementation of IIRSA, but, more significantly, it adopted the Declaration on Making South America a Zone of Peace and signed the Consensus of Guayaquil on Integration, Security and Infrastructure for Development. The aim was to gradually reduce military spending in the continent so as to release more resources for the fight against poverty.

Inspired by this prefatory consensus, in 2004, the third South America Summit produced the Cusco Declaration, a two-page statement of intent announcing the foundation of a South American Community. The community aimed to provide the basis for political, social, and cultural cooperation, economic commercial and financial integration, and the development of physical, energy, and communication infrastructure in the region. The First Community of Nations of South America (CASA) Summit was held in Brasilia on 29-30 September 2005, endorsing the mechanisms for this new entity. At the Second Summit in 8-9 December 2006 in Cochabamba, Bolivia, the implementation of an executive commission and a strategic plan for deepening South American integration were agreed upon by the member states. They also called for further discussions in order to establish the Parliament of South America in the Bolivian city. In April 2007 at the First Summit of Energy of South America Nations it was agreed to rename the institution to Union of South America Nations (UNASUR) with a Constitutive Treaty and a Treaty of Energy programmed initially to be approved at the Third Summit in Cartagena de las Indias, Colombia, in 2008. The name change was suggested by Hugo Chávez to whom South America should aim at a "union" and not a "community" or a mere "integration" project.

The adoption of UNASUR's Constitutive Treaty took place in Brasília in May 2008. The launch was heralded as a historical event by Brazil's President Lula da Silva who also declared that its establishment showed that South America was becoming a "global player."[2] But to become a global player, UNASUR needed to show internal consistency, and that did not occur. The foundational meeting in Brasilia was held only two months after Colombian forces bombed a site just within Ecuador's territory in which a secret camp occupied by the FARC had been laid out. The episode sparked a very tense diplomatic crisis that permeated the backstage negotiations leading up to the formation of UNASUR. On the docket was also a plan to create a military coordinating component of UNASUR, the South American Defense Council (CDS). But Colombia refused to go along with it because it regarded the Council as a continental military force, aimed at countering U.S. influence. Indeed Chávez signaled with enthusiasm that the alliance would help in the formation of a "big South America." To Chávez and the like-minded leaders, the CDS meant greater autonomy for South America from the United States.

Brazil, the mastermind behind UNASUR and the CDS, had a different view. It mostly hoped to use the CDS to strengthen regional ties across highly sensitive boundaries – polarized between right- and left-wing regimes. Lula's foreign policy stance was based on the determination to maintain cordial relations with all parties, while trying to promote the country's emergence as a military and economic power. The withdrawal of Bogotá, however, with one of the region's most advanced militaries, significantly weakened the pact from its onset. Nevertheless, after Colombia refused to join the CDS, the other eleven member states agreed to establish a task force to present a revised proposal to Colombia within three months. And the country ended up joining the Council some months later.

Despite these internal divergences UNASUR went ahead. The Constitutive Treaty declares boldly that the objective of the organization is to seek an "integration and union among its peoples in the cultural, social, economic and political fields, prioritizing political dialogue, social policies, education, energy, infrastructure, financing and the environment" (Art. 2). Although the security domain seems to be absent, UNASUR has accorded itself a strong legal capacity in this area.

Legal Capacity

UNASUR's treaty (in effect since February 2011) endows it with the capacity to operate in both traditional and nontraditional security issues. It includes, for instance, the following objectives:

- Coordination among specialized bodies of the Member States, taking into account international norms, in order to strengthen the fight against corruption, the global drug problem, trafficking in persons, trafficking in small and light weapons, terrorism, transnational organized crime and other threats as well as for disarmament, the nonproliferation of nuclear weapons and weapons of mass destruction, and elimination of landmines (Art. 3-r);
- The exchange of information and experiences in matters of defense (Art. 3-t);
- Cooperation for the strengthening of citizen security (Art. 3-u);

At the Fourth Summit of Heads of State (in November 2010), UNASUR adopted an additional protocol to the organization's Constitutive Treaty, which added a democratic clause to the charter. The democratic clause imposes sanctions on any member country of UNASUR that breaks or attempts to break constitutional rule or the democratic system. The clause establishes sanctions, such as shutting down borders and the suspension of trade, against the country that suffers an attempted coup. Yet, UNASUR lacks an explicit set of guidelines regarding democratic accountability among member states, as its electoral observer missions to both 2013 elections in Venezuela and Paraguay quickly validated the results despite other accredited international monitors reporting widespread irregularities such as voter intimidation.

Beyond the Constitutive Treaty and the additional Protocol, several UNASUR declarations have reiterated similar principles and objectives, namely the intention to strengthen South America as a zone of peace, the need to prevent conflicts and respect the territorial sovereignty of each state, or the aim to enhance cooperative efforts in the fight against terrorism and drug trafficking (see Georgetown Declaration/2010, Bariloche Declaration/2009, Presidential Declaration of Quito/2009, or the Declaration on Bolivia/2008).

Within the context of the South American Community of Nations, South American leaders had already adopted in Fortaleza, in 2005, the Declaration on Citizen Security in South America. The bulk of the document is a checklist of good intentions, but at the conceptual level it provides some food for thought. The focus on "citizen" and not "state" security is not a novelty (see for instance the OAS Declaration on Security in the Americas), but it is a significant breakthrough in the South American context. Although the declaration never explicitly defines "citizen security" it provides some hints. It spells out, for instance, that its aim is to guarantee "the citizens the full exercise of their rights and freedom, as well as the fulfilling of their duties in an environment free of threats and risks, allowing the recovery of institutional confidence within the community" (Preamble). Earlier, the declaration stated that, "security is a necessary condition for freedom. . . There is no democracy without freedom, and no freedom without security" (Preamble). Citizen security seem thus to be related not only to living in an environment with no military threats, but also to having access to democracy and freedom. Also interestingly, the Declaration highlights that "in many countries, historically, the security provided by the Government to its citizens has been insufficient, focused only on police forces and dissociated from the civil society" (Preamble). Security declarations adopted by regional organizations are very common, but it is rare to see a regional organization positioning itself so explicitly as an alternative to States.

However, the analysis of the declaration in contrast to the political practice of UNASUR/CASA permits us to say that its emphatic tone was perhaps lightly handled. In the Presidential Declaration and Priority Agenda adopted in Brasilia, in September 2005, security was not included in the eight priority action areas, which gives room for some doubts on the resolve and capacity of the organization in serving as an alternative provider of security. Moreover, the Declaration on Citizen Security was adopted under the CASA frame, and UNASUR political declarations remain vague on whether the Declaration is still part of the juridical apparatus of the organization or not.

Organizational Capacity

UNASUR organic structure is anchored in five main bodies: the Summit of Heads of State and Government (see Table 13.1.), the pro tempore Presidency, the Council of Ministers of Foreign Affairs, the Council of Delegates, and the General Secretariat (in Quito). These organs hold the decision-making capacity of the organization, namely to plan, implement and supervise initiatives. But the core of the security apparatus of UNASUR lies with the South American Defense Council and the South American Council on the World Drug Problem.

According to then Brazilian Minister Nelson Jobim (2007-2011), the CDS is meant to serve as an internal conflict resolution platform as well as a medium to encourage multilateral defensive collaborations and consensus building. Jobim was the moving force behind the CDS in Lula's government, and traveled the continent meeting with local leaders to promote CDS's maturation. At the inaugural meeting of the CDS, held in Santiago in March 2009, the ministers issued a joint declaration declaring that the Council was aimed at creating a mechanism of integration, dialogue, and cooperation among South American countries and should focus on (i) defense policies; (ii) military cooperation, humanitarian actions, and peace operations; (iii) defense industry and technology; and (iv) training. The ministers also announced their intention to reduce the asymmetry of military spending among the member countries. In fact, for a long time now analysts have suggested that regional defense agreements, such as CDS, would foster military professionalism through cost sharing, joint problem solving, and refocusing military attention and training away from internal warfare and toward external threats (Pion-Berlin, 2000:59). But even if it is clear that the CDS was not formed to become a regional security force or amass an international army, its conceptual and operative objectives are not clearly defined – except for the intention to coordinate military technology and resources, which is on the top of its objectives. Brazil, the major weapons producer in the region is set to be the primary beneficiary from renewed shipment of weapons to its neighbors. Brasília hopes that increasing arms sales to nontraditional markets around the world, and the coordination of technology resulting from this newly formed alliance, will in the long run lessen dependence on the United States.

Table 13.1: UNASUR Heads of State Meetings, 2005–2013

Meeting	Locality and Date	Output
First CASA Meeting of Heads of State	Brasília, 29-30 September 2005	Adoption of a priority agenda
Second CASA Meeting of Heads of State	Cochabamba, 8-9 December 2006	Cochabamba Declaration
Extraordinary Meeting of Heads of State	Brasília, 23 May 2008	UNASUR Constitutive treaty
Extraordinary Meeting of Heads of State	Santiago, 15-16 September 2008	UNASUR Declaration on Bolivia ("Declaración de la Moneda")
Extraordinary Meeting of Heads of State	Salvador, 16 December 2008	Salvador Declaration
Third Meeting of Heads of State	Quito, 10 August 2009	Presidential Declaration of Quito
Extraordinary Meeting of Heads of State	Bariloche, 28 August 2009	UNASUR Declaration on Peace in South America
Extraordinary Meeting of Heads of State	Manaus, 26 November 2009	--
Extraordinary Meeting of Heads of State	Quito, 9 February 2010	Support for Haiti's reconstruction (earthquake)
Extraordinary Meeting of Heads of State	Los Cardales, 4 May 2010	Election of Néstor Kirchner as UNASUR's Secretary General

Extraordinary Meeting of Heads of State	Buenos Aires, 1 October 2010	Discussion of the 2010 Ecuador crisis
Fourth Meeting of Heads of State	Georgetown, 26 November 2010	Georgetown Declaration
Extraordinary Meeting of Heads of State	Mar del Plata, 4 December 2010	Kirchner's successor after his death
Extraordinary Meeting of Heads of State	Lima, 28 July 2011	UNASUR Commitment Against Inequality
Fifth Meeting of Heads of State	Asunción, 29 October 2011	Asunción Declaration
Extraordinary Meeting of Heads of State	Mendoza, 29 June 2012	Discussion on the impeachment of President Fernando Lugo of Paraguay
Sixth Meeting of Heads of State	Lima, 30 November 2012	- Special Communiqué on Terrorism - Special Declaration on the Malvinas - Declaration on the Peace Process in Colombia - Lima Declaration - Declaration of South America as a Peace Zone
Extraordinary Meeting of Heads of State	Lima, 18 April 2013	Recognition of Venezuelan presidential elections results
Extraordinary Meeting of Heads of State	Cochabamba, 5 July 2013	Discussion on the Evo Morales aircraft incident in Europe
Seventh Meeting of Heads of State	Paramaribo, 30 August 2013	- Declaration of Paramaribo - Declaration on the Situation in Syria

The Action Plan of the CDS was adopted in November 2011, at an extraordinary meeting of the ministers of defense held in Lima. It was an attempt to amalgamate all the initiatives presented to establish a common, accepted, compatible methodology to assess military spending in the region. The Plan also includes defense training and the full endorsement of the Center of Strategic Studies on Defense (CEED), which was launched also in 2011. The CEED was created to consolidate South America in terms of defense, and is based at Argentina's "Casa Patria Grande Néstor Kirchner," a research center dedicated to Latin American integration idealized by former President Kirchner. Despite the adoption of plans, guidelines, and charters, the operational capacity of the CDS is still low and the deliverables are not impressive. As pointed out by Hackett "the South American Defence Council, could do more to create a long-term agenda resistant to hijacking by subregional and single-issue concerns." (Hackett, 2010: 6).

When the first signs of the crises related to the U.S. bases in Colombian territory arose, Presidents Lula da Silva, Tabaré Vázquez, and Michelle Bachelet called for a CDS meeting. But the Council was overpowered by South American heads of state and government who assumed responsibility for tackling the crisis. Moreover, an important apparent limitation of the CDS is that it does not take positions on internal affairs, and as a result, crucial domestic issues (some of them with regional implications such as the Colombian civil war) will not fall under the Council's competence. As we saw in Chapter 3, the overwhelming majority of conflicts afflicting the region are internal and not bilateral. In several CDS meetings, attendees agreed to make the military stock of South American countries more transparent, but as pointed out by a report issued in 2012 by the leading research institute on the topic, off-budget spending and secrecy are still limiting the democratic accountability of the military sector in the region (Bromley and Solmirano, 2012).

UNASUR leaders have also created a South American Council on the World Drug Problem. Aware that the region is the largest producer of drugs in the world (Peru, Colombia, and Bolivia produce almost all of the world's coca leaf) and conscious of its detrimental impact on the welfare and security of their citizens, the establishment of the Council marked UNASUR's baptism in human security issues. The decision to constitute the new organ was taken in August 2009 during the third UNASUR Summit in Quito and later operationalized during a ministerial meeting of UNASUR members' representatives held in Montevideo, Uruguay, in October the same year. Peruvian Minister Alfredo Rada, the spokesperson for that meeting, declared that, "operations in border areas made possible through binational agreements are the most successful and practical way of advancing towards the regionalization of the drugs trade combat."[3] The Statutes of the Council were, however, only approved in April 2010 after three rounds of negotiations on the objectives and agreements of the regional body. According to the press, in the preparation of the document differences in approach surfaced, particularly among representatives of the Andean governments. Whereas the Bolivian delegation opposed any reference to legal coca leaf, Colombian representatives stressed the need to combat drug trafficking with military means.[4] Despite the different political views, the Council went ahead and gained a new name. The original "South American Council of Struggle Against Drug Trafficking" was replaced by "South American Council on the World Drug Problem" in order to reflect the Andean countries' view that the war on drugs should contemplate both the issues of production and demand. The Action Plan was also adopted in 2010. It seeks to help countries reduce the demand for narcotics by researching prevention programs and treatment plans. It also promotes social inclusion and rural projects to prevent "at-risk" populations from becoming involved in illegal activities. Despite the good will, the Council has not yielded any effective result beyond political declarations and administrative technical working groups.

Notwithstanding the setting up of internal organs, the overall organizational capacity of UNASUR is low. Its institutional structure is feeble and the decision-making process obeys a strict intergovernmental approach. Member states have also acknowledged that UNASUR needs to make an effort to strengthen its institutional apparatus. In 2010, the spokesperson of President Lula declared that it hoped that the election of former Argentina President Néstor Kirchner as UNASUR Secretary General would set a new phase in the process of consolidation of UNASUR, "an organization that is undergoing a period of indefinition of its institutional architecture."[5] Policy analysts have also claimed that UNASUR has so far confined itself to a series of summits and declarations driven by personalities.[6]

Operational Experience in Traditional Security

UNASUR's only tangible intervention has been in Bolivia. The violence, that erupted in September 2008, was rooted in the standoff between President Evo Morales' leftist government and opposition governors who controlled four of the country's nine regions – some of which hold the country's valuable natural gas reserves (see Chapter 3).

The governors demanded more energy revenue and opposed Morales plan to distribute land to the poor and rewrite the constitution. As opposition leaders spoke openly of secession, President Morales tried to maintain central control. Clashes erupted between the army and opponents of the government resulting in at least thirty deaths. In Pando alone, twenty pro-Morales farmers were killed. The National Ombudsman's office, which carried out an initial investigation into the incident, stated that the deaths were the result of a planned massacre. The Bolivian government referred to the crisis as a civil coup d'état.

UNASUR reacted to the civil unrest by having President Michelle Bachelet of Chile, pro-tempore president of UNASUR, call an emergency meeting to discuss the situation in Bolivia (held on 15 September 2008). The Summit expressed its "fullest and decided" (Art. 1) support for the government of President Evo Morales, condemned the groups that "look for the destabilization of Bolivia's democracy" (Art. 3), and expressed the firmest condemnation of the massacre that took place in the department of Pando. It also decided to set up a commission to investigate and report the Pando incident, and to formulate recommendations "in such a way that it is not left unpunished" (Art.5). According to the head of inquiries – Argentine Rodolfo Mattarollo – the deaths in the province of Pando were "a massacre under the UN definition of the word."[7] In addition, Mattarollo claimed that local authorities including Pando's former Mayor were implicated in the massacre and other acts of violence. Amnesty International also traced the civil unrest to "civilians linked to some regional authorities opposed to President (Evo) Morales."[8]

UNASUR backing of Morales was instrumental to force opposition leaders to the negotiation table. There was genuine surprise when the opposition realized that their business partners (namely Brazil) had supported Morales instead of backing their traditional oil and gas clients in the rich provinces. Their only choice was thus to negotiate. UNASUR (and OAS) was invited to take part in the negotiations between the government and opposition leaders, with Morales expressing his preference for UNASUR's participation. Marco Aurélio Garcia, the international relations adviser of President Lula da Silva, asserted that, "with no UNASUR intervention, that country [Bolivia] would have plunged into civil war with unpredictable consequences" (Garcia, 2010:30). It may be claimed, on the other hand, that UNASUR's driving force was not a supranational intention to mitigate conflicts, but the work of President Bachelet of Chile. As pointed out by Detsch, if UNASUR gave signs of its effectiveness in the Bolivian conflict, that was due to "the intelligent mediation of the Chilean government, who was holding the pro-tempore presidency."[9] Once again, individuals or states, not regional organizations, made the difference.

UNASUR has also taken some measures to mitigate the conflict sparked by Colombia's plan to allow the U.S. military to use air bases on Colombian soil to track drug traffickers and even rebels (see Chapter 8). The issue was omnipresent in the Third UNASUR Summit (August 2009), although South American leaders decided not to include it in the final Declaration. Even so, all South American countries (except Peru, which held a more compromising approach), expressed their antagonism towards the Colombian plan. Bolivia, Ecuador, and Venezuela, imbued with anti-Americanism, vehemently reproved an expanded U.S. military presence in the region. In his flamboyant style, President Chávez even said that the issue "could cause a war in South America."[10] Brazil also opposed the plan because it feared strong U.S. presence close to the strategic Amazon rainforest. But it was mostly apprehensive with the idea that the Colombia-U.S. pact was not in tune with UNASUR's purposes, since the organization was meant to prioritize intraregional security relations and generate intraregional defense strategies. The other countries had a more conciliatory tone but criticized the plan nonetheless. Only Peru, due to its strategic relation with the United States, declared that it would respect Colombia's decision. In such difficult terrain, the UNASUR Summit failed to abate tensions and reach compromises. The best it could do was to postpone the thorny discussion to the Extraordinary Summit held in the same month in Argentina.

In the mean time, a handful of proposals were put on the table. Ernesto Samper, former Colombian president, suggested that UNASUR could set up its first military bases in Colombia. Evo Morales of Bolivia proposed that a regional referendum should be carried out to consult South Americans on whether they wished to have U.S. military in the region. And Lula da Silva advanced the idea of organizing a UNASUR Summit with President Obama.[11] But the solution was found in the old way South American conflicts are traditionally solved – presidential diplomacy. Uribe was indeed reluctant to use UNASUR or any other multilateral organization to solve the crisis. He declined the invitation to take part in the Third UNASUR Summit and, forced by Brazil to partake in the Extraordinary Summit in Argentina, he conceded saying that he would go only to *inform* and not *consult* his partners. And once there, Uribe demanded consistency with the other South American countries as some of them had also signed very large military contracts with nonregional powers. In 2009 Brazil signed a U.S.$ 12 billion contract with France and Venezuela and had ongoing military cooperation with

Russia, Iran, and Cuba.[12] Uribe also justified Colombia's cooperation with the U.S. on narcotrafficking by "the lack of support of South American countries" on this matter.[13] After seven hours of intense debate and accusations, the Summit produced a vague final declaration, which did not openly condemn the U.S. bases.[14] The somehow-conciliatory tone was nonetheless a product of the background work conducted by governments, not institutions. Before the Summit, Uribe had gone on a tour to seven different South American capitals to announce and discuss Colombia's cooperation with the U.S. Hence, although the crisis was contained *at* a UNASUR Summit, one could not infer that it was *by* UNASUR.

In fact, the crisis was only temporarily contained. In three subsequent meetings held in September and November (2009) and July (2010), UNASUR ministers of defense and foreign affairs attempted to band-aid the Andean dispute but no major agreements were reached. In the second meeting held in Quito, Colombia even decided to stay out "to prevent itself from listening to insults that could hurt its national dignity."[15] UNASUR's contribution to problem-solving was therefore not successful. The result of the third meeting is also symptomatic and is well reflected in the words of the Ecuadorian Foreign Minister Ricardo Patino who declared at the end of the five-hour meeting that "it was not possible to draw up a final accord [on the political-diplomatic crisis between Venezuela and Colombia] that all agreed on" and added rhetorically that participants stressed that "to maintain peace in the region and harmony in interstate relations, it is necessary to make a clear effort against the presence of illegal groups in the nations of the region."[16]

UNASUR has also been quick in condemning attempts to change constitutional order in the region. In October 2010, a group of soldiers from the national police in Ecuador kidnapped President Correa and held him in a hospital in Quito. He was rescued following an operation led by military forces and a group of special operations forces (see Chapter 3). UNASUR released a statement declaring that it "heavily condemned the attempted coup" and warning that the governments of the region "would not tolerate any further challenges to constitutional authority, or attempts to overthrow a legitimately elected civil power." Ricardo Patiño, Ecuador's Foreign Minister declared in an interview that UNASUR's support, along with a declaration of the Armed Forces supporting democratic institutions, was detrimental to stop the rebellion from escalating.[17] In May 2010, UNASUR heads of state also manifested their solidarity with the government of Paraguay, stating their "total and absolute support for the constitutional government of

Fernando Lugo" in its "fight against the criminal violence that affects five departments in the country," referring to activities in northern Paraguay of the Paraguayan People's Army (EPP).. And in 2012, UNASUR (along with Mercosur) suspended the country after President Lugo was impeached, accused of "poor performance" on his presidency administration. According to the bloc, Lugo's fast-track trial indicated that the "democratic order was broken" in Paraguay. The president was impeached by the country's Congress in a trial lasting just hours; his removal from office was sparked by clashes over a land eviction in which seventeen police and landless peasants died. Vice-President Federico Franco, who was inaugurated as president immediately after the impeachment, defended the constitutionality of the impeachment trial, saying the transition of power was carried out according to the law. The decision of UNASUR looked, however, like a necessary and convenient step once Mercosur leaders – gathered in the same city and in the same day – decided to first oust Paraguay. Pushed by Argentina, this move enabled the integration of Venezuela into Mercosur since full membership in the trade bloc had been opposed by Paraguayan lawmakers as the sole obstacle. Finally, in April 2013 UNASUR heads of state were also quick to meet extraordinarily in Lima to issue a joint statement supporting the election of Nicolas Maduro as the new president in the midst of accusations of fraud made by opposition leader Henrique Capriles who demands a recount of votes. A UNASUR observers' mission during the electoral process in Venezuela did not question the vote or results.

Despite these interventions, UNASUR has stayed aloof from most conflicts in the region. As it functions on a strict intergovernmental basis, thorny issues are only discussed under its auspices when and if conflict-affected states wish UNASUR to do so. This limits the organization immensely and renders it unable to serve as an alternative conflict resolution actor. This includes, for instance, the resolution of the controversy between Bolivia, Chile, and Peru for the sovereignty of certain maritime areas in a conflict that started at the beginning of the nineteenth century (see Chapter 3). The president of Ecuador, Rafael Correa, proposed discussion of the conflict as part of the UNASUR Extraordinary Summit in Bariloche agenda or to be the central topic at another Extraordinary Summit; but his proposal was rejected by the parties in the conflict. Chilean Minister of Foreign Affairs, Mariano Fernández, declared then that, "this is not a topic to be discussed in multilateral organizations, less so for Chile who is not willing to go on an Inquisition trial by third countries."[18]

UNASUR's track-record with democracy is also questionable. If member countries often highlight the role the organization plays in defending the principles of democracy and often illustrate their speeches with Paraguay's suspension in 2012 after President Lugo's impeachment or with the adoption of an Additional Protocol to its treaty in 2010 to specifically protect democratically elected governments from non-democratic forms of usurpation, several countries in the region – such as Bolivia, Argentina, Venezuela or Ecuador – have no high democratic credentials according to international rankings. Symbolically, in 2010 Dési Bouterse, Suriname's military dictator from 1980 to 1987 was elected to power. Accused of drug trafficking, Europol issued in 1999 an arrest warrant for him, but since he is president he enjoys immunity. In 2013, he took over as UNASUR's chair.

Operational Experience in Human Security

UNASUR has not made significant headway on this front. In November 2009 Brazil's President Lula da Silva proposed that UNASUR countries organize a meeting in Manaus ahead of the United Nations Climate Change Conference in Copenhagen the following month, to devise a united front on climate-change-related issues. But the meeting was far from successful. Besides Lula, only French President Nicolas Sarkozy (representing French Guiana) and Bharrat Jagdeo of Guyana attended. At the end, even the official photo session was canceled. A meeting in Georgetown the following year produced better results. The Georgetown Declaration addressed the critical issue of climate change stating that responsibility "must be assumed by the Member States that are party to the United Nations Framework Convention on Climate Change, based on their common yet differential responsibilities and their respective capabilities" (Art. 26). UNASUR's contribution to environmental protection has been, however, declaratory and no major breakthrough has been reached. Other nontraditional security threats have also been addressed only timidly. In the Bariloche Declaration of 2009, member states reaffirmed their "commitment to strengthen the fight and cooperation against terrorism and transnational organized crime and its related crimes: narcotrafficking, small and light arms trafficking, in addition to the rejection of the presence or action of illegal armed groups" (Para. 2). A similar disposition was conveyed in the Special Communiqué on Terrorism, adopted in November 2012. But no significant action has been taken.

Conclusions

In South America, fraternal wishes are often overshadowed by political differences. For UNASUR to even begin to realize many of its ambitious aims, it may have to overcome a series of significant hurdles. First, South America is fraught with historical animosity. Despite much bonhomie, regional harmony remains elusive. Symbolically, the foundational meeting of UNASUR (originally scheduled for 28 March 2008), had to be canceled due to the disputes between Ecuador and Colombia. It took two months of backstage work and heavy diplomatic pressure for the meeting to actually happen (on 23 May 2008). And when it finally did, Chilean President Michelle Bachelet, instead of Colombia's Alvaro Uribe, accepted the rotating presidency. Uribe declined because of the conflict between his country and Ecuador and Venezuela. This was also his justification to turn down the invitation to take part in the third UNASUR Summit in Quito (10 August 2009). Also symbolically, the election of former Argentine President Kirchner as UNASUR's first Secretary General had to face the initial opposition of Uruguay. Back then Argentina and Uruguay were at loggerheads over the construction of a pulp mill at their common border.

Second, evidence from elsewhere in the world points strongly toward what could be the futility of UNASUR's attempts at defense integration. The European Union, whose members first developed economic cooperation, before establishing a political and monetary union, has still, after more than fifty years, failed to negotiate a common defense policy, despite its largely peaceful internal relations. The African Peace and Security Architecture (APSA), established by the African Union (AU) in collaboration with the Regional Economic Communities (RECS), deals with the prevention, management, and resolution of conflicts in Africa. Its core organ is the African Union Peace and Security Council, whose operational capacity remains tentative and reactive. The underachievement of some organizations does not necessarily dictate the failure of UNASUR's defense integration, but it certainly calls attention to the inherent complexity of multilateral cooperation on such sensitive issues as defense.

Third, the region is not likely to be able to adopt a common approach on drug combating. The South American Council on the World Drug Problem has its scope restricted because the overlap between terrorism and drug producers is not acknowledged by everyone. Venezuela, Ecuador and Bolivia have often labeled the FARC as "insurgents". But together with the Shining Path in Peru, these organizations, regardless of their political purposes, are narcoagents that will keep having some room for maneuvers as long as their political agenda is supported by some neighboring states.

Fourth, although there are undoubtedly some prospects for progress that have the potential to further integrate the region, the group's set of aspirations are too ambitious. Indeed, UNASUR aims to encourage cooperation in the cultural, social, economic, and political fields. If the group is to advance all these goals it will be difficult to prevent duplication with other South American regional organizations. At the first meeting of Heads of State of CASA, a presidential declaration was issued where leaders declared that the establishment of CASA "will be based on existing institutions, preventing duplication and overlapping of efforts, as well as new expenditures" (Art.7), but the opposite is happening.

Finally, UNASUR still operates on a strong intergovernmental basis. The process of continuous integration cannot rely solely on the political will of the governments involved, however, which is strongly influenced by specific political circumstances of each member country. Permanent supranational institutions with decision-making capacity are needed to quickly remove the obstacles that arise on the path towards deeper integration (Junquera, 2008:64). As pointed out by Malamud, the higher the concentration of power in the national executives and the lower the degree of regional institutionalization, the greater the ability of heads of state and government to influence – be it to drive or stop – the integration process (Malamud, 2008:141).

Notes

[1] UNASUR is formed by Argentina, Brazil, Bolivia, Chile, Colombia, Ecuador, Guyana, Paraguay, Peru, Uruguay, Venezuela and Suriname (twelve members).

[2] "South American Nations Found Union" (*BBC News*, 28 May 2009).

[3] "UNASUR agrees to create a council to combat drugs' trade" (*Mercopress*, 7 October 2009).

[4] "Unasur Crea Organismo de Lucha Contra el Narcotráfico" (*El Día*, 9 April, 2010).

[5] "Unasul se Reúne Para Eleger Kirchner Seu Secretário Geral" (*Folha de São Paulo*, 4 May 2010)

[6] This opinion has been conveyed for example by Chris Sabatini, senior policy director at the Council of the Americas in New York. See "UNASUR in Guyana: democratic charta, fight drug trafficking and no names to substitute Kirchner" (*The Americas Post*, 28 November 2010).

[7] Bolivian Unrest Ruled "Massacre" (*BBC News*, 4 December 2008)

[8] Bolivia's Constitution – Civil Conflict and Social Progress (*Amnesty International News*, 21 November 2008).

[9] Claudia Detsch, Friedrich Ebert Foundation in Quito, quoted in "Cúpula da UNASUL: Perspectivas em Meio a Graves Divergências?" (*Deutsche Welle*, 10 August 2008)

[10] "Colômbia Inclui Acordos da Venezuela Com a Rússia em Debate Sobre Bases" (*Folha de São Paulo*, 24 August 2009).

[11] Lula Propõe que Unasul Discuta com Obama a Segurança na Região (*O Estado de São Paulo*, 11 August 2009).

[12] "Uribe Cobrará Coerência de Paises da UNASUL" (*O Estado de São Paulo*, 23 August 2009).

[13] "Impasse na Cúpula Favorece Uribe" (*O Estado de São Paulo*, 29 August 2009).

[14] It merely decided "To reaffirm that the presence of foreign military forces cannot, with its means and resources linked to its own goals, threaten the sovereignty and integrity of any South American nation and as a consequence, the peace and security of the region."

[15] Colômbia Cancela Participação em Reunião em Quito" (*O Estado de São Paulo*, 27 November 2009).

[16] UNASUR Makes Efforts to Restore Colombia-Venezuela Ties (*Guyana Journal*, 31 July 2010).

[17] "Para Chanceler, Pode Haver Nova Rebelião," interview with Ricardo Patiño (*O Estado de São Paulo*, 3 October 2010).

[18] "Conflicto de Bolívia com Peru y Chile Será Tema Fuera de Agenda" (*El Deber*, 28 August 2009).

14

The Ibero-American Summit

"The Iberoamerican community will have a great improvement in the coming years and will play an important role in the world." —Mariano Rajoy, prime minister of Spain, 2012

The Iberian Peninsula and South America share obvious historical ties but it was only in the early 1990s that the two sides of the Atlantic Ocean forged an arrangement for political harmonization on matters concerning the region. In the context of the 500th anniversary of the discovery of the Americas, Spain and Mexico made the joint decision to develop the Ibero-American Summits System.[1] In 1991, the First Summit of Heads of State and Government was held in Guadalajara, Mexico, establishing the Ibero-American Summit as a forum for political and diplomatic consensus and cooperation for development among its members. Its aim was also to correct the asymmetry in diplomatic and cultural relations between Spain and the Spanish-speaking world as epitomized by the concepts of *Hispanidad* (the Hispanic World) and *Madre Patria* (Mother Country), which were mostly cultivated during Francisco Franco's dictatorial regime.[2]

From its inception, the Ibero-American Summit also incorporated a security role, expressed explicitly at the First Summit. In the final declaration, states pledged to "actively promote negotiations for the settlement of conflicts and support regional initiatives on the control, reduction and trafficking of arms . . . and to refrain from any action or measure which could hinder the prompt resolution of conflicts and urge all members of the international community to do the same" (Art. 1b).

A key development in 2003 was the strengthening of the Ibero-American Summits process by the creation of an Ibero-American General Secretariat (SEGIB) in Madrid. The establishment of a secretariat was an important pillar of Spain's foreign policy toward Latin America and an attempt to foster and capitalize on historical ties.

The establishment of the SEGIB came at a challenging time for the inter-American system. The OAS was facing financial difficulties, hemispheric free trade negotiations had been suspended, and many countries were instead seeking bilateral trade agreements with Europe. There was concern that the OAS could be further weakened by a shift of member states' preferences in favor of the Ibero-American Summits – a venue where they can work without the overbearing presence of the United States, without the complexities posed by the Anglo and Franco Caribbean States, without a strong focus on democracy and democratic institutions, and with the inclusion of Cuba.

Despite the opportune environment, the Ibero-American Community still faces major challenges. The most pronounced is the need for each state to define its individual role in the subregional schemes to which it belongs (Mercosur, UNASUR, CAN, etc.).[3] They need to set the bloc aims and limitations, before embarking into an intercontinental linkage that could contradict the requirements and limitations of both the EU and the inter-American or South American frameworks. Second, the Ibero-American arrangement needs to tackle the resistance for institutionalization and supranationality so customary in South America, condemning regionalism (or interregionalism) to a set of periodical intergovernmental events (as highlighted in Chapter 10).

Legal Capacity

At each summit a declaration is issued named after the city where the meeting was held. The Guadalajara (1991) and Madrid (1992) declarations are considered to be foundational, as they set out the aims of the Ibero-American group. Since the arrangement has not adopted a constitutional treaty, its legal capacity can only be inferred by the summit declarations. Although security is a not a priority area of intervention (unlike education, health, culture, tourism, media), the subject has pervaded most meetings. In the first summit member states pledged to "actively promote the process of negotiation leading to the settlement of regional conflicts and support initiatives regarding the control, reduction, and trafficking of armaments" (Art. 1-b). The first declarations have also condemned terrorism as a political tool and expressed the commitment of all countries in cooperating on combating drug trafficking. These principles were reiterated in Santiago y Viña del Mar (1996), Isla Margarita (1997), San José (2004), Salamanca (2005), Montevideo (2006), Santiago de Chile (2007), San Salvador (2008), Estoril (2009), Mar de la Plata (2010), Asunción (2011), and Cádiz (2012). Traditional and nontraditional security issues have been simultaneously addressed. According to Dabène, 28 percent of all Ibero-American's Summit decisions between 1990 and 1999 were dedicated to international issues, the second most discussed topic (after politics with 33 percent) (2009:204). In 2010, the Mar de la Plata Summit also represented a significant step to the organization with the adoption of the so-called "democratic clause" that would suspend from the Ibero-American conference any country that breaks away from institutional democracy. For the Ecuadorian Rafael Correa, one of the champions of the idea, the meeting marked "a before and after" in the history of the region, because "we are establishing procedures so that never again in our America will those unable to win at the polls be able to conspire against legitimately elected governments."[4]

Organizational Capacity

What is popularly known as the "Ibero-American Summit" is simply an annual meeting of heads of state and government, lasting only two days (from 2014 onwards, it will become biennial). The Summit provides political guidance and coordination but the technical and institutional work is carried out by the Ibero-American General Secretariat (SEGIB). It assists in the preparations of the Annual Summits and executes the guidelines agreed upon by the Summit. SEGIB also facilitates the ministerial meetings, which are held on a regular basis and on a wide range of topics such as youth, justice, labor, culture, health, agriculture or urban development. At the 2013 Panamá Summit, Ibero-American states issued a resolution on the renovation of the Summit, calling for a more results-oriented entity and underlining the need to focus on the topics on which the Summit may have a comparative advantage, such as culture, social issues, economic development and research and development.

For lack of a comprehensive treaty, experts have suggested that the Ibero-American system has been composed of two "high-level structures" (the summits of the Heads of States and Government, and the meetings of Ministers of Foreign Affairs), three "continuity" structures (Pro Tempore Secretariat, Troika, Extended Troika), "management structures" (national coordinators, cooperation officers, joint meetings), "permanent organs" (the Ibero-American General Secretariat) and "Conference Forums" (ministerial meetings, cooperation programs).

None of the postsummit organs (including ministerial meetings) are tailored to debate security issues, and the subject has been absent in the postsummit decision-making process. The only exception is the establishment of the Virtual Iberoamerican Center for Peace and

International Security Studies (*Centro Virtual Iberoamericano de Estudios para la Paz y Seguridad Internacionales*). In the spring of 2007, Spain submitted an initiative to the rest of the Latin American Community to create a Virtual Ibero-American Security and Defence College. This initiative was included in the Action Plan adopted by the Santiago de Chile Summit (2007). The goal was to facilitate "the transfer of information, studies and academic experiences and the ongoing contacts between the Ibero-American Defense Colleges, taking advantage of the virtual network and new information technologies" (Art.33). The issue was further discussed at the 2008 and 2009 Summits (Rio de Janeiro and Santo Domingo) paving the way for the presentation of the "Website of the Association of Ibero-American Defense Colleges" at the 2010 Summit (Mexico City).

Operational Capacity in Traditional Security

The Ibero-American group's experience with security issues is confined to discussions or declarations at the annual Summits. Although, as it may be inferred by the first and second summits, states have enumerated security as one of the areas of possible intervention, the group has most of the time shied away from any intervention. One of the first times it did so was at the Estoril Summit (2009), which set off some internal tension. The wide consensus surrounding the summit's central theme of "Innovation and Knowledge" was missing, however, in relation to the political crisis in Honduras, a parallel and controversial matter of discussion. With the Latin American leaders divided over the legitimacy of Honduras' postcoup presidential election, the Portuguese summit presidency issued a statement, condemning the coup that deposed President Manuel Zelaya in June 2009. It called for Zelaya's reinstatement, for "national dialogue" to restore the "democratic regime" and for Honduran security forces to end the encirclement of the Brazilian embassy in Tegucigalpa, where Zelaya had taken refuge. The involvement of the Ibero-group did not contribute, however, to crisis abatement.

It is also worth noticing that all Summits since Costa Rica in 2004 have adopted special communiqués on terrorism. They all are very similar and repetitive, generally condemning all acts of terrorism and committing states to fight it "in all its forms and manifestations." The declarations are declamatory and euphuistic and thereby carry very low political weight. It is telling that in a region where the very concept of terrorism is far from being universal (see, for instance, the contrastive way FARC is regarded by different states), the adoption of these declarations sparks no major controversy. The Ibero-American Summit has also systematically called for the reactivation of the negotiations between Argentina and the United Kingdom over the Falklands/Malvinas (e.g., Estoril, Mar de La Plata, Asunción and Panamá Summits), and supported the Alliance of Civilizations process (e.g., at Estoril Summit). The Alliance is an initiative proposed by Spain's former Prime Minister José Luis Rodríguez Zapatero, at the fifty-ninth General Assembly of the United Nations in 2005. It was cosponsored by the Turkish Prime Minister, Recep Tayyip Erdoğan. The initiative seeks to galvanize international action against extremism through the forging of international, intercultural and interreligious dialogue and cooperation. At the Panamá Summit in 2013, Ibero-American states have also issued a special communiqué supporting the President of Colombia for his efforts in ending the internal conflict with the FARC. It was a mere political statement as no instruments were identified to assist Colombia in that endeavor.

Beyond issuing declarations, the Summits have also witnessed important backstage negotiations that paved the way for bilateral and multilateral cooperation. For example, Argentina, Brazil, and Paraguay reached an agreement during the Ibero-American Summit of October 1995, regarding the eventual implementation of measures to coordinate security in the trilateral boundary region. Yet, the agreement emanated largely from the goodwill of these leaders at the Summit and not from any background and preparatory work carried out by the institution itself. The Ibero-American Sumit provided only the *momentum* for the handshake to take place. The lack of institutional capacity of the Summit in the security field was also patent at the Seventeenth Summit in 2007, where Argentinean President Néstor Kirchner and Uruguay's President Tabaré Vázquez engaged in a war of words over the installation of a pulp mill (see Chapter 3). Although the conflict stained and largely paralyzed political relations between both countries, the Ibero-American Summit had no contribution to its mediation or resolution.

Operational Capacity in Human Security

The Summit's contribution to nontraditional security problems is weak. In 1998, the Ibero-American Supreme Justice Courts and Tribunals met to design policies and judgments oriented to developing the principles contained in the Margarita Declaration of November 1997, in which the Ibero-American Chiefs of State and of Government pointed out aspects relative to the administration of justice in these countries. Special importance was awarded to the enforcement and revision of the sanctioning system against offenses such as corruption and drug trafficking, whose solutions were to be addressed from an interjurisdictional perspective. In fact, drug trafficking has been discussed at the Sixth Summit held in Santiago y Viña del Mar (1996) and at the Eighth Summit held in Oporto, Portugal (1998). The issue has also been debated at youth forums facilitated by the General Secretariat, but no major program, accord, or guidelines have yet been established. The main reason for this is because the organization has neither sufficient political capital nor institutional capacity to generate any distinct discussion or methodology on the issue. And also because the visions of the problem are so different that reaching a consensus would be difficult to achieve. A sign of this impassivity was the resolution adopted at the 2011 Summit in Asunción recognizing the coca leaf – which can be processed into cocaine – as an official part of Bolivian heritage, for its cultural significance as a medicinal leaf used for teas and indigenous medical treatment. Although the vast majority of the countries have serious issues with this light-handed treatment of the coca leaf, they ended up espousing the resolution with no discussion. Realistically, they knew that the firing range of the resolution was very short.

Conclusions

The inertia and lukewarm enthusiasm that settle in afterward is the main negative obstacle towards the strengthening of the Summit. Very little emanates from South America in the direction of creating a supranational unit with a minimum of autonomy to represent the bloc in world forums. In recent years, high-level attendance has also been declining. At the 2011 Summit, for instance, only eleven of twenty-two leaders participated, which prompted one Spanish newspaper to write that the causes of the failure were "an unconvincing Spanish foreign policy, the way the Ibero-American group secretariat is managed or its penchant for bureaucracy full of good intentions, ad infinitum rhetoric and no follow up of the pompous cooperation programs which many times compete directly with bilateral or multilateral Spanish cooperation."[5]

Also, funding appears to be insufficient. If the body really wants to overcome the perception of Spanish dependency, it has to drastically alter its budgetary arrangements. Up until 2005, Spain responded for approximately 80 percent of the General Secretariat's budget. In 2005 it struck a deal with Portugal so that both could take the responsibility for 70 percent of the budget, but it remained by far the largest contributor. It currently accounts for 61 percent of the budget, followed by Mexico (11 percent), Portugal (9 percent), and Brazil (8 percent).[6]

And how does Portugal, the other colonial power, react to Spanish dominance? Portugal's estrangement with Spain dates back to 1640 when the Iberian Union was dismantled and Portugal started to consolidate its commercial and political alliance with England. Although both countries share strong diplomatic and trade ties within the framework of the EU, and heads of state often have very cordial (even personal) relations, there is still in Portugal a sense of vulnerability and reticence over Spain's projection in the world. On the other hand, Portugal has been aware of its limited political and economic capacity in South America (even in Brazil). And therefore Lisbon has been careful not to increase the dependency on Spanish investment and the overpowering presence of its big neighbor, and in addition, it was moved to participate in the Ibero-American Summit by the need to balance a forum that it is believed to be more Hispanic than Lusophone (Prados, 2002:156). In the first Summit in Guadalajara, Portuguese president Mário Soares (1986-1996) talked about the "reunion of Spain and Portugal in Latin America, achieved so brilliantly in the Guadalajara Summit" (cited in Prados, 2002:157). Second, Portugal has also been pulled into the Ibero-American Summit by the magnetic power of Brazil – its historic entrance door into the region – and by its interest in consolidating its ties with countries such as Venezuela, where there is a large Portuguese colony; Uruguay, a country with whom it shared historical and colonial ties; or with Mexico, an important economic hub in the region. Despite these apparent interests and the rhetoric displayed by the Portuguese in the Oporto Summit of 1998 and the Panama Summit of 2000, the Ibero-American Summit has never been on the top of the Portuguese agenda. Willing to look cooperative, Portuguese leaders appeared to accept the Ibero-American project with unpretentious enthusiasm without showing any resistance. Priming its European presence and the advantageous alliance with the United States, Africa had taken precedence over South America.

Notes

[1] Take part in the Summit 22 Spanish and Portuguese-speaking countries in Latin America and the Iberian Peninsula.

[2] This idea of "iberophone" culture, was made explicit by the Declarationa adopted at the end of the Bariloche Summit of 1995, which underlined "la existência de una base lingüística común entre todas lãs naciones

iberoamericanas producto de dos lenguas afines, el espanol y el português; así como sus substratos históricos, culturales, morales y educativos."

[3] Canadian Foundation for the Americas (2006), "Strengthening of the Ibero-American Conference: Likely Impact on the Inter-American System and Canada's influence in the Americas," FOCAL Strategy Paper, p.21.

[4] Wikileaks Messages Generate Rift at Mar del Plata's Summit on Education and Democracy (*Mercopress*, 6 December 2010).

[5] "IberoAmerican summit a 'failure': Latam has its own voice in world affairs" (*Mercopress*, 1 November 2011).

[6] Portugal é Terceiro Contribuinte da Cimeira" (*Diário de Notícias*, 23 November 2009).

15

The Community of Latin American and Caribbean States

"The purpose of the countries of Latin America and the Caribbean is to make the Community of Latin American and Caribbean States replace the Organization of American States." —Evo Morales, president of Bolivia, 2012

The Community of Latin American and Caribbean States (CELAC) was officially crated in 2011 by thirty-three countries, "to promote and project a unified voice for Latin America and the Caribbean."[1] The inaugural summit, held in Caracas, Venezuela, displayed the intention of some of its leaders to establish a block in opposition to the OAS, which includes the United States and Canada. In his inauguration speech, President Chávez described the new regional bloc as a tribute to his idol Simón Bolívar, saying the time has come to put an end to U.S. hegemony. Cuban President Raúl Castro added in the same cerimony that if it is successful, the creation of the new organization will be the biggest event in 200 years. *The New York Times* has also quoted President Daniel Ortega of Nicaragua who said that it it was time for the region to sentence "the Monroe Doctrine to death."[2]

The CELAC is heir to (and officially replaces[3]) an older group, the Permanent Mechanism of Political Consultation and Coordination (Rio Group), which was created – with equal fanfare – in 1986, in Rio de Janeiro, as the result of the fusion of the Contadora Group (Mexico, Colombia, Venezuela, and Panama) and the Support Group (Argentina, Brazil, Uruguay, and Peru). These groups had been formed to analyze and propose solutions to the political crises in Central America.

Although the relevance of the Rio Group was up and down, South American leaders often used its Summits to raise red flags or to break deadlocks in international affairs. According to Dabène (2009:204), 31 percent of all Rio Group's Summit decisions between 1990 and 1999 were dedicated to international issues, the most discussed topic. In fact, the Group represented one of the first attempts at multilateral regional cooperation in South America. *The New York Times* wrote on the first Presidential Summit (Acapulco, 1987), that it was the "first large-scale Latin American summit conference without the participation of the United States" and quoted Mexican Foreign Minister, Bernardo Sepulveda Amor, who said with pomp that "This is the first opportunity in the entire history of the region in which eight Latin American heads of state are meeting through their own convocation and having determined the agenda themselves" (i.e. without U.S. interference).[4]

In fact, when it was founded, and similarly to CELAC, the group was perceived by some observers as an alternative body to the OAS, since the latter was dominated by the United States during the Cold War. The Punta del Este Declaration, issued at the end of the Second Summit in 1988, openly stated that "US–Latin American relations are undergoing a period of challenges. . . . Differences of interests and perceptions have not allowed [the parties] to take full advantage of opportunities for ample and equitable cooperation" (Art.III-5). This idea was reinforced by some of its member countries throughout the years. For instance, in the ceremony that formalized the adherence of Cuba to the Rio Group, held in 2008, Cuban President Raúl Castro professed that the OAS should come to an end and that the Rio Group is the only legitimate representative of the region.

In practice however, the group never filled these high expectations and operated simply as a multilateral forum that discussed issues of common concern. In the final Declaration of the Eighteenth Summit, held in Rio in 2004, member states reaffirmed that "only the multilateral treatment of global problems and of the threats to international peace and security along with the full respect for International Law will enable us, in a new spirit of international cooperation, to achieve peace and development with social inclusion. Similarly, we recognize the urgent need to strengthen multilateralism in order to solve and handle effectively the issues on the global agenda" (art. 2). This was as far as it could go.

At its core there was also a concern about democracy promotion. As the Peruvian Minister of Foreign Affairs Allan Wagner Tizón (2003) highlighted, the Rio Group "was born under the imprint of democracy at a time when we were fighting not just for democracy and peace in Central America, but also for the consolidation of our own democracies after decades of dictatorial military governments" (cited in Oelsner, 2009:201). So central was democracy to the Rio Group that it became "an association of democratic countries" in Latin America. Practice, however, showed otherwise, as we will see below.

Not surprisingly, over time the Group started having difficulties in showing its purpose beyond the usual summit get-together discussions. And in order to provide it with new strengths, regional leaders have therefore decided to merge the Rio Group and the Latin American and Caribbean Summit on Integration and Development (CALC) to form a new multilateral organization. This is how CELAC was formed. The name of the organization was not consensual: whereas Venezuela prefered the term "Organization" (to make the opposition with the OAS more obvious), and Mexico suggested "Union," Brazil proposed the more palatable "Community."[5] The idea to create a mechanism that could "be the foundation of a genuine conference of Latin American and Caribbean peoples" was initially proposed by Mexico's President Calderón at the Santo Domingo Twentieth Rio Group Summit in 2008, and reinforced in December 2008 in Costa do Sauípe, Brazil, where the First CALC took place. The formal announcement came at the Twenty-First Summit of the Rio Group and the Second CALC in Playa del Carmen, México, in February 2010. According to the Summit Declaration, CELAC should as a priority (Art. 5):

- Encourage, the regional integration, aiming toward the promotion of our sustainable development.
- Promote political coordination, the enhancement of the Latin-American and Caribbean agenda in global forums and a better positioning of Latin America and the Caribbean in the face of relevant international developments.
- Encourage the dialogue processes with other states, groups of countries, and regional organizations, in order to strengthen the presence of the region in the international arena.
- Promote the communication, cooperation, articulation, coordination, complimentarity, and synergy among the subregional organisms and institutions.
- Increase our ability to develop specific programs on dialogue and international cooperation both within the region and with other states and international actors.
- Strengthen cooperation on the issues and take into account both the CALC Declaration of Salvador-Bahia mandate, and the Montego Bay Action Plan, and other documents

that could be incorporated, based on the broadest
integration efforts.
- Promote the implementation our own mechanisms for
  peaceful conflict resolution. [6]

The announcement of a new regional organization was welcomed
with hesitation by policy analysts. An editorial in Brazil's *O Estado de
São Paulo* newspaper said, "CELAC reflects the disorientation of the
region's governments in relation to its problematic environment and its
lack of foreign policy direction, locked as it is into the illusion that
snubbing the United States will do for Latin American integration what
200 years of history failed to do."[7] The same newspaper, one of the most
widely read in Brazil, wrote sarcastically at the end of the First CELAC
Summit in 2011 that the leaders of the three largest economies (Brazil,
Mexico, and Argentina) had not even bothered to attend the second day
of the event.[8]

To a large extent, CELAC embodies the impulse of Mexico to
reunite with Latin America and its attempt to create windows of
opportunity beyond the traditional focus on NAFTA and North America.
CALC, whose membership is identical to CELAC, was the proud
creation of Brazil; and by proposing the merger of CALC and the Group
of Rio, Mexico effectively became a founder in its own right. The two
regional powers – the largest in the Latin American and Caribbean
region both in terms of economy and population – have competed before
for regional influence. And there are no indications why they will not
continue to do so under CELAC.

Legal Capacity

The Community lacks a constitutional framework that would grant it the
status of an international organization with international legal
personality. It should hence be regarded as an arrangement. In fact, the
Caracas Declaration "In the Bicentenary of the Struggle for
Independence Towards the Path of Our Liberators" of 2011, which
established the Community, calls it simply a "mechanism for dialogue
and consensus" (Art. 28) or as a "representative mechanism for political
consultation, integration and cooperation of Latin America and
Caribbean States" (Art. 32). There is no evolution in this regard from the
Rio Group.[9]

The juridical similarity of both groups ends, however, when we look
at their legal capacity to engage in security issues. Whereas the
Declaration of Rio de Janeiro established as main objectives of the

Group, inter alia, "To present appropriate solutions to the problems and conflicts affecting the region" (art. d), and "To promote initiatives and actions with the objective to improve, through dialogue and cooperation, international relations" (art. e), CELAC's inaugural declarations, the Caracas Action Plan 2012 and the CELAC Statute of Proceedings – approved at the first Summit – endow the Community with no clear mandate in security. The legal competence of the Community in this field derives therefore from the legal principles that had been adopted by the Rio Group over the years. As CELAC Declaration of 2011 points out recurrently, "CELAC is based on [the] legacy of the shared principles and adopted by consensus" of the Rio Group (and of CALC) (Art. 32). What was then the legal capacity of the Group in security matters? The first Presidential Summit in 1987 adopted the Acapulco Commitment to Peace, Development and Democracy,[10] which included one chapter on "The security of our region: peace, democracy and development," through which states vowed to:

- Encourage initiatives in favor of international disarmament and security;
- Foster mutual trust and our own solutions to the problems and conflicts affecting the region;
- Contribute, through cooperation and consultation, to the defense, strengthening and consolidation of democratic institutions;
- Promote and broaden political dialogue with other states and groups of states, within and outside the region;
- Coordinate positions in order to strengthen multilateralism and democracy in international decision-making;
- Promote the establishment of zones of peace and cooperation;
- Encourage processes of integration and cooperation in order to strengthen the region's autonomy;
- Embark on an active, coordinated struggle to eradicate extreme poverty;
- Reinforce cooperation against drug trafficking and also against terrorism.

These objectives were reiterated by several other declarations.[11] Most importantly, in March 1999, the Veracruz Act consolidated the positions and principles shared by Rio Group members on those topics. The Group also adopted numerous declarations and statements reiterating the conviction that in order to overcome the global problem of drugs, efforts had to be based on a comprehensive and balanced approach and on the principle of shared responsibility. In the declarations, the Group also tended to stress that a collective action was needed on the part of the international community at the different stages of production, marketing, and consumption of illicit drugs, as well as the criminal offenses associated with this phenomenon. Moreover, the Group's statements generally underscored the need to overcome exclusive punitive strategies. As the Declaration on the Tenth Anniversary of the Rio Group, adopted in Cochabamba, Bolívia, in 1996, stated:

> "We reiterate that a comprehensive strategy in the fight against drugs must include the social and economic aspects of the phenomenon, to which end efforts must be directed towards alternative social and regional development programmes designed to help improve the living conditions of the rural families affected."

The only legal instrument adopted directly by CELAC that might endow it with competence in the security field is the Special Statement on the Defense of Democracy and Constitutional Order, adopted at the First Summit. The document establishes the mechanisms for CELAC to act vis-à-vis any breach of the constitutional order in a member state. It stresses that when the constitutional government of a member state believes that the democratic order is threatened or disrupted seriously, the member state may notify the Pro-tempore president. The Statement is based on the clauses adopted by UNASUR and the Ibero-American Summit (both were proposed by Ecuador after the events of September 2010 that threatened the life of President Rafael Correa), as it seeks to protect governments from any coup attempt. CELAC's instrument is, however, weaker than the Inter-American Democratic Charter of the OAS, which clearly states the values to be respected by its members: holding of periodic, free and fair elections based on universal vote and secret ballot; a system of plural parties and political organizations; and the separation and independence of public powers. At the Second Summit held in Havana in 2014, CELAC leaders adopted a symbolic Declaration on Latin America as a Zone of Peace, but it turned out to be content-less, serving as a repository of good wishes and not providing legal instruments in the security field.

Organizational Capacity

The CELAC does not have a secretariat or permanent body (similar to the former Rio Group), and relies instead on yearly summits of heads of states. No organ is set up for handling the routine affairs; and consultative meetings of foreign ministers or ministers in charge of other special matters are held irregularly and generally in response to events in South America. Every year, the foreign ministry of the host state for the summit meeting carries out the Community's liaison work. Its organizational capacity is therefore low and dependent on the political will and administrative capacity of its pro-tempore secretariat. It is symbolic that the official website of the organization is hosted in the official portal of the Venezuelan government.[12]

Operational Experience in Traditional Security

As a recently formed organization, CELAC does not yet have a legacy of its own, apart from issuing bureaucratic communiqués as was the case on the 2013 tense Venezuela's election, on the situation in Syria, or the one adopted at the 2014 Summit expressing support to Argentina in the island sovereignty dispute. The same, however, cannot be said about its progenitor. The Rio Group's intergovernmental nature and all-encompassing composition was regarded as a natural asset. Indeed, the Group was generally regarded as "a privileged interlocutor of the region vis-à-vis other countries and groups of countries."[13] It was in this capacity that the Group held annual meetings with the European Union. Others claim that the Group's role was deeply rooted in the idea that it had the opportunity and the capability to build the consensus that is required for a regional security accord (Aravena, 1998a:113). But there was the other side of the coin as the Group was *only* that, an interlocutor or a representative of the region. The Group had neither political muscle, decision-making capacity nor organizational capacity to be a compelling actor in the field of security (or any other). Its operational experience was therefore low and was confined to the issuing of political declarations, such as about the situation in the Middle East (July 2006), Haiti (June 2006), Falklands/Malvinas (November 1987, November 2004, May 2005, November 2009), the terrorist attacks in Egypt (July 2005) and London (July 2005), the political situation in Nicaragua (July 2005), the Colombian conflict (July 2008), or the political crisis in Bolivia (April 2008).

The Group was even more straightjacketed because it obeyed the principle of nonintervention. In fact, formal adherence to such principles by most regional organizations (namely the OAS) has not impeded them from intervening in the domestic affairs of a member state. But the Rio Group was able to uphold those principles – not for a marked conviction but due to the incapacity to do otherwise.[14]

Despite all these constraints, the Rio Group had some initiatives to showcase. It was the first South American regional organization to include democracy as criteria for membership and participation. On two occasions it has suspended members who did not meet this requirement:

Panama in 1986 and Peru in 1992. After the Fujimori *autogolpe*, the Rio Group prohibited Peru from attending its meetings, but accepted it back in 1993, as a result of the measures adopted by Fujimori to restore democracy. The Group also reacted quickly to the 2002 coup in Venezuela. The incident coincided with the annual meeting of the Group, held in Costa Rica, and therefore, member states did not hesitate in condemning "the interruption to constitutional order" in Venezuela. They asked the secretary general of the OAS, Cesar Gaviria, to call a special meeting of the organizations' Permanent Council to discuss the situation in Venezuela, following Article 20 of the Democratic Charter. The initial declaration of the Group called on reestablishing full democracy and holding elections soon. The Group reacted quicker and more determinately than the United States to preserve democracy in the region. But this good track record was nonetheless sullied in 2008, when the Group formally accepted Cuba, which in any optimistic view can be regarded a democracy. The distinctiveness of the Group became harder to grasp.

The body ventured also into other terrains. In May 2003, the Heads of State and Government of the Group, the president of the Caribbean Community (CARICOM) and Haiti called on the UN Secretary General to use his good offices to promote with rigor a peace process in Colombia, exhorting the guerrilla movements to engage in dialogue. This call was supported in June by the OAS member states' meeting in the XXXIII session of the General Assembly.

Years later, in 2008, the Group brought together the presidents of Ecuador and Colombia, Rafael Correa and Álvaro Uribe, shortly after Colombian soldiers raided a camp belonging to the FARC on Ecuadorian territory, triggering the suspension of diplomatic relations between the two. The Rio Group issued a declaration expressing its rejection of the Colombian raid, described in the document as a violation of Ecuador's territorial integrity, and reaffirmed the principle that the territory of a nation cannot be the target of military occupation or other measures of force by other states, whatever the reason. During the meeting Colombia's President Álvaro Uribe promised no similar actions would occur again, while Ecuadorian President Rafael Correa dropped his call for a sanction against Bogotá putting, therefore, an end to the crisis. At the end of that meeting, in the Dominican Republic capital Santo Domingo, Correa and Uribe shook hands for the first time after the incident. Brazil's presidential adviser in international affairs, Marco Aurélio Garcia, claimed that the Group's role in managing the Andean crisis led to its reinvigoration after going through an agonizing phase.[15] One may wonder, however, why the Rio Group has been chosen to mediate the crisis at the highest level rather than other more capable and experienced organizations, such as the OAS or UNASUR. In the words of the OAS Secretary General, it was a "happy coincidence" (Insulza, 2008-2009:26). The twentieth Meeting of the Group had long been scheduled for March 7th, only six days after Colombia's incursion, and therefore it would have been implausible to keep the issue off the agenda.

Operational Experience in Human Security

The Group's Uruguay Summit of 1988 specifically included drug trafficking as a security issue. The presidents approached this point on the agenda with a clear and transparent goal: the creation of an international regime, of a functional nature, to combat and control the trade, smuggling, and consumption of illegal narcotics. The aim was the establishment of integrated regional policies. A mechanism was proposed to this end: the International Convention Agaînt Drug Trafficking. Eight-point "Guidelines for Action" were established regarding the constitution of an international regime for dealing with drug trafficking and related issues (Aravena, 1998a:120). The drug problem was brought up systematically in following summits. For instance in Caracas (1990), member states produced a joint statement on the war against the illegal trade in narcotics reaffirming the need for an integral approach, able to encompass not only the policing aspects but essentially, the political, economic, and social dimensions of the problem (Aravena, 1998a:122). It is symptomatic, however, that these declarations served both as the legal framework that legitimized the Group to act and, ironically, were the action itself. The operational capacity and experience in dealing with security issues – beyond presidential summit activities and declaratory statements – was feeble.

Conclusions

CELAC's goal is to conduct consultations over the important political, economic, and social issues of the South American areas and coordinate the positions of the member states so as to take corresponding actions to accelerate the development of the Latin American integration. But if we look at past experiences in the region coordination may be difficult to achieve. The difficulty in having relations between some of CELAC's members improve, and the political and ideological split in the region, have led to a sentiment of distrust and pursuit of opposed geopolitical strategies. With no strong identity or robust institutional capacity,

CELAC has some hey challenges ahead. As just one example, the CELAC 2013 Summit in Santiago was supposed to be an experiment in regional cohesion, but it was marked by a spat between Chilean and Bolivian officials over the longstanding territorial dispute (see chapter 3).

But expectations still run high. As summarized by Ambassador José Antonio Zabalgoitia, Mexico's National Coordinator for the Rio Group:

> "The Community will draw upon the Rio Group and CALC experiences in fostering coordinated actions and harmonization with the several subregional integration institutions and mechanisms in LAC. By establishing clear priorities, promoting communication and taking advantage of synergies, it is possible to achieve greater efficiency and proper allocation of scarce resources, and to avoid duplication of efforts by seeing convergence as a main long-term goal."[16]

There is, however, a difference between expectations and reality. If on the drawing board, leaders expect the OAS to provide a hemispheric approach – CELAC to serve as the main Latin American and Caribbean interlocutor, and UNASUR to lead South American affairs – in practice the demarcations will likely be erased by the complex and paradoxical interests of all members that compose the Americas.

Notes

[1] Caracas Declaration "In the Bicentenary of the Struggle for Independence towards the Path of Our Liberators" (Art. 9).

[2] "Venezuela: New Regional Group Meets" (*The New York Times*, 3 December 2011).

[3] Caracas Declaration "In the Bicentenary of the Struggle for Independence towards the Path of Our Liberators" (Art. 33).

[4] "8 Latin Presidents in Acapulco for Summit Talks" (*The New York Times*, 27 November 1987).

[5] "Communicado Final Cria 'OEA do B' Sem EUA" (*O Estado de São Paulo*, 24 de Fevereiro, 2010).

[6] Online at http://www.europarl.europa.eu/intcoop/eurolat/key_documents/cancun_declaration_2010_en.pdf. Visited 3 January 2010.

[7] "A Retórica da Integração" (*O Estado de São Paulo*, 25 February 2010).

[8] "Uma OEA Sem os Gringos" (*O Estado de São Paulo*, 6 December 2011).

[9] The Declaration of Rio de Janeiro of 1986, which established the Group, calls it simply "a process of regular consultations," or a "mechanism for political concertation".

[10] Available online at http://www2.ohchr.org/english/law/ compilation_democracy/grio.htm. Visited 3 March 2012.

[11] See Declaration of Mar Del Plata by the Rio Group's Heads of State and Government (November 2005); Rio Group Declaration – Eighteenth Summit (November 2004); Fifth Summit Latin America and the Caribbean-European Union, Declaration of Lima (May 2008).

[12] http://www.celac.gob.ve/

[13] Declaration of Mar del Plata by the Rio Group's Heads of State and Government (November 2005).

[14] See Rio Group's Communiqué on Bolívia (June 2005); Fifth Summit Latin America and the Caribbean-European Union, Declaration of Lima (May 2008).

[15] "Calderón Quer Região 'À Imagem de Bolívar'" (*O Estado de São Paulo*, 23 de Fevereiro 2010).

[16] Online in http://www.focal.ca/publications/focalpoint/236-april-2010-jose-antonio-zabalgoitia-en. Visited 20 March 2011.

PART 4

CONCLUSION

16

The Dynamics of South American Security

South America forms a regional cluster or security complex, where regional securitization and desecuritization processes are "so interlinked that security problems [of a set of units] cannot reasonably be analyzed or resolved apart from one another" (Buzan and Wæver, 2003: 491). Thus, ensuring security to South Americans states and citizens means accounting for the regional factors that affect it. As the sources of insecurity are difficult to be contained within the confines of a state, "regional conflict complexes" (Wallensteen and Sollenberg, 1998), "regional conflict formations" (Rubin, Armstrong, and Ntegeye, 2001), "regional peace and security clusters" (Tavares, 2008), or "regional security complexes" (Buzan, Wæver, and de Wilde, 1998; Buzan and Wæver, 2003) (as academics like to call this regional mutually reinforcing linkages) have emerged.

To understand the dynamics of South America's security, the book examined two central variables. First, it looked at the type of threats and conflicts that affect the region, and second it assessed the role played by states and international organizations to ensure the security of South American citizens.

What Threats to Security?

If we were to trust obediently the word of South American leaders, we could easily believe that South America is an island of stability standing isolated in a world of confrontation. Indeed, on at least nine top-level occasions since the end of the Cold War, South American heads of state have officially declared the region to be a peace zone:

- Establishment of the South Atlantic Peace and Cooperation Zone (ZPCSA) (1986) (adopted by twenty-four members, including Argentina, Uruguay, and Brazil);
- Declaration of Mercosur, Bolivia, and Chile as a Zone of Peace (1998) (signed by six countries);
- Declaration regarding a South American Peace Zone (27 July 2002) (signed by twelve countries);
- OAS Recognition of the South American Zone of Peace and Cooperation (10 June 2003) (adopted by all OAS members);
- Declaration of San Francisco de Quito on the Establishment and Development of an Andean Peace Area (12 July 2004) (signed by five countries);
- UNASUR Declaration on Peace in South America (28 August 2009) (signed by twelve countries);
- UNASUR Declaration of South America as a Peace Zone (30 November 2012) (signed by twelve countries);
- CELAC Declaration on Nuclear Disarmament (20 August 2013) (signed by thirty-three countries).
- CELAC Declaration on Latin America as a Zone of Peace (29 January 2014) (signed by thirty-three countries).

The persistent way the term is solemnly used seems to indicate that there is some grain of self-induction. North American or European leaders, for instance, do not need to retell that their regions are peace zones. But despite this apparent fragility, a significant number of academic publications have also conceived South America as a "pluralistic security community" (Kacowicz, 2000:216; Kacowicz, 1998:121; Dominguez, 2007:111-112; Jervis, 2002:9; Hurrell, 1998; Oelsner, 2003), i.e., a transnational region comprising sovereign states whose people maintain dependable expectations of peaceful change (Deutsch et. al., 1957). In fact, this proposition is not totally false because it is predicated on the idea that the threats that affect the region are of a military type, and it stresses the view that no interstate conflict has been waged since 1995 (Peru-Ecuador). Traditionally, the concept of security has generally been addressed in the context of "national security" and "public security." National security involves defense of the sovereignty both with respect to the state's role as an independent actor in interstate relations and the ultimate expression of legitimate coercion in internal affairs. The legitimate defense of territorial boundaries, internal order and sufficient political and economic stability to permit functioning of state institutions are also matters of national security. If viewed in this way, South America could possibly be regarded as a zone of peace.

The book demonstrated that this view, although not false, is certainly incomplete. And it is so for three main reasons. First, because the original premise only looks at interstate conflicts. It is true that as the Cold War ideologies waxed and waned in the late 1980s, the support they lent to both interstate conflicts eroded. Moreover, the integration processes in the region, even if they involve mostly political leaders and not the people, have contributed to the cementing of regional norms of cooperation. Interstate violence has decreased dramatically, and the only interstate conflict waged after the end of the Cold War was the one between Peru and Ecuador. The book highlighted, however, that in addition to this armed conflict, eight other armed conflicts occurred – all of them intrastate (Table 16.1.). An evolution of the political organizations and practices involved a change of the methods to make conflicts. Practice changed, but armed conflict remained a commonplace.

The second reason is because nonarmed conflicts – territorial disputes and domestic political crises – are also a major feature in the region. It is difficult to envisage a peace zone where thirty-two nonarmed conflicts (encompassing eleven territorial disputes, nineteen domestic political crises, and two other nonarmed disputes) have occurred since the end of the Cold War (Table 16.1). A coup d'etat is always a violent challenge to the state, analogous to a rebellion. It directly impacts the quality of living of a population.

Thirdly, as the book brought out, any conceptualization of the security framework of South America needs to encompass both the security of the twelve South American states and the security of 390 million people. Both traditional and human security are integral parts of the equation. In fact, this is a view that, at least at a declaratory level, has already set root. As we saw, several official declarations emphasize the need to integrate a comprehensive notion of security, such as:

- OAS Declaration on Security (2003);
- CAN Guidelines of the Andean Policy on External Security (2004);
- CASA Declaration on Citizen Security in South America (2005);
- UNASUR Constitutive Treaty (2008), Art. 3-u

All these legal instruments recognize that security threats and other challenges in the South American context are of a diverse nature and have a multidimensional scope; and that the traditional concept should also be expanded to encompass new and nontraditional threats, which include political, economic, social, health, and environmental aspects. Therefore, state security and citizen security – or traditional security threats and human security threats – should be conceived in an integrated way. They complement each other, and no analysis of security would be complete if it focused exclusively on one or the other. Security is a comprehensive and multidimensional concept. Threats are varied and labyrinthine. Paradoxically, the very same leaders that declare South America to be a peace zone since there is no active interstate armed conflict, also advance the idea that security is indeed multidimensional and based on human needs.

Table 16.1: Traditional Security Threats Since the End of the Cold War

Armed Conflicts (9)		• Colombia (since 1964) • Ecuador-Peru (1995) • Paraguay (1989) • Peru (1981-1999, 2007-2010) • Suriname (1986-1992) • Venezuela (1989) • Venezuela (1992) • Bolivia (2008) • Brazil (2010)
Non-Armed Conflicts (32)	**Territorial Disputes (11)**	Venezuela-Guyana, Venezuela-Colombia, Suriname-Guyana, Suriname-French Guiana, Chile-Bolivia, Chile-Peru, Peru-Ecuador, Bolivia-Paraguay, Argentina-Chile (Southern Fields + Laguna del Desierto) Argentina-UK (Falkands/ Malvinas)
	Domestic Political Crises (19)	Suriname (1990), Argentina (1990 and 2001), Peru (1992 and 2000), Brazil (1992), Venezuela (1993 and 2002), Paraguay (1996, 1999, 2000, and 2012), Ecuador (1997, 2000, 2005, 2007, and 2010), Bolivia (2003 and 2005)
	Other (bilateral or intrastate) (2)	• Argentina-Uruguay (pulp mill and Martín García Canal) • Paraguay (EPP guerrilla)

As the book showed, the region is battling against human security threats such as drug trafficking, urban criminality, illegal small arms trade, Islamic terrorism, and environmental threats. How can we conceive of a "security community" when urban violence and homicide rates are some of the highest in the world? The narrative of violence is still present. As we saw, it may be argued that the most fundamental threats to South American citizens are not related to internal and external armed aggression, but to drug-trafficking and urban criminality. The fear of crime and anxiety about personal security is crossing boundaries of class, political preference, and ideology. This problem generates social, political, and economic costs: it affects the quality of life of large sections of population; obstructs economic development and discourages investment; erodes the capabilities of government and the public credibility of institutions; affects the performance of the courts and the police; has negative effects for the promotion human rights; and prevents democratic principles from being fully realized. Many of these new menaces, concerns, and other challenges to hemispheric security are transnational in nature and require appropriate hemispheric cooperation.

The South American "peace" that regional leaders celebrate does not entirely reflect empirical reality. In fact, the lack of effective security institutions and efficient mechanisms for conflict resolution in the region make it difficult to make substantial progress in the development of international regimes centered around the concept of security community (Aravena, 1998b:80-81). Hence, South America is better described as a form of security cooperation. Countries do not depend on the build-up of dissuasive forces to deter aggression from others. They strengthen international institutions to maintain peace, resolve disputes, and promote collaboration to address joint problems, and they develop bilateral cooperation to address specific joint problems. Deterrence is achieved through the transparency of military procedures and information and through confidence-building measures that engage the armed forces of the region (Domínguez, 1988:12). But unlike "security communities," the region is still not depicted by the sharing of identities, values, and meaning (Hirst, 1996:176). Democratization has led to cooperative and shared experiences but has not led to a process of security integration. Whereas there has been a growing convergence regarding economic policies, differences have persisted with respect to security and defense policies. As we saw, Santiago and La Paz, for instance, have had no diplomatic ties since 1962. In addition, differences over border delimitation and sovereignty along the Pacific coast led to a complicated chess game by four South American countries — Chile, Bolivia, Peru, and Ecuador — in which all are moving their pieces at a snail's pace while keeping an eye on their neighbor's chessboard. Colombia and Venezuela have also long viewed each other as potential threats, and geopolitically driven conflicts have periodically flared up.

Who Handles the Threats?

Threats could be handled by forces outside the region, by international organizations, or by states themselves. Let us pause on the first option. Throughout history, South American states have shown a high level of reluctance towards extraregional interventions. Indeed, the wider South American defense of noninterventionism – first articulated by Argentine Foreign Minister Luis Drago in 1902 – sought to counter the U.S. and European official view that they had the right to armed intervention to compel states to honor their public debts. The Calvo Doctrine was also prevalent in the region. It was advanced by the Argentine diplomat and legal scholar Carlos Calvo (1824-1906) and affirmed that rules governing the jurisdiction of a country over aliens and the collection of indemnities should apply equally to all nations, regardless of size. The book has shown that this posture is still prevalent in the region. The establishment of the Union of South American Nations (UNASUR) and the Community of Latin American and Caribbean States (CELAC) is explained, to a large extent, by the need to keep the United States off the marrow of regional politics.

International Organizations

Given this resistance to extraregional security actors, the second available option is to delegate competences to local organizations. Historical institutionalism claims that national preferences are (partly) endogenous to the institutional setting, and that the entrenchment of institutional arrangements may obstruct an easy reversal of initial choices and involve high costs. As Pierson argues, "actors may be in a strong initial position, seek to maximize their interests, and nevertheless carry out institutional and policy reforms that fundamentally transform their own positions (or those of their successors) in ways that are unanticipated" (Pierson, 1996:126). But in South America, international organizations have little room for maneuver. Liberal intergovernmentalism, on the other hand, inspired by neorealist and liberal theory, argues that any international agreement requires that the interests of the dominant domestic groups in the participating countries converge (Moravcsik, 1998). From this perspective, there is an inherent tendency towards lowest common denominator outcomes, and new supranational solutions in South America are only put in place when necessary to make credible commitments (e.g.. to constrain and control the other governments).

Indeed, the book highlighted that the current security system in South America puts low value and low credibility in the existing formal instruments of conflict resolution covering the region. There are abundant initiatives but they do not lead to the institutionalization of a common normative framework or to coordinated action. Existing institutions lay down guidelines either for potential collective action to resolve disputes among states or for building a regional response to extracontinental threats. But these objectives remain mostly at the level of the rhetoric of meetings and resolutions; very few concrete measures were taken to ensure, under their auspices, the ending of conflicts in the region (da Costa, 1998:47-48). In fact, it has been shown that heads of state and government are the only available driver of regional integration (Malamud, 2010:651). The underdevelopment of common institutions cannot persist for long if integration is to move ahead. Beyond poor institutional integration, regional bodies are also affected by the persistence and renovation of interstate disputes, and by the differences in defense doctrines and the conflicting strategies to handle regional threats. Finally, the division of labor between regional organizations is far from being consensual. There are no regular meetings between them to agree on guidelines or on a pan-regional strategy of burden sharing.

It has been argued that the emergence of new regionalist projects, such as UNASUR and CELAC, are currently redefining new geographical and ideological boundaries while fostering new consensus at the regional level. Some note that, "although embryonic, these consensuses are setting new regional frontiers beyond the historical hub of what defined U.S.- and market-led regionalism" (Riggirozzi and Tussie, 2012:6). We have demonstrated, however, that there is little room for excitement, as these new regional creations follow the same parameters of older constructions.

The analysis in the book has shown that out of the forty-one disputes registered in the region since the end of the Cold War (including armed and nonarmed conflicts), international organizations have intervened in twenty-two of them through forty-three different actions. These actions include: (a) issuing a declaration/resolution or call to action, (b) fact-finding or observer missions, (c) mediation/good offices, (d) peacekeeping, (e) peacebuilding activities, or (f) membership suspension. Quantity differs from quality, however, and four specific conclusions can be reached:

- The OAS accounts for twenty-nine of these actions (67 percent), whereas the UNASUR intervened six times; Rio Group/CELAC, six; CAN, one; and the Ibero-American Summit, one. It becomes evident that there is an unbalance between the operational capacity of OAS and the other organizations.
- Out of the forty-three actions, twenty-four (or 56 percent) are limited to calls to action or issuing of declarations/resolutions supporting or condemning specific events. There were seven mediation/good offices actions (16 percent), seven fact-finding or observer missions (16 percent), two peacebuilding activities (5 percent), two membership suspensions (5 percent), and one peacekeeping operation (2 percent). Thus, the majority of the interventions still have low-fire capacity.
- Out of all these interventions it may be claimed that only four contributed significantly to the prevention or the resolution of conflicts: OAS peacebuilding mission in Colombia (OAS/MAPP), OAS peacekeeping operation in Suriname (OAS Special Mission to Suriname), OAS mediation in Bolivia (2008), and UNASUR good offices in Bolívia (2008). International organizations are still weak security players.
- International organizations have been conspicuously absent from intervening in the eleven territorial conflicts in the region. The only exception is the resolutions and declarations issued frequently, at Argentina's request, to condemn British presence in the Falklands/Malvinas. Interestingly, the contenders are more prone to request the intervention of the ICJ (such as Peru-Chile or Bolivia-Chile) than to expect support from local organizations.

The low capacity of local organizations to handle traditional security issues is also visible when the threats are nontraditional. Although in theory these organizations would be better positioned to cope with challenges that extrapolate state borders – such as drug trafficking, small-arms trade, Islamic terrorism or environmental threats – their operational experience in this regard is still tenuous. There is in fact a discrepancy between the declaratory capacity of these organizations and their operational might. With no exception, member states have gathered to adopt vigorous declarations or to agree on action plans that provide a good first step to cooperate on issues such as terrorism or drug trafficking. The OAS has for instance adopted the Inter-American Convention Against Terrorism, and the Andean Community signed the Andean Plan to Prevent, Combat and Eradicate Illicit Trade in Small Arms and Light Weapons in all its Aspects. But these general instruments have not led to concrete, long-lasting and determining actions.

It is interesting to note that although international organizations have low operational experience and capacity, they ironically have strong legal capacity to handle security issues (both traditional and human security). All of them, and mainly the CAN, UNASUR and the OAS have adopted a broad legal framework that leaves no doubt about their power under law to operate in the security field. These organizations have adopted specific treaties, charters or declarations that explicitly bestow them with legal capacity. But on the other hand, the organizational capacity is low. With the exception of the OAS, none of the security organizations in South America have a permanent secretariat, and their institutional capacity is grounded on the regular two-day presidential summits.

Indeed, most countries are not interested in giving up sovereignty to a supranational agency that would weaken their ability to make decisions and defend national interests. The argument of most regional leaders over the last decades is that the low level of institutionalization and the intergovernmental character of the regional integration process – driven and controlled by the executive branches of the member countries – would ensure rapid progress, bypassing heavy bureaucracies (Vigevani and Cepaluni, 2009). But this is not the case. Intergovernamentalism facilitates the personalization of the institutions and often allows for domestic problems to paralyze an organization's capacity to offer an autonomous and definitive solution to a conflict. Indeed, one key challenge faced by policy-makers in the construction and reform of the South American institutional order is the so-called *negotiator's dilemma*, which – in devising or reforming institutional order – mirrors the collective search for a solution that leaves all participants better off, and a struggle to realize individual distributive goals (Lindner and Rittberger, 2003). There is a constant tension between realizing the "common good" and securing the distribution of gains from institutionalized cooperation.

Although we have not detected a tendency to inject institutional robustness to South American organizations, there is an emerging propensity to merge some of these institutions. South America has the thickest network of intergovernmental institutions in the world, and thereby it is almost mandatory to have some of them terminated. In

2011, the Latin American and Caribbean Summit (created in 2008) and the Rio Group (established in 1986) merged to form the Community of Latin American and Caribbean States. There is also a strong movement to having CAN subsumed by UNASUR. Although symbolic, these developments are not likely to lead to any progress in the road towards supranationality.

States

The third option is thereby the most recurrently used. States still call upon themselves the near exclusivity to ensure traditional and human security. Although there has been an increase in convergence around particular threat-clusters, and this has led to the establishment of regional and subregional bilateral and multilateral arrangements for policy coordination, cooperation, and regulation; even in these processes, states have retained the central role. States are still the agents through which the structures of governance are instituted and financed, and the agents through which the efforts of these structures are largely realized.

Yet, the book has shown that South American states, with the probable exception of Chile, have regularly failed to establish their institutional autonomy; their scale and scope remain a part of daily political debate, and their legitimacy is often called into question (Centeno, 2002:2). We consistently found that the South American state has not had the required institutional capacity to ensure civil order and protection. Most of the deaths and the threats to South Americans have resulted from the inability of the state to impose its authority in a definitive and permanent manner. If we look at specific countries, however, we naturally spot variances. In Argentina and Chile the state as an institution has managed to establish some administrative norms and it has relatively institutional capacity; whereas in other countries such as Brazil, Venezuela, and Colombia, the viability of the state, as an actor of protection and security, has been questioned. Paradigmatically, when in 2011 the Secretary General of the OAS criticized a law that gave President Chávez the power to govern by decree – which is contrary to the Inter-American Democratic Charter – the president dismissed the remarks as "shameful" and condemned OAS's "interference." Chávez wanted to make sure that the state was still in control.[1]

Moreover, most threats affecting South American citizens are transnational, borderless, and migratory demanding for states to cooperate. Indeed, security concerns in the region would require institutional and multilateral forms of cooperation, yet states in the region tend to rely on traditional diplomatic means. As Llenderrozas (2007: 15–18) highlighted, the obstacles are of a political, infrastructural, and budgetary nature. Governments have frequently perceived the extent of the threats posed by organized crime and terrorism differently. In addition, the domestic legal competence of the armed forces and the police varies from state to state, making coordination sometimes difficult. In this sense, the gap between formal agreements and intentions, on the one hand, and effective adoption and implementation of policy, on the other, is sometimes wider than it might first appear (Oelsner, 2009). Second of all, state-to-state cooperation is also curbed by ideological rifts. It is interesting to notice that in the same way transnational cooperation by military governments in the 1970s was facilitated by adherence to common political principles (Operation Condor is a good illustration), so today leftist South American countries are priorizing cooperation among themselves to strengthen their own principles (e.g., ALBA). Cooperation can sometimes be hijacked by ideology. South America may become, but it is not yet, an island of peace.

---

[1] "Chavez Condemns OAS 'Interference' in Venezuela" (*BBC News*, 10 January 2011).

Bibliography

Abbott, Philip K., (2004), "Terrorist Threat in the Tri-Border Area: Myth or Reality?" in *Military Review*.

Acharya, Amitav, (2001), "Human Security: East versus West" in *International Journal*, Vol. 56 (3), p. 442-460.

Alagappa, M., & Inoguchi, T. (Eds.), (1999), *International Security Management and the United Nations*. Tokyo: United Nations University Press.

Albuquerque, José Augusto Guilhon (2003), "Brazil: From Dependency to Globalization" In Frank O. Mora and Jeanne A.K. Hey (Eds.), *Latin American and Caribbean Foreign Policy*. Lanham: Rowman and Littlefield Publishers.

Alkire, Sabina (2003), *A Conceptual Framework for Human Security, Working Paper 2*. Oxford: Centre for Research on Inequality, Human Security and Ethnicity, CRISE.

Amaral, Arthur Bernardes, (2008), Guerra ao Terror e a Tríplice Fronteira na Agenda de Segurança dos Estados Unidos, Dissertação de Mestrado PUC-Rio Janeiro.

———, (2010), "Novo Rumo na Tríplice Fronteira" in *O Globo* (2 March 2010).

Arancibia-Clavel, Felipe, (2007), "Chile and Argentina: From Measures of Trust to Military Integration" in *Military Review*, Vol. 87 (5).

Aravena, Francisco Rojas, (1998a), "The Rio Group and Regional Security in Latin America" in Olga Pellicer (Ed.), *Regional Mechanisms and International Security in Latin America*. Tokyo and New York: United Nations University Press.

———, (1998b) "Transition and Civil Military Relations in Chile: Contributions in a New International Framework" in Jorge I. Domínguez (Ed.), *International Security and Democracy: Latin America and the Caribbean in the Post-Cold War Era*. Pittsburgh: University of Pittsburgh Press.

———, (2005), "Panorama de la Seguridad en la América del Sur" in Klaus Bodemer and Francisco Rojas Aravena (Eds.), *La Seguridad en las Américas: Nuevos e Viejos Desafíos*. Madrid and Frankfurt am Main: Iberoamericana and Vervuert Verlag.

Arceneaux, Craig and David Pion-Berlin, (2005), *Transforming Latin America: The International and Domestic Origins of Change*. Pittsburgh: University of Pittsburgh Press.

———, (2007), "Issues, Threats, and Institutions: Explaining OAS Responses to Democratic Dilemmas in Latin America" in *Latin American Politics & Society*, Vol. 49 (2).

Ardila, Martha, (2005), "Seguridad e Integracíon en el Marco dela Comunidad Andina de Naciones" in Klaus Bodemer and Francisco Rojas Aravena (Eds.), *La Seguridad en las Américas: Nuevos e Viejos Desafíos*. Madrid and Frankfurt am Main: Iberoamericana and Vervuert Verlag.

Arias, Aimee, (2011), "Human Security in the Andean Community," Paper presented at the annual meeting of the *International Studies Association Annual Conference* "Global Governance: Political Authority in Transition", Le Centre Sheraton Montreal Hotel, Montreal, Canada.

Atkins, G. Pope, (1990), "South America in the International Political System" in G. Pope Atkins (Ed.), *South America into the 1990s: Evolving International Relationships in a New Era*. Boulder and London: Westview Press.

Avilés, William, (2009), "Policy Coalitions, Economic Reform and Military Power in Ecuador and Venezuela" in *Third World Quarterly*, Vol. 30 (8).

Axworthy, Lloyd, (1997), "Canada and Human Security: the Need for Leadership"in *International Journal*, Vol. 11 (2), p. 183-196.

Baburkin, Sergei; Andrew C. Danopoulus; Rita Giacalone; and Erika Moreno, (1999), "The 1992 Coup Attempts in Venezuela: Causes and Failure" in *Journal of Political and Military Sociology*, Vol. 27 (1).

Bagley, Bruce Michael, and Juan Gabriel Tokatlián, (1985), "Colombia Foreign Policy in the 1980s: The Search for Leverage" in *Journal of Internamerican Studies and World Affairs* Vol. 30 (1), pp. 161-82.

———, (1987), *"La Política Exterior de Colombia Durante la Década de los Ochenta: los Límites de un Poder Regional"* in Monica Hirst (ed.), Continuidad y Cambio en las Relaciones América Latina-Estados Unidos, Buenos Aires: GEL, pp. 151-176.

Banega, Cyro, Björn Hettne and Fredrik Söderbaum, (2001), "The New Regionalism in South America" in Michael Schulz, Fredrik Söderbaum and Joakim Öjendal (Eds.), *Regionalization in a Globalizing World: A Comparative Perspective on Forms, Actors and Processes*. London and New York: Zed Books.

Baud, Michiel, (2004), "Fronteras y la Construcción del Estado en América Latina" in Gustavo Torres Cisneros (Ed.), *Cruzando Fronteras*. Quito: Ediciones Abya-Yala.

Bernal-Meza, Raúl, (2007), "Cambios y Continuidades en la Política Exterior Brasileña. El Consejo de Seguridad: ¿El Retorno del Realismo? Sus Impactos en el Cono Sur" in Sérgio Costa, Hartmut Sangmeister and Sonja Steckbauer (Eds.), *O Brasil na América Latina: Interações, Percepções, Interdependencias*. São Paulo: Annablume Editora.

Bodemer, Klaus; Sabine Kurtenbach and Andreas Steinhauf, (2001), *El Nuevo Escenario de (In)seguridad en América Latina*. Hamburgo: IIK.

Bond, Robert D., (1981), "Venezuela, Brazil, and the Amazon Basin" in Elizabeth B. Ferris and Jennie K. Lincoln (Eds.), *Latin American Foreign Policies*. Boulder: Westview Press.

Bonilla, Adrián, (1999), "The Ecuador-Peru Dispute: The Limits and Prospects for Negotiation and Conflict" in Gabriel Marcella and Richard Downes (Eds.), *Security Cooperation in the Western Hemisphere: Resolving the Peru-Ecuador Conflict*. Coral Gables: North-South Center Press at the University of Miami.

Boulden, J. (Ed.), (2003). Dealing with Conflict in Africa: The United Nations and Regional Organizations. London: Palgrave Macmillan.

Bourguignon, François, (1999), "Crime, Violence, and Inequitable Development" in Boris Pleskovic and Joseph Stiglitz, (editors). *Annual World Bank Conference on Development Economics 1999/2000*, Washington DC, World Bank.

Bourne, Richard, (2008), *Lula of Brazil: The Story So Far*. Berkeley and Los Angeles: University of California Press.

Brecher, Michael and Jonathan Wilkenfeld, (2000), *A Study of Crisis*. Ann Arbor: University of Michigan Press.

Briceno-Leon, Andres Villaveces, and Alberto Concha-Eastman, (2008), "Understanding the Uneven Distribution of the Incidence of Homicide in Latin America" in *International Journal of Epidemiology*, Vol. 37, No. 4, pp. 751-757.

Bromley, Mark and Carina Solmirano, (2012), *Transparency in Military Spending and Arms Acquisitions in Latin America and the Caribbean*, SIPRI Policy Paper no. 31. *Stockholm: SIPRI*.

Bruntland, G., (Ed) (1987). *Our Common Future: The World Commission on Environment and Development*. Oxford: Oxford University Press.

Buitrago, Francisco Leal, (1989), *Estado y Política en Colombia* (2nd edition) Bogotá: CEREC/Siglo Veintiuno de Colombia.

———, (2008), "Una Mirada a la Seguridad en la Región Andina" in Roberto Russell (Ed.), *América Latina:¿Integracíon o Fragmentación?* Buenos Aires: Edhasa.

Burges, Sean W., (2009), *Brazilian Foreign Policy after the Cold War*. Gainesville: University Press of Florida.

Buzan, B., and Wæver, O., (2003), *Regions and Powers: The Structure of International Security*. Cambridge: Cambridge University Press.

Buzan, B., Wæver, O., and de Wilde, J., (1998), *Security: A New Framework for Analysis*. Boulder: Lynne Rienner.

Calderón, Ernesto Garcia, (2001), "Peru's Decade of Living Dangerously" in *Journal of Democracy*, Volume 12 (2).

Calvert, Peter, (1983), *Boundary Disputes in Latin America*. London: Institute for the Study of Conflict.

Campbell, Zélia, (2009), "IBSA: Overview and Perspectives" in *II Conferência Nacional de Política Externa e Política Internacional – IBAS*. Brasília: MRE/Fundação Alexandre de Gusmão.

Campos Mello, Flávia de, (2000), Regionalismo e Insercão Internacional: Continuidades e Transformacão da Política Externa Brasileira nos anos 90. Sao Paulo: FFLCH/USP. Ph.D. Dissertation.

Cardoso, Fernando Henrique, (2006), *The Accidental President of Brazil: A Memoir*. New York: PublicAffairs.

Carpenter, Ted Galen, (2003), *Bad Neighbor Policy: Washington's Futile War on Drugs in Latin America*. Houndmills and New York: Palgrave Macmillan.

Cason, Jeffrey, "Resisting Free Trade: Brazil and the FTAA" Paper presented at the annual meeting of the International Studies Association 48th Annual Convention, Hilton Chicago, Chicago, IL, USA, February 28, 2007

Caviedes, César N., (1988), "The Emergence and Development of Geopolitical Doctrines in the Southern Cone Countries" in Philip Kelly and Jack Child

(Eds.), *Geopolitics of the Southern Cone and Antarctica*. Boulder and London: Lynne Rienner.

Cárdenas, Miguel Eduardo and Melanie Höwer, (2004), "La Comunidad Andina: Ventajas y Obstáculos Respecto al Libre Comercio y a la Seguridad Humana" in Miguel Eduardo Cárdenas (Ed.), *El Futuro de la Integración Andina*. Bogotá: CEREO.

Centeno, Miguel Angel, (2002), *Blood and Debt: War and the Nation-State in Latin America*. University Park: Pennsylvania State University Press.

Cervo, Amado Luiz, (2010), "Brazil's Rise on the International Scene: Brazil and the World" in *Revista Brasileira de Política Internacional*, Vol. 53 (special edition).

Charvériat, Céline, (2000), Natural Disasters in Latin America and the Caribbean: An Overview of Risk. Inter-American Development Bank Working Paper Nr. 434. Washington: Inter-American Development Bank.

Chicago Council on Global Affairs, (2010), Constrained Internationalism: Adapting to New Realities – Results of a 2010 National Survey of American Public Opinion. Chicago: Chicago Council on Global Affairs.

Child, Jack, (1985), Geopolitics and Conflict in South America: Quarrels Among Neighbors. New York: Praeger.

Collier, Paul, (2003), Natural Resources, Development and Conflict: Channels of Causation and Policy Interventions. Washington: World Bank.

Coelho, Pedro Motta Pinto and José Flávio Sombra Saraiva (Eds.), (2004), *Brazil-Africa Forum on Politics, Cooperation and Trade*. Brasília: Instituto Brasileiro de Relacoes Internacionais.

Connell-Smith, Gordon, (1966), *The Inter-American System*. Oxford: Oxford University [hanging indent as above needed here]Press.

Cooper, Andrew F. and Thomas Legler, (2001), "The OAS in Peru: A Model for the Future?" in *Journal of Democracy*, Vol. 12 (4).

———, (2005), "A Tale of Two *Mesas*: The OAS Defense of Democracy in Peru and Venezuela" in *Global Governance*, Vol 11 (4).

———, (2006), Intervention Without Intervening? The OAS Defense and Promotion of Democracy in the Americas. Basingstoke, U.K.: Palgrave Macmillan.

Corporación Latinobarómetro, (2011), *Informe Latinobarómetro 2011*. Santiago de Chile: Latinobarómetro.

Crandall, Russell C., (2008), *The United States and Latin America after the Cold War*. Cambridge and New York: Cambridge University Press.

———, (2008b), *Driven by Drugs: U.S. Policy Toward Colombia*. Boulder and London: Lynne Rienner.

Cruz, Giovanni Molano, (2010), "Regionalismo y Seguridad en América Latina. La Construcción de la Cooperación Regional de Lucha Contra la Droga en los Andes" unpublished paper.

Currea-Lugo, Victor de, (2007), *Poder Y Guerrillas en América Latina: Una Mirada a la Historia del Guerrillero de a Pie*. Málaga: Sepha.

Da Costa, Thomaz Guedes, (1998), "Latin America and the New Challenges for a New International Security Regime in the Post-Cold War Period" in Olga Pellicer (Ed.), *Regional Mechanisms and International Security in Latin America*. Tokyo and New York: United Nations University Press.

————, (2001), "Strategies for Global Insertion: Brazil and the Regional Partners" in Joseph S. Tulchin and Ralph H. Espach (Eds.), *Latin America in the New International System*. Boulder: Lynne Rienner.

————, (2006), "Em Busca da Relevância: Os Desafios do Brasil na Segurança Internacional do Pós-Guerra Fria" in Henrique Altemani and Antônio Carlos Lessa (Eds.), *Relações Internacionais do Brasil: Temas e Agendas*. São Paulo: Editora Saraiva.

Da Silva, Elsa Cardoso and Richard S. Hillman, (2003), "Venezuela: Petroleum, Democratization, and International Affairs" in Frank O. Mora and Jeanne A.K.Hey (Eds.), *Latin American and Caribbean Foreign Policy*. Lanham: Rowman and Littlefield Publishers.

De Almeida, Paulo Roberto, (2009), "O Brasil no Contexto da Governação Global" in Wilhelm Hofmeister (Ed.), *Governança Global*. Rio de Janeiro: Fundação Konrad Adenauer.

————, (2002), Os Primeiros Anos do Século XXI: O Brasil e as Relacões Internacionais Contemporâneas. São Paulo: Editora Paz e Terra.

De Lima, Maria Regina Soares, (1996), "Brazil's Response to the "New Regionalism" in Gordon Mace and Jean-Philippe Thérien (Eds.), *Foreign Policy and Regionalism in the Americas*. Boulder: Lynne Rienner.

————, (2005), "A Política Externa Brasileira e os Desafios da Cooperação Sul-Sul" in *Revista Brasileira de Política Internacional*, Vol. 48 (1).

De Souza, Amaury, (2009), A Agenda International do Brasil: A Política Externa Brasileira de FHC e Lula. Rio de Janeiro: Elsevier Editora.

————, (2002), A Agenda International do Brasil: Um Estudo sobre a Comunidade Brasileira de Política Externa. Rio de Janeiro: CEBRI.

Dabène, Olivier, (2009), *The Politics of Regional Integration in Latin America: Theoretical and Comparative Explorations*. New York: Palgrave Macmillan.

Dahl, Robert, (1971), *Polyarchy: Participation and Opposition*. New Haven: Yale University Press.

Dammert, Lucía, (2007), Perspectivas y Dilemas de la Seguridad Ciudadana en América Latina. Quito: FLASCO.

Danese, Sérgio, (2009), A Escola da Liderança: Ensaios sobre a Política Externa e a Inserção Internacional do Brasil. Rio de Janeiro and São Paulo: Editora Record.

DeRouen Jr., Karl and Uk Heo, (2005), Defense and Security: A Compendium of National Armed Forces and Security Policies. Santa Barbara: ABC-CLIO.

Deutsch, Karl, Sidney Burrell, Robert Kann, Maurice Lee Jr., Martin Lichterman, Raymond Lindgren, Francis Loewenheim and Richard Van Wagenen, (1957) *Political Community and the North Atlantic Area*. Princeton: Princeton University Press.

Diehl, P. F., & Lepgold, J., (2003). *Regional Conflict Management*. Oxford: Rowman & Littlefield.

Diniz, Eugenio, (2006), "O Brasil e as Operações de Paz" in Henrique Altemani and Antônio Carlos Lessa (Eds.), *Relações Internacionais do Brasil: Temas e Agendas*. São Paulo: Editora Saraiva.

Domínguez, Jorge I., (1998), "Security, Peace, and Democracy in Latin America and the Caribbean: Challenges for the Post-Cold War Era" in Jorge I. Domínguez (Ed.), *International Security and Democracy: Latin*

America and the Caribbean in the Post-Cold War Era. Pittsburgh: University of Pittsburgh Press.

———, (2003a), "Boundary Disputes in Latin America" in *Peaceworks* Nr. 50. Washington: United States Institute of Peace.

———, (2003b), "Conflictos Territoriales y Limítrofes en América Latina y el Caribe" in Jorge I. Domínguez (Ed.), *Conflictos Territoriales y Democracia en América Latina*. Buenos Aires: Siglo XXI Editores Argentina.

———, (2008), "Internacional Cooperation in Latin America: the Design of Regional Institutions by Show Accretion" in Amitav Acharya and Alastair Iain Johnston (Eds.), *Crafting Cooperation: Regional Internacional Institutions in Comparative Perspective*. Cambridge: Cambridge University Press.

Duran, W. Andrew, (1996), "Democracy and Regional Multilateralism in Chile" in Gordon Mace and Jean-Philippe Thérien (Eds.), *Foreign Policy and Regionalism in the Americas*. Boulder: Lynne Rienner.

Ebel, Roland H., Raymond C. Taras and James D. Cochrane, (1991), *Political Culture and Foreign Policy in Latin America: Case Studies from the Circum-Caribbean*. Albany: State University of New York.

Ehrenfeld, Rachel, (1990), *Narco-terrorism*. New York: Basic Books.

Elizondo, José Rodríguez, (2009), *De Charaña a la Haya*. Santiago de Chile: La Tercera Ediciones.

Escudé, Carlos, (1988), "Argentine Territorial Nationalism" in *Journal of Latin American Studies*, Vol. 20.

Escudé, Carlos and Andrés Fontana, (1998), "Argentina's Security Policies: Their Rationale and Regional Context" in Jorge I. Domínguez (Ed.), *International Security and Democracy: Latin America and the Caribbean in the Post-Cold War Era*. Pittsburgh: University of Pittsburgh Press.

Fajnzylber, Pablo, Daniel Lederman, and Norman Loayza, (2002), "What Causes Violent Crime?" in *European Economic Review*, Vol.46 (7), p. 1323-57.

Farías, Carolina Rosales, (2008), The Andean Community in the International Context: Difficulties of Integration and Importance of Its Common Foreign Policy. Saarbrücken: VDM Verlag.

Fawcett, Louise, (2005), "The Origins and Development of the Regional Idea in the Americas" in Louise Fawcett and Monica Serrano (Eds.), *Regionalism and Governance in the Americas: Continental Drift*. Houndmills and New York: Palgrave Macmillan.

Fermandois, Joaquín, (2005), *Mundo y Fin de Mundo. Chile en la Política Mundial. 1900-2004*. Santiago: Ediciones Universidad Católica de Chile.

———, (2011), "Pragmatism, Ideology, and Tradition in Chilean Foreign Policy since 1990" in Gian Luca Gardini and Peter Lambert (Eds.), *Latin American Foreign Policies: Between Ideology and Pragmatism*. Houndmills and New York: Palgrave Macmillan.

Fernandes, Tiago Coelho, (2008), "Entre Bolívar e Monroe: o Brasil nas Relações Interamericanas" in Luis Suárez Salazar and Tania García Lorenzo (Eds.), *Las Relaciones Interamericanas: Continuidades y Cambios*. Buenos Aires: Clacso Libros.

Fier, Florisvaldo, (2010), "A Política Externa e a Integração Regional" in Kjeld Jakobsen (Ed.), *2003-2010: O Brasil em Transformação - A Nova Política Externa* (Vol. 4). São Paulo: Editora Perseu Abramo.

Filho, Joao R. Martins and Daniel Zirker, (2000), "The Brazilian Military under Cardoso: Overcoming the Identity Crisis" in *Journal of Interamerican Studies and World Affairs*, Vol. 42 (3).

Fishlow, Albert, (1999), "The Western Hemisphere Relation: Quo Vadis?" In Albert Fishlow and James Jones (Eds.), *The United States and the Americas: a 21st Century View*. New York and London: W.W. Norton & Company.

Fórum Brasileiro de Segurança Pública, (2012), *Anuário Brasileiro de Segurança Pública 2012*. São Paulo: Fórum Brasileiro de Segurança Pública.

Fox, Gregory H. and Brad R. Roth, (2000) Democratic Governance and International Law. Cambridge: Cambridge University Press.

Franco, Andrés, (1998), "La cooperación fragmentada como una nueva forma de diplomacia: Las relaciones entre Colombia y Estados Unidos en los noventa," in Andrés Franco, ed., *Estados Unidos y los países andinos, 1993-1997. Poder y desintegración*, Bogotá: CEJA, pp. 37-80.

Franko, Patrice, (1999),"Patterns of Military Procurement in Latin America: Implications for U.S. Regional Policy" in Gabriel Marcella and Richard Downes (Eds.), *Security Cooperation in the Western Hemisphere: Resolving the Peru-Ecuador Conflict*. Coral Gables: North-South Center Press at the University of Miami.

Fuentes, Claudio A., (2000), "After Pinochet: Civilian Policies toward the Military in the 1990s Chilean Democracy" in *Journal of Interamerican Studies and World Affairs*, Vol. 42 (3).

Garcia, Marco Aurélio, (2010), "A Política Externa Brasileira" in Kjeld Jakobsen (Ed.), *2003-2010: O Brasil em Transformação - A Nova Política Externa* (Vol. 4). São Paulo: Editora Perseu Abramo.

Gardini, Gian Luca, (2010), The Origins of Mercosur: Democracy and Regionalization in South America. New York: Palgrave Macmillan.

Garreton, Manuel Antonio, (1995), "Redemocratization in Chile" in *Journal of Democracy*, Vol. 6 (1).

Geneva Declaration on Armed Violence and Development, (2011), *Global Burden of Armed Violence 2011*. Geneva: Geneva Declaration Secretariat.

Gerth, H.H. and C. Wright Mills, (Ed. and Trans.) (1946), *From Max Weber: Essays in Sociology*. Oxford: Oxford University Press.

Gordon, Dennis R., (1984), "Argentina's Foreign Policies in the Post-Malvinas Era" in Jennie K. Lincoln and Elizabeth Ferris (Eds.), *The Dynamics of Latin American Foreign Policies: Challenges for the 1980s*. Boulder and London: Westview Press.

Goucha, Moufida and John Crowley, (Eds.) (2009), *Rethinking Human Security*. Chichester, UK: Wiley-Blackwell and UNESCO.

Graduate Institute of International and Development Studies, (2010), *Small Arms in Brazil: Production, Trade and Holdings*. Geneva: Small Arms Survey/Graduate Institute of International and Development Studies.

———, (2012). *Small Arms Survey 2012*. Cambridge: Cambridge University Press.

Graham, Kennedy, and Tânia Felício, (2006), Regional security and global governance: A study of interactions between regional agencies and the UN Security Council with a proposal for a regional–global security mechanism. Brussels: VUB Brussels University Press.

Grandin, Greg, (2007), Empire's Workshop: Latin America, the United States, and the Rise of the New Imperialism. New York: Holt Paperbacks.

Greenpeace, (2009), *Amazon Cattle Footprint*. São Paulo and Manaus: Greenpeace Brazil.

Griffith, Ivelaw L., (1993-1994), "From Cold War Geopolitics to Cold War Geonarcotics" in *International Journal* (Canada), Vol. 49, p. 1-36.

Grugel, Jean, (1996), "Latin America and the Remaking of the Americas" in Andrew Gamble and Anthony Payne (Eds.), *Regionalism and World Order*. Basingstoke and London: Macmillan Press.

Guimarães, Samuel Pinheiro, (2010), "Uma Política Externa Para Enfrentar as Vulnerabilidades e Disparidades" in Kjeld Jakobsen (Ed.), *2003-2010: O Brasil em Transformação - A Nova Política Externa* (Vol. 4). São Paulo: Editora Perseu Abramo.

Guizado, Álvaro Camacho and Andrés López Restrepo, (2007), "From Smugglers to Drug Lords to *Traquetos*: Changes in the Colombian Illicit Drug Organization" in Christopher Welna and Gustavo Gallón (Eds.), *Peace, Democracy, and Human Rights in Colombia*. Notre Dame: University of Notre Dame Press.

Hackett, James, (Ed.) (2010), Military Balance 2010 - The International Institute for Strategic Studies. London and New York: Routledge.

Halperin, Morton H. and Mirna Galic, (2005), *Protecting Democracy: International Responses*. Lanham: Lexington Books;

Haq, Mahbub ul., (1995), "New Imperatives of Human Security" in U. Kirdar and L. Silk (Eds.), *From Impoverishment to Empowerment*. New York: NYU Press.

Harmon, Christopher C., (2000), *Terrorism Today*. London and Portland: Frank Cass Publishers.

Hayes, Margaret Daly, (2003), "The New Security Agenda for the Americas: Focus on "Insecurity" in Riordan Roett and Guadalupe Paz (Eds.), *Latin America in a Changing Global Environment*. Boulder: Lynne Rienner.

———, (2007), "Building Consensus on Security: Toward a New Framework" in Gordon Mace, Jean-Philippe Thérien, and Paul Haslam (Eds.), *Governing the Americas: Assessing Multilateral Institutions*. Boulder: Lynne Rienner.

Hazleton, William A., (1984), "The Foreign Policies of Venezuela and Colômbia: Collaboration, Competition, and Conflict" in Jennie K. Lincoln and Elizabeth Ferris (Eds.), *The Dynamics of Latin American Foreign Policies: Challenges for the 1980s*. Boulder and London: Westview Press.

Heredia, Edmundo Aníbal, (2006), *Relaciones Internacionales Latinoamericanas (Vol. 1: Gestación y Nacimiento)*. Buenos Aires: Grupo Editor Latinoamericano.

Herz, Mônica, (2003), "Managing Security in the Western Hemisphere: The OAS's New Activism," in Michael Pugh and Waheguru Pal Singh Sidhu (eds.) *The United Nations and Regional Security: Europe and Beyond*. Boulder, Colo. and London: Lynne Rienner.

————, (2011), *The Organization of American States (OAS)*. London and New York: Routledge.

Hirst, Mônica, (1996), Democracia, Seguridad e Integración: América Latina en un Mundo en Transición. Buenos Aires: Grupo Editorial Norma.

————, (1996b) "The Foreign Policy of Brazil: From the Democratic Transition to Its Consolidation" in Heraldo Muñoz and Joseph S. Tulchin (Eds.), *Latin American Nations in World Politics* (second edition). Boulder: Westview Press.

————, (1998), "Security Policies, Democratization, and Regional Integration in the Southern Cone" in Jorge I. Domínguez (Ed.), *International Security and Democracy: Latin America and the Caribbean in the Post-Cold War Era*. Pittsburgh: University of Pittsburgh Press.

————, (2006), "Os Cinco 'As' das Relações Brasil-Estados Unidos: Aliança, Alinhamento, Autonomia, Ajustamento e Afirmação" in Henrique Altemani and Antônio Carlos Lessa (Eds.), *Relações Internacionais do Brasil*. São Paulo: Editora Saraiva.

————, (2008), "Seguridad en América del Sur: La Dimensión Regional de sus Desafios Políticos" in Roberto Russell (Ed.), *América Latina:¿Integracíon o Fragmentación?* Buenos Aires: Edhasa.

Hirst, Mônica and Leticia Pinheiros, (1995), "A Política Externa do Brasil em Dois Tempos" in *Revista Brasileira de Política Internacional*, Vol. 38 (1).

Hodell, D.A., J.H. Curtis, and M. Brenner, (1995) "Possible Role of Climate in the Collapse of Classic Maya Civilization" in *Nature*, Vol. 375 (6530), p.391-393.

Hofmeister, Wilhelm, (2007), "No Obediencia, Pero Mayor Interdependencia: La Relación del Brasil con sus Vecinos" in Sérgio Costa, Hartmut Sangmeister and Sonja Steckbauer (Eds.), *O Brasil na América Latina: Interações, Percepções, Interdependencias*. São Paulo: Annablume Editora.

Homer-Dixon, Thomas F., (1994), "Environmental Scarcities and Violent Conflict" in *International Security*, Vol. 19, p.5-40.

Hoskin, Gary and Gabriel Murillo-Castaño, (2001), "Colombia's Perpetual Quest for Peace" in *Journal of Democracy*, Volume 12 (2).

Hudson, Rex, (2003), *Terrorist and Organized Crime Groups in the Tri-Border Area (TBA) of South America*. Report Prepared by the Federal Research Division, Library of Congress under an Interagency Agreement with the United States Government. Washington: Library of Congress.

Hufty, Marc, (1996), "Argentina: The Great Opening Up" in Gordon Mace and Jean-Philippe Thérien (Eds.), *Foreign Policy and Regionalism in the Americas*. Boulder: Lynne Rienner.

Hunter, Wendy, (1997), *Eroding Military Influence in Brazil: Politicians against Soldiers*. Chapel Hill: University of North Carolina Press.

Huntington, Samuel P., (1991), The Third Wave: Democratization in the Late Twentieth Century. *Oklahoma:* University of Oklahoma Press.

Human Rights Watch, (HRW) (2009), Lethal Force: Police Violence and Public Security in Rio de Janeiro and Sao Paulo. New York: HRW.

Hurrell, Andrew, (1995), "Regionalism in the Americas" in Louise Fawcett and Andrew Hurrell (Eds.), *Regionalism in World Politics: Regional Organization and International Order*. Oxford and New York: Oxford University Press.

————, (1998). "An Emerging Security Community in South America?" in Emanuel Adler & Michael Barnett, (Eds.), Security Communities. Cambridge: Cambridge University Press (228–264).

Hurell, A., (1998b), "Security in Latin America" in *International Affairs*, Vol. 74 (3).

Independent Commission on Disarmament and Security Issues, (1982), Common Security: A Programme for Disarmament, Report of the Independent Commission on Disarmament and Security Issues. London: Pan.

Instituto de Relações Internacionais, (IRI) da Universidade de São Paulo (USP) (2013), "Brasil, as Américas e o Mundo: Opinião Pública e Política Externa". São Paulo: IRI-USP.

Insulza, José Miguel, (1990), "La Seguridad de América del Sur: Posible Contribución Europea" in Carlos Contreras Q. (Ed.) *Despues de la Guerra Fria: Los Desafíos a la Seguridad de América del Sur*. Santiago de Chile and Caracas: Comisión Sudamericana de Paz and Editorial Nueva Sociedad.

————, (2008-2009), "A OEA e a Solução da Crise Colômbia-Equador" in *Política Externa*, Vol. 17 (3).

Inter-American Commission on Human Rights, (2009), *Democracy and Human Rights in Venezuela*. Washington: OAS (Doc. 54).

International Institute for Strategic Studies, (IISS) (2011), *The FARC Files: Venezuela, Ecuador and the Secret Archive of 'Raúl Reyes.'* London: IISS.

Jervis, Robert, (2002), "Theories of War in an Era of Leading-Power Peace" in *American Political Science Review*, Vol. 96.

Johnson, Kenneth L., (2001), "Regionalism Redux? The Prospects for Cooperation in the Americas" in *Latin American Politics and Society*, Vol. 43.

Junquera, Fernando Rueda, (2008), "Las Debilidades de la Integración Subregional en América Latina y el Caribe" in Philippe de Lombaerde, Shigeru Kochi and José Briceño Ruiz (Eds.), *Del Regionalismo Latinoamericano a la Integración Interregional*. Madrid: Fundación Carolina.

Kacowicz, Arie M., (1998), Zones of Peace in the Third World: South America and West Africa in Comparative Perspective. Albany: State University of New York Press.

————, (2000), "Stable Peace in South America: The ABC Triangle, 1979-1999" in Arie M. Kacowicz, Yaacov Bar-Siman-Tov, Ole Elgström, and Magnus Jerneck (Eds.), *Stable Peace among Nations*. Boulder and Oxford: Rowman and Littlefield.

————, (2005), The Impact of Norms in International Society: The Latin American Experience, 1881-2001. Notre Dame: University of Notre Dame Press.

Kaldor, Mary, (2007), *Human Security*. Cambridge: *Polity* Press

Kay, Bruce H., (1999), "The Rise and Fall of 'King Coca' and Shining Path" in *Journal of Interamerican Studies and World Affairs*, Vol. 41 (3).

Kelly, Philip, (1988), "Traditional Themes of Brazilian Geopolitics and the Future of Geopolitics in the Southern Cone" in Philip Kelly and Jack Child (Eds.), *Geopolitics of the Southern Cone and Antarctica*. Boulder and London: Lynne Rienner.

Kelly, Philip and Child, Jack, (1988), "An Overview: Geopolitics, Integration, and Conflict in the Southern Cone and Antarctica" in Philip Kelly and Jack Child (Eds.), *Geopolitics of the Southern Cone and Antarctica*. Boulder and London: Lynne Rienner.

Keohane, Robert O., (2001), "Between Vision and Reality: Variables in Latin American Foreign Policy" in Joseph S. Tulchin and Ralph H. Espach (Eds.), *Latin America in the New International System*. Boulder: Lynne Rienner.

Klare, Michael T., (2001), Resource Wars: The New Landscape of Global Conflict. New York: Henry Holt.

Krause, Keith and Michael C. Williams, 1996. "Broadening the Agenda of Security Studies: Politics and Methods," Mershon International Studies Review 40 (2): 229–254.

Krause, Keith and Michael C. Williams, (Eds.), 1997. Critical Security Studies: Concepts and Cases. Minneapolis, MN: University of Minnesota Press.

Kurth, James R., (1986), "The United States, Latin America, and the World: The Changing International Concept of U.S.-Latin American Relations," in Kevin J. Middlebrook and Carlos Rico (Eds.), *The United States and Latin America in the 1980s: Contending Perspectives on a Decade of Crisis*. Pittsburgh: University of Pittsburgh Press.

Leaning, Jennifer and Sam Arie, (2000). Human Security: A Framework for Assessment in Conflict and Transition. Washington: USAID/CERTI.

Lima, Maria Regina Soares de and Regina Kfuri, (2007), "Política Externa da Venezuela e Relacões com o Brasil" in *Papeis Legislativos* 6. Rio de Janeiro: Observatório Político Sul-Americano.

Lindner, Johannes and Berthold Rittberger, (2003), "The Creation, Interpretation and. Contestation of Institutions – Revisiting Historical Institutionalism" *in Journal of Common Market Studies*, Vol. 41 (3), p. 445–73.

Linz, Juan J., and Alfred C. Stepan, (1996), Problems of Democratic Transition and Consolidation: Southern Europe, South America, and Post-Communist Europe. Baltimore: Johns Hopkins University Press.

Lombaerde, Philippe de, Shigeru Kochi and José Briceño Ruiz, (2008), "Introducción" in Philippe de Lombaerde, Shigeru Kochi and José Briceño Ruiz (Eds.), *Del Regionalismo Latinoamericano a la Integración Interregional*. Madrid: Fundación Carolina.

Londoño, Juan Luis and Rodrigo Guerrero, (1999). "Violencia en América Latina –
Epidemiología y Costos." Office of the Chief Economist's Research Network, Documento de Trabajo R-375. Washington, D.C.: Inter-American Development Bank.

Malamud, A., (2005) "Spillover in European and South American Integration: an Assessment", LASA 2001 meeting paper, Lisboa, Portugal: Centre for Research and Studies in Sociology (CIES-ISCTE).

———, (2008), "Jefes de Gobierno y Procesos de Integración: Las Experiencias de Europa y América Latina" in Philippe de Lombaerde, Shigeru Kochi and José Briceño Ruiz (Eds.), *Del Regionalismo Latinoamericano a la Integración Interregional*. Madrid: Fundación Carolina.

———, (2011), "Argentine Foreign Policy under the Kirchners: Ideological, Pragmatic or Simply Peronist?" in Gian Luca Gardini and Peter Lambert

(Eds.), *Latin American Foreign Policies: Between Ideology and Pragmatism.* Houndmills and New York: Palgrave Macmillan.

Mares, David, (2001a), "Boundary Disputes in the Western Hemisphere: Analyzing their Relationship to Democratic Stability, Economic Integration and Social Welfare" in *Pensamiento Propio* 14, p. 31-59.

———, (2001b), Violent Peace: Militarized interstate Bargaining in Latin America. New York: Columbia University Press.

———, (2003) "Conflictos Limítrofes en el Hemisferio Occidental: Análisis de su Relación con la Estabilidad Democrática, la Integración Económica y el Bienestar Social" in Jorge I. Domínguez (Ed.), *Conflictos Territoriales y Democracia en América Latina.* Buenos Aires: Siglo XXI Editores Argentina.

———, (2007), "Confidence- and Security-Building Measures: Relevance and Efficiency" in Gordon Mace, Jean-Philippe Thérien, and Paul Haslam (Eds.), *Governing the Americas: Assessing Multilateral Institutions.* Boulder: Lynne Rienner.

Mares, David R. and Steven A. Bernstein, (1998), "The Use of Force in Latin American Interstate Relations" in Jorge I. Domínguez (Ed.), *International Security and Democracy: Latin America and the Caribbean in the Post-Cold War Era.* Pittsburgh: University of Pittsburgh Press.

Marighella, Carlos, (1974), "Minimanual of the Urban Guerrilla" in James Kohl and John Litt (Eds.) *Urban Guerrilla Warfare in Latin America.* Cambridge and London: MIT Press.

Márquez, Martha Lucía, Lucas Sánchez and Mariana Quevedo, (2006), "La Política Exterior del Gobierno de Chávez: La Ingración y la Política Energética" in Heinrich Meyer and Consuelo Ahumada Beltrán (Eds.), *Gobiernos Alternativos de la Región Andina y Perspectivas de la CAN.* Bogotá: Observatorio Andino.

Martín, Félix E., (2006), *Militarist Peace in South America: Conditions for War and Peace.* Houndmills and New York: Palgrave Macmillan.

McClintock, Cynthia, (2001), "The OAS in Peru: Room for Improvement" in *Journal of Democracy*, Vol. 12 (4).

McCormick, Gordon H., (2001), "The Shining Path and Peruvian Terrorism" in David C. Rapoport (Ed.), *Inside Terrorist Organizations.* London and Portland: Frank Cass.

Milenky, Edward, (1978), *Argentina's Foreign Policies.* Boulder: Westview Press.

Miller, Benjamin, (2007) States, Nations, and the Great Powers: the Sources of Regional War and Peace. Cambridge: Cambridge University Press.

Millett, Richard L., (2009), "Introduction: Democracy in Latin America: Promises and Perils" in Richard L. Millett, Jennifer S. Holmes and Orlando J. Pérez (Eds.), *Latin American Democracy: Emerging Reality or Endangered Species?* Abingdon and New York: Routledge.

Ministério das Relacoes Exteriores, (2007), *Repertório de Política Externa: Posicoes do Brasil.* Brasília: MRE and Fundacao Alexandre de Gusmao.

Montenegro, Silvia and Verónica Giménez Béliveau, (2006), *La Triple Frontera: Globalización y Construcción Social del Espacio.* Buenos Aires: Miño y Dávila Editores.

Morandé José A., (2003), "Chile: The Invisible Hand and Contemporary Foreign Policy" in Frank O. Mora and Jeanne A.K.Hey (Eds.), *Latin*

American and Caribbean Foreign Policy. Lanham: Rowman and Littlefield Publishers.

Moravcsik, Andrew, (1998), The Choice for Europe: Social Purpose and State Power from Messina to Maastricht. Ithaca, Cornell University Press.

Mullenbach, Mark J. and Matthews, Gerard P., (2008), "Deciding to Intervene: An Analysis of International and Domestic Influences on United States Interventions in Intrastate Disputes" in *International Interactions*, Vol. 34 (1).

Mullins, Martin, (2006), In the Shadow of the Generals: Foreign Policy Making in Argentina, Brazil and Chile. Aldershot: Ashgate.

Muro M., R. Cohen, D. Maffei, M. Ballesteros, L. Espinosa, (2003), "Terrorism in Argentina" in *Prehospital* and *Disaster Medicine*, Vol. 18 (2).

Muñoz, Heraldo, (1994), "A New OAS for the New Times" in Abraham F. Lowenthal and Gregory F. Treverton (Eds.), *Latin America in a New World*. Boulder: Westview Press.

Naím, Moisés, (2001), "The Real Story Behind Venezuela's Woes" in *Journal of Democracy*, Vol. 12 (2), p. 17-31.

Narich, R., (2003) "Traditional and Non-traditional Security Issues in Latin America: Evolution and Recent Developments" in *Occasional Paper Series*, Nr. 42. Geneva: Geneva Centre for Security Policy (GCSP).

Nel, Philip and Marjolein Righarts, (2008), "Natural Disasters and the Risk of Violent Civil Conflict" in International Studies Quarterly, Vol. 52.

Nepstad, Daniel; Britaldo S. Soares-Filho; Frank Merry; André Lima; Paulo Moutinho; John Carter; Maria Bowman; Andrea Cattaneo; Hermann Rodrigues; Stephan Schwartzman; David G. McGrath; Claudia M. Stickler; Ruben Lubowski; Pedro Piris-Cabezas; Sergio Rivero; Ane Alencar; Oriana Almeida and Osvaldo Stella, (2009), "The End of Deforestation in the Brazilian Amazon" in *Science*, Vol. 326 (5958).

Norden, Deborah L., (1995), "Keeping the Peace, Outside and In: Argentina's UN Missions" in *International Peacekeeping* Vol. 2 (3).

Norden, Deborah L. And Roberto Russell, (2002), *The United States and Argentina: Changing Relations in a Changing World*. New York and London: Routledge.

Noriega, Roger, (2011), *Neutralizing the Iranian Threat in Latin America*. Washington: American Enterprise Institute. Online at http://www.aei.org/article/foreign-and-defense-policy/terrorism/hezbollah/neutralizing-the-iranian-threat-in-latin-america/

Oelsner, Andréa, (2003), "Two Sides of the Same Coin: Mutual Perceptions and Security Community in the Case of Argentina and Brazil" in Finn Laursen (Ed.), *Comparative Regional Integration: Theoretical Perspectives*. Aldershot: Ashgate.

————, (2005), International Relations in Latin América: Peace and Security in the Southern Cone. London and New York: Routledge.

————, (2009), "Security Agenda Consensus and Governance in Mercosur: The Evolution of the South American Security Agenda" in Security Dialogue, Vol. 40(2).

Oliveira, Eliézer Rizzo de, (1999), "Brazilian Diplomacy and the 1995 Ecuador-Peru War" in Gabriel Marcella and Richard Downes (Eds.), *Security Cooperation in the Western Hemisphere: Resolving the Peru-Ecuador*

Conflict. Coral Gables: North-South Center Press at the University of Miami.

Oxfam, (2008), Shooting Down the MDGs: How Irresponsible Arms Transfers Undermine Development Goals. Oxfam Briefing Paper 120. Oxford: Oxfam International.

Pardo, Rodrigo and Juan Gabriel Tokatlian, (1989), *Politica exterior colombiana. De la subordinacion a la autonoma?* Bogota: Tercer Mundo Editores-Ediciones Uniandes.

Parodi, Carlos A., (2002), *The Politics of South American Boundaries*. Westport: Praeger Publishers.

Pastor, Robert A., (2005), "North America and the Americas: Integration among Unequal Partners," in Mary Farrell, Björn Hettne, and Luk Van Langenhove (Eds.), *Global Politics of Regionalism: Theory and Practice*. Ann Arbor, Mich. and London: Pluto Press.

Pastrana, Andrés and Camilo Gómez, (2005). *La Palabra Bajo Fuego*. Bogotá: Editorial Planeta Colombiana.

Peck, Connie, (1998), Sustainable Peace: The Role of the UN and Regional Organizations in Preventing Conflict. Lanham, Md.: Rowman and Littlefield.

Peeler, John, (2009), *Building Democracy in Latin America*. Boulder: Lynne Rienner.

Penna, José Osvaldo de Meira, (1988), "Brazilian Geopolitics and Foreign Policy" in Philip Kelly and Jack Child (Eds.), *Geopolitics of the Southern Cone and Antarctica*. Boulder and London: Lynne Rienner.

Peña, Féliz, (2008), "Relações Brasil-Arrgentina" in *Política Externa*, Vol. 16 (4).

Pierson, Paul, (1996), "The Path to European Integration: A Historical Institutionalist Analysis" in *Comparative Political Studies*, Vol. 29 (2), pp. 123-163.

Pion-Berlin, David, (2000), "Will Soldiers Follow? Economic Integration and Regional Security in the Southern Cone" in *Journal of Interamerican Studies and World Affairs*, Vol. 42 (1).

——, (2005), "Sub-Regional Cooperation, Hemispheric Threat: Security in the Southern Cone" in Louise Fawcett and Monica Serrano (Eds.), *Regionalism and Governance in the Americas: Continental Drift*. Houndmills and New York: Palgrave Macmillan.

Pittman, Howard T., (1981), "Geopolitics and Foreign Policy in Argentina, Brazil, and Chile" in Elizabeth B. Ferris and Jennie K. Lincoln (Eds.), *Latin American Foreign Policies*. Boulder: Westview Press.

——, (1984), "Chilean Foreign Policy: The Pragmatic Pursuit of Geopolitical Goals" in Jennie K. Lincoln and Elizabeth Ferris (Eds.), *The Dynamics of Latin American Foreign Policies: Challenges for the 1980s*. Boulder and London: Westview Press.

——, (1988), "Harmony or Discord: The Impact of Democratization on Geopolitics and Conflict in the Southern Cone" in Philip Kelly and Jack Child (Eds.), *Geopolitics of the Southern Cone and Antarctica*. Boulder and London: Lynne Rienner.

——, (1988b), "From O'Higgins to Pinochet: Applied Geopolitics in Chile" in Philip Kelly and Jack Child (Eds.), *Geopolitics of the Southern Cone and Antarctica*. Boulder and London: Lynne Rienner.

Prada, Fernando and Alvaro Espinoza, (2008), "Monitoring Regional Integration and Cooperation in the Andean Region" in Philippe de Lombaerde, Antoni Estevadeordal and Kati Suominen (Eds.), *Governing Regional Integration for Development: Monitoring Experiences, Methods and Prospects*. Aldershot and Burlington: Ashgate.

Prados, Frigdiano-Álvaro Durántez, (2002), "La Dilatación Lusófona del Iberismo Hispánico" in *Análisis, Estratégia y Prospectiva de la Comunidad Iberoamericana. Cuadernos de Estratégia 118*. Madrid: Ministério de Defensa, Secretaría General.

Prieto, Alberto, (2007), *Las Guerrillas Contemporáneas en América Latina*. Bogotá and Mexico D.F.: Ocean Sur.

Pugh, M., & Sidhu, W. P. S., (2003). *The United Nations and Regional Security*. Boulder, CO: Lynne Rienner.

Rabasa, Angel, Peter Chalk, Kim Cragin, Sara A. Daly, Heather S. Gregg, Theodore W. Karasik, Kevin A. O'Brien, and William Rosenau, (2006), *Beyond al-Qaeda: the Outer Rings of the Terrorist Universe*. Santa Monica: RAND Corporation.

Raby, Diana, (2011), "Venezuelan Foreign Policy under Chávez, 1999-2010: The Pragmatic Success of Revolutionary Ideology?" in Gian Luca Gardini and Peter Lambert (Eds.), *Latin American Foreign Policies: Between Ideology and Pragmatism*. Houndmills and New York: Palgrave Macmillan.

Randall, Stephen J., (2011), "The Continuing Pull of the Polar Star: Colombian Foreign Policy in the Post-Cold War Era" in Gian Luca Gardini and Peter Lambert (Eds.), *Latin American Foreign Policies: Between Ideology and Pragmatism*. Houndmills and New York: Palgrave Macmillan.

Reboratti, Carlos E., (2007), "América del Sur, Brasil y la Cuestión Ambiental" in Sérgio Costa, Hartmut Sangmeister and Sonja Steckbauer (Eds.), *O Brasil na América Latina: Interações, Percepções, Interdependencias*. São Paulo: Annablume Editora.

Resende-Santos, João, (2002), "The Origins of Security Cooperation in the Southern Cone" in *Latin American Politics and Society, Vol.* 44 (4), pp. 89-126.

Ricupero, Rubens, (2009), "As Linhas Mestras da Atual Política Externa do Brasil" in Paulo Gouvêa da Costa (Ed.), *A Política Externa do Brasil: Presente e Futuro*. Brasília: Fundação Liberdade e Cidadania.

Riggirozzi, Pía and Diana Tussie, (Ed.) (2012), *The Rise of Post-Hegemonic Regionalism: The Case of Latin America*. Dordrecht and London: Springer.

Roett, Riordan, (2003), "Brazil's Role as a Regional Power" in Riordan Roett and Guadalupe Paz (Eds.), *Latin America in a Changing Global Environment*. Boulder: Lynne Rienner.

Romero, M. T., (2002), "U.S. Policy for the Promotion of Democracy: the Venezuelan Case" in R. Hillman, J.A. Peeler and E. Cardozo Da Silva (Eds.), *Democracy and Human Rights in Latin America*, Westport, CT: Praeger.

Rubin, B. R., Armstrong, A., and Ntegeye, G. R., (Eds.). (2001). *Regional Conflict Formation in the Great Lakes Region of Africa: Structure, Dynamics and Challenges for Policy*. Center on International Cooperation, New York and the African Peace Forum, Nairobi. Available at http://www.cic.nyu.edu/peacebuilding/oldpdfs/RCF_NAIROBI.pdf. Accessed on 10 February 2010).

Russell, Roberto, (1988), "Argentina: Ten Years of Foreign Policy toward the Southern Cone" in Philip Kelly and Jack Child (Eds.), *Geopolitics of the Southern Cone and Antarctica*. Boulder and London: Lynne Rienner.

Saavedra, Boris, (2004), "Confronting Terrorism in Latin America: Building up Cooperation in the Andean Ridge Region" in *Low Intensity Conflict & Law Enforcement*, Vol.12 (3).

Sachs, Jeffrey D. and Andrew Warner, (1997), "Fundamental Sources of Long-Run Growth" in *American Economics Review*, Vol. 87 (2), pp. 184-188.

Sánchez, Rubén; Juan Carlos Ruiz; Stéphanie Lavaux; Francesca Ramos; Manuel José Bonett; Rocío Pachón; Federmán Rodríguez; Andrés Otálvaro; Ivonne Duarte; Rubén Machuca; and Carlos Suárez , (2005), *Seguridades en Construcción en América Latina. Tomo 1: el círculo de Colombia, Brasil, Ecuador, Panamá, Perú y Venezuela*. Bogotá: Centro Editorial Universidad del Rosario.

Waiselfisz, Julio Jacobo, (2013), *Mapa da Violência 2013: Homicídios e Juventude no Brasil*. Rio de Janeiro: CEBELA and FLACSO Brasil.

Sanjuán, Ana Maria, (2004), "La Agenda de Seguridad de Venezuela: ¿Ruptura o Continuidad del Paradigma? Una Análisis Preliminar" in Marco Cepik and Socorro Ramírez (Eds.), *Agenda de Seguridad Andino-Brasileña: Primeras Aproximaciones*. Bogotá: Friedrich-Ebert Stiftung.

———, (2008), "América Latina y el Bolivarianismo del siglo XXI: Alcances y Desafios de la Política Venezolana Hacia la Región" in Roberto Russell (Ed.), *América Latina: ¿Integracíon o Fragmentación?*. Buenos Aires: Edhasa.

Santa Cruz, Arturo, (2005), "Constitutional Structures, Sovereignty, and the Emergence of Norms: The Case of International Election Monitoring" in *International Organization*, Vol. 59 (3), p. 663-693.

Santiso, Carlos, (2003), "The Gordian Knot of Brazilian Foreign Policy: Promoting democracy while respecting sovereignty" in *Cambridge Review of International Affairs*, Vol. 16 (2).

Santoro, Maurício and Leonardo Valente, (2006), *A Diplomacia Midiática do Governo Hugo Chávez*. Rio de Janeiro: Observatório Político Sul-Americano.

Saraiva, Miriam Gomes, (2011), "Brazilian Foreign Policy: Causal Beliefs in Formulation and Pragmatism in Practice" in Gian Luca Gardini and Peter Lambert (Eds.), *Latin American Foreign Policies: Between Ideology and Pragmatism*. Houndmills and New York: Palgrave Macmillan.

Schirm, Stefan A., (2007), "Indicadores de Liderança e Modelos de Análise para a Nova Política Internacional do Brasil" in Sérgio Costa, Hartmut Sangmeister and Sonja Steckbauer (Eds.), *O Brasil na América Latina: Interações, Percepções, Interdependencias*. São Paulo: Annablume Editora.

Scott, James Brown, (1931), The International Conferences of American States, 1889-1928: A Collection of the Conventions, Recommendations, Resolutions, Reports, and Motions Adopted by the First Six International Conferences of the American States, and Documents Relating to the Organization of the Conferences. Oxford: Oxford University Press.

Seelke, Clare Ribando; Liana Sun Wyler, and June S. Beittel, (2010), *Latin America and the Caribbean: Illicit Drug Trafficking and U.S. Counterdrug Programs*. Congressional Research Service report for U.S. Congress.

Serbin, Andrés, (1996), "Venezuela, *el Gran Viraje*, and Regionalism in the Caribbean Basin" in Gordon Mace and Jean-Philippe Thérien (Eds.), *Foreign Policy and Regionalism in the Americas*. Boulder: Lynne Rienner.

Shai, Shaul, (2004), *The Axis of Evil: Hezbollah and the Palestinian Terror*. Brunswick: Transaction Publishers.

Shaw, Carolyn M., (2003), "Conflict Management in Latin America," in Paul F. Diehl and Joseph Lepgold (Eds.) *Regional Conflict Management*. Lanham, Md.: Rowman and Littlefield.

———, (2004), Cooperation, Conflict and Consensus in the Organization of American States. Basingstoke: Palgrave Macmillan.

Sicker, Martin, (2002), The Geopolitics of Security in the Americas: Hemispheric Denial from Monroe to Clinton. Westport: Praeger Publishers.

Smith, Peter, (1996), Talons of the Eagle: Dynamics of U.S.-Latin American Relations. Oxford: Oxford University Press.

Snyder, Jack, (1984), "Civil-Military Relations and the Cult of the Offensive, 1914 and 1984" in *International Security*, Vol. 9 (1), p. 108-146.

Soares, Rodrigo R. and Joana Naritomi, (2007), "Understanding High Crime Rates in Latin America: The Role of Social and Policy Factors," paper presented at the conference *Confronting Crime and Violence in Latin America: Crafting a Public Policy Agenda*, organized by the Instituto Fernando Henrique Cardoso (iFHC) at the John F. Kennedy School of Government, Harvard University, July.

Solís, Javier Elguea, (1990), "Las Guerras de Desarrollo en América Latina" in *Nueva Sociedad*, Vol. 105.

Stohl, Rachel and Doug Tuttle, (2008), "The Small Arms Trade in Latin America" in *NACLA Report on the Americas*, Issue March/April.

Strange, Susan, (1996), The Retreat of the State: The Diffusion of Power in the World Economy. Cambridge: Cambridge University Press.

Sullivan, Mark P., (2007), "Latin America: Terrorism Issues," Congressional Research Service Report for Congress RS21049; available at http://fpc.state.gov/documents/organization/81364.pdf (accessed 15 March 2008).

Sznajder, Mario and Luis Roniger, (2003), "Trends and Constraints of Partial Democracy in Latin America" in *Cambridge Review of International Affairs*, Vol. 16 (2).

Tacsan, Joaquín, (1998), "Searching for OAS/UN Task-Sharing Opportunities in Central America and Haiti," in Thomas G. Weiss (Ed.), *Beyond Subcontracting: Task-Sharing With Regional Security Arrangements and Service Providing NGOs*. Houndmills, U.K. and London: Macmillan Press.

Tavares, R., (2008), "Regional Peace and Security: A Framework for Analysis" in *Contemporary Politics*, 14 (2), 107–127.

———, (2010). Regional Security: The Capacity of International Organizations. London and New York: Routledge.

Tavares, Rodrigo and Vanessa Tang, (2011), "Regional Economic Integration in Africa: Impediments to Progress?" in *South African Journal of International Affairs*, Vol. 18 (2), p. 217 233.

The White House, (2010), *National Security Strategy 2010*. Washington: The White House.

Themnér, Lotta and Peter Wallensteen, (2013), "Armed Conflicts, 1946-2012" in *Journal of Peace Research*, 50 (4).

Thies, Cameron G., (2008), "The Construction of a Latin American Interstate Culture of Rivalry" in *International Interactions*, Vol. 34 (3).

Thomas, Christopher R. and Juliana T. Magloire, (2000), *The Organization of American States in a Global Changing Environment*. Norwell and Dordrecht: Kluwer Academic Publishers.

Tickner, Arlene B., (2001), "Colombia: An Ambiguous Foreign Policy," paper presented at the Congress Latin American Studies Association Washington, D.C. 6-8 September 2001.

———, (2003), "Colombia: U.S. Subordinate, Autonomous Actor, or Something in Between" in Frank O. Mora and Jeanne A. K. Hey (Eds.), *Latin American and Caribbean Foreign Policy*. Lanham: Rowman and Littlefield Publishers.

Tickner, J. Ann, (1995), "Re-Visioning Security" in Ken Booth and Steve Smith (Eds.) *International Relations Theory Today*. Oxford: Polity.

Tokatlian, Juan Gabriel and Arlene B. Tickner, (1996), "Colombia's Assertive Regionalism in Latin America" in Gordon Mace and Jean-Philippe Thérien (Eds.), *Foreign Policy and Regionalism in the Americas*. Boulder: Lynne Rienner.

Transnational Institute, (2010*), Systems Overload: Drug Laws and Prisons in Latin America*. Washington: Transnational Institute and Washington Office in Latin America.

Trinkunas, Harold A., (2000), "Crafting Civilian Control in Emerging Democracies: Argentina and Venezuela" in *Journal of Interamerican Studies and World Affairs*, Vol. 42 (3).

Tulchin, Joseph S., (1996), "Continuity and Change in Argentine Foreign Policy" in Heraldo Muñoz and Joseph S. Tulchin (Eds.), *Latin American Nations in World Politics* (second edition). Boulder: Westview Press.

Tulchin, Joseph S. and Heather A. Golding, (2003), "Introduction: Citizen Security in Regional Perspective" in Hugo Frühling, Joseph S. Tulchin and Heather A. Golding (Eds.), *Crime and Violence in Latin America: Citizen Security, Democracy, and the State*. Baltimore and London: The Johns Hopkins University Press.

Ullman, Richard, (1983), "Redefining Security," International Security 8 (1): 129–153.

Ulloa, Fernando Cepeda, (1998), "Introduction" in Elizabeth Joyce and Carlos Malamud (Eds.), *Latin America and the Multinational Drug Trade*. New York and Houndmills: St. Martin's Press and Macmillan Press.

UNDP (2013), *Citizen Security with a Human Face: Evidence and Proposals for Latin America*. New York: UNDP.

Ungar, Mark, (2006), "Crime and Citizen Security in Latin America" in Eric Hershberg and Fred Rosen (Eds.*), Latin America after Neoliberalism: Turning the Tide in the 21st Century*. New York: North America Congress on Latin America.

UNODC, (2010), *World Drug Report 2010*. New York and Vienna: UNODC.

———, (2010a), Crime and Instability: Case Studies of Transnational Threats. New York and Vienna: UNODC.

————, (2011), *World Drug Report 2011*. New York and Vienna: UNODC.
————, (2011a), *2011 Global Study on Homicide*. New York and Vienna: UNODC.
————, (2012), *World Drug Report 2012*. New York and Vienna: UNODC.
————, (2013), *UNODC Homicide Statistics 2013*. Available online in http://www.unodc.org/unodc/en/data-and-analysis/homicide.html.
————, (2013a), *World Drug Report 2013*. New York and Vienna: UNODC.
Urrutia, Edmundo González, (2006), "Las Dos Etapas de la Política Exterior de Chávez" in *Nueva Sociedad*, 2005, p. 158-171.
U.S. Department of State, (2010), *Country Reports on Terrorism 2009*. Washington: U.S. Department of State.
————, (2011), *Country Reports on Terrorism 2010*. Washington: U.S. Department of State.
Vacz, Aldo C., (2003), "Argentina: Between Confrontation and Alignment" In Frank O. Mora and Jeanne A.K.Hey (Eds.), *Latin American and Caribbean Foreign Policy*. Lanham: Rowman and Littlefield Publishers.
Valenzuela, Arturo, (1997), "Paraguay: The Coup That Didn't Happen" in *Journal of Democracy*, Vol. 8 (1).
Van Klaveren, Alberto, (1996), "Understanding Latin American Foreign Policies" in Heraldo Muñoz and Joseph S. Tulchin (Eds.), *Latin American Nations in World Politics* (second edition). Boulder: Westview Press.
————, (2000), "Chile: The Search for Open Regionalism" in Björn Hettne, András Inotai, and Osvaldo Sunkel (Eds.), *National Perspectives on the New Regionalism in the South*. New York and Houndmills: St. Martin's Press and Macmillan Press.
Vanderschueren, Franz, (2000), "The Prevention of Urban Crime," paper presented at the *Africities 2000 Summit*, Windhoek, May.
Varas, Augusto, (1998), "Cooperative Hemispheric Security after the Cold War" in Olga Pellicer (Ed.), *Regional Mechanisms and International Security in Latin America*. Tokyo and New York: United Nations University Press.
Velázquez, Arturo C. Sotomayor, (2010), "Why Some States Participate in UN Peace Missions While Others Do Not: An Analysis of Civil-Military Relations and Its Effects on Latin America's Contributions to Peacekeeping Operations" in *Security Studies*, Vol. 19 (1).
Vigevani, Tullo and Gabriel Cepaluni, (2009), *Brazilian Foreign Policy in Changing Times*. Lanham: Lexington Books.
Vizentini, Paulo Fagundes, (2008, first edition in 2003), *Relacoes Internacionais do Brasil: De Vargas a Lula*. Sao Paulo: Editora Fundacao Perseu Abramo.
Wiarda, Howard J., (1990), "South American Domestic Politics and Foreign Policy" in G. Pope Atkins (Ed.), *South America into the 1990s: Evolving International Relationships in a New Era*. Boulder and London: Westview Press.
————, (2005), Dilemmas of Democracy in Latin América: Crises and Opportunity. Lanham: Rowman & Littlefield.
Wilpert, Gregory, (2007), Changing Venezuela by Taking Power: The History and Policies of the Chávez Government. London and New York: Verso.
Wood, Bryce, (1966), *The United States and Latin American Wars, 1932-1942*. New York: Columbia University Press.

WHO [World Health Organization], (2002). *World Report on Violence and Health*. Geneva: WHO.

Wallensteen, Peter, and Sollenberg, M., (1998). Armed conflict and regional conflict complexes 1989-1996. Journal of Peace Research, 35 (5), 621–634.

Webber, Mark; Stuart Croft, Jolyon Howorth, Terry Terriff & Elke Krahmann, (2004), "The Governance of European Security," Review of International Studies 30 (1): 3–26.

Weiss, T. G., (Ed.) (1998). Beyond UN subcontracting: Task-sharing with regional security arrangements and service-providing NGOs. Houndmills: Macmillan.

World Bank, (2001), *World Development Indicators*. Washington: World Bank.

Youngers, Coletta A., (2006), "Dangerous Consequences: The U.S. 'War on Drugs' in Latin America" in Eric Hershberg and Fred Rosen (Eds.), *Latin America after Neoliberalism: Turning the Tide in the 21ˢᵗ Century*. New York: North America Congress on Latin America.

Zacher, Mark W., (1979), International Conflicts and Collective Security, 1946-1977: The United Nations, Organization of American States, Organization of African Unity, and Arab League. New York: Praeger.

Index

About the Book

What types of threats and conflicts affect the countries of South America? What roles can and should states and regional organizations play in maintaining both traditional and human security in the region? Ranging from armed conflicts, terrorism, and the arms trade to political crises, drug trafficking, and environmental concerns, Rodrigo Tavares provides a comprehensive discussion of the issues and actors that affect South American security.

Rodrigo Tavares is associate research fellow at United Nations University and assistant professor of international relations at the Getúlio Vargas Foundation. His publications include *Regional Security: The Capacity of International Organizations* and *Regional Organizations in African Security* (with Fredrik Söderbaum).